ROB SCHENCK

THE · TEN
WORDS
THAT · WILL
CHANGE
A · NATION

THE · TEN
COMMANDMENTS

ALBURY
PUBLISHING
Tulsa, Oklahoma

THE TEN WORDS THAT WILL CHANGE A NATION: THE TEN COMMANDMENTS
ISBN 1-57778-128-7
COPYRIGHT © 1999 BY ROBERT L. SCHENCK
8813 COMMERCE COURT
MANASSAS, VIRGINIA 20110

PUBLISHED BY ALBURY PUBLISHING
P. O. BOX 470406
TULSA, OKLAHOMA 74147-0406

CONTENTS

◤

DEDICATION

I dedicate this book first "to God our Savior, who alone is wise" (Jude 25).

Second, to Cheryl, the woman with whom I am made complete; to my children, Anna and Matthew, whom I love with all my soul; and to my parents and sisters who have suffered with me more than they deserve.

Last, to the people who have given selflessly so that together we can carry on the Lord's work. To name just a few: David Anderson, Sam and Cherri Benson, Greg and Bonnie Cox, Greg Brandt, Brad Dobeck, the Hunters, the Martinkes, John McCall, the Magnificent Moffits of Philadelphia, my soulmate Charles Nestor and his bride, Belinda, Stan and Hope Parks, Jan Peterson, Karen Prior (whose command of English always makes me look better in print than I really am), Sam Smucker, Don and Nancy Wilson, Don and Gayle Wright, Jim and Christine Tennies, and the endlessly inspiring Dexter and Birdie Yager.

To my editor *par excellence* and a great writer from whom I've learned so much, Richard Exley, and to Elizabeth Sherman from Albury Publishing, thank you, and thank you again!

Special thanks goes to my brother, Paul C. Schenck, for his many contributions to the text, and to my incomparable ministry team and *Family Circle* for their tireless work and prayers. May they bear much fruit!

AN OPEN LETTER FROM BETH NIMMO, MOTHER OF COLUMBINE HIGH SCHOOL MURDER VICTIM, RACHEL JOY SCOTT

July 21, 1999

In June of 1962 legislation was enacted which stripped our public schools of prayer. The prayer which was banned by this unwise decision was simply: "Almighty God, we acknowledge our dependence upon Thee, and beg Thy blessing upon us, our parents, our teachers, and our country." This action sabotaged the safety and future well-being of generations to come. We have now inherited the bitter fruit. Teen violence, crime, and pregnancies rose dramatically, while academic scores have plummeted. The Duke of Wellington once said, "If you divorce religion from education, you produce a race of clever devils." Nowhere have we seen this more clearly demonstrated than here in Littleton, Colorado.

For years now, our children have been fed on a constant diet of violence through television, movies, and video games. They have been exposed to an entirely new set of values, which glorify hedonism, sexual promiscuity, and violence as a means of conflict management. Some of our youth have learned these new values well, and are now acting out their frustrations and anger in the most horrible acts of murder and violence.

Where do we go from here? We must recapture our nation's great spiritual inheritance of Judeo-Christian values. We must have a change of heart, which of necessity must begin with the nurture of the family unit. Support and encouragement must be given to fathers and mothers to raise their children with godly values and respect for human life, beginning at conception. New legislation and more laws cannot guarantee a changed society, only a true change of heart will insure that. Government should merely encourage and empower what we the people, as a nation conceived under God, must be responsible to uphold. Most importantly, the laws of our land should never be in contradiction to the laws of God.

The down payment for the change we so desperately need in our nation has been paid by the blood of my daughter, Rachel, and the other precious children killed or wounded at Columbine. The grim spiritual darkness which now covers our nation has been challenged by the light of our children, several of whom willingly laid down their lives for the cause of Jesus Christ. Our nation must come to grips with the fact that Almighty God, our Creator, will call us into account for the elimination of His Word and counsel. It's time for those God-honoring leaders of our nation to once again rise to the challenge before us and let their voice be heard. May that voice rise to a chorus, refusing to be turned away or once again intimidated into silence!

My daughter, Rachel, had the courage to stand for godly truth even at the cost of her life because she also had a deep understanding of the despair of her generation, a generation who has been deprived of the knowledge of God. Here are her own words, penned in her personal journal only a few days before her untimely death on April 20, 1999.

I'm drowning
In my own lake of despair;
I'm choking
My hands wrapped around my neck;
I'm dying . . .
Quickly my soul leaves, slowly my body withers;
It isn't suicide . . .

I consider it homicide;
The world you have created has led to my death.

As a mother of a slain child, slaughtered in the tragedy at Columbine High School, I plead for public repentance from our nation's leaders for removing God's influence from our schools. Please, I beg you, do not let my daughter's sacrifice be in vain. I conclude with these immortal words drawn from President Abraham Lincoln's speech at Gettysburg, Pennsylvania, on November 19, 1863, who stated so eloquently: "It is rather for us to be here dedicated to the great task remaining before us . . . that from these honored dead we take increased devotion to that cause for which they gave the last full measure of devotion . . . That we here highly resolve that these dead shall not have died in vain."

Sincerely,

Beth Nimmo
(Mother of Rachel Joy Scott)

INTRODUCTION

More Than Just Words

"[I]f people can gather inspiration from this particular action . . . it will be to the benefit of us all."

—Senator Edward Kennedy

John F. Kennedy would have turned eighty years old on that day in May 1997. Instead, his birthday was being celebrated posthumously by his youngest brother, Senator Edward M. Kennedy, who hosted Judge Charles Price of Montgomery, Alabama, at the Kennedy Library in Boston, Massachusetts.

As he makes his way to the podium, Senator Kennedy appears relaxed, if only for the number of times he has had to address these types of small political gatherings. He clears his throat once and begins to speak in the familiar Kennedy brogue. "This is a special day for our family," he says, his eyes alternately glancing to the floor, then scanning his audience.

"First of all, it's President Kennedy's birthday. It's hard to imagine, but Jack would have been eighty years old today, and this special anniversary reminds us again how much we miss him. Today is also the day that the annual Profile in Courage Award is presented. Our family established this award several years ago in honor of my brother and the famous book he wrote while still a Senator."

The Senator then turns towards a small man with a mustache standing nearby. "This year's winner is Judge Charles Price of Alabama, and he's being honored for his courage in defending the First Amendment and freedom of religion. President Kennedy would be proud that Judge Price . . . stood up for one of the important constitutional provisions."

The Senator compares Judge Price's actions to President Kennedy's support of the Supreme Court's 1963 decision to take prayer out of public schools. He concludes by giving Judge Price a silver lamp crafted by Tiffany and Company along with a $25,000 check. Following the presentation ceremony, Kennedy tells reporters, "[I]f people can gather inspiration from this particular action . . . it will be to the benefit of us all."

Judge Charles Price was being feted by the Kennedy family on the hallowed day of JFK's birthday for ordering fellow Alabaman Judge Roy Moore to stop inviting the prayers of pastors in his courtroom before jury selection—and for demanding that Judge Moore take down the Ten Commandments plaque that hangs on his courtroom wall. The fact that the honor conferred was the Profile in Courage Award was especially ironic. It was Judge Moore who now faced contempt charges and possible legal sanctions if he did not obey Judge Price's ruling.

The day after the event, Judge Moore called me to express his frustration over what the Kennedys had done. "Reverend Schenck," he said, "you know I've been attacked by the media and accused of taking money and everything else. But you know, Reverend, that I've never taken a dime for any public appearance I've made. In fact, it's actually cost me money to travel to a lot of these places. And my lawyers aren't getting paid for all the time they're putting into this."

The hypocrisy betrayed by the press, who never questioned the money flowing from the Kennedys to Judge Price, was so painfully obvious that it amused us. In fact, several weeks later the same wire service that questioned Judge Moore's ethics in regard to travel reimbursements waited until the end of a very long article to mention Judge Price's trip to Boston at the Kennedys' expense, and that a judicial ethics commission had approved it. This is just one of the more recent glaring indictments American culture and media have pronounced on God's ten unchangeable rules.

"TEN WORDS"

In the Hebrew language in which they were first delivered, the Ten Commandments are called *Aseret Dev'rote,* "Ten Words." These are not just any ten words. They are THE TEN WORDS, because there are no ten words like them. The Ten Commandments are the most enduring and universal of all ancient law codes. They transcend time and space, as well as language, culture, and religion. Jews, Christians, and Moslems agree that they are words from God. In fact, virtually all religious belief systems consider the majority of the Ten Commandments as good for the human race. Only one religious group, the Church of Satan, Inc., is on record as opposing them.

Of course, these words are more than just words. They are as powerful as the supernatural force that first cut them into stone. They have already changed history. Yet, they are surprisingly ordinary. Simple and to the point, they don't leave room for the luxury of multiple interpretations. They were not given to be venerated as a mystery, but were meant to be literally interpreted and followed—*to the letter!*

When most people think of Moses carrying the tables of the Law down the mountain, they envision Charlton Heston with two giant stone slabs in his arms. While this is an impressive image, it is probably not the way the Commandments originally looked. Biblical archeologists and scholars believe the stones upon which the Commandments first appeared were slightly larger than the palm of your hand.[1] We also know from Scripture that they were written on both sides (see Exodus 32:15), indicating that they were probably exact copies of each other, with a complete listing of the Commandments on either side. This would be in keeping with the Ten Words as *covenant,* or as an agreement between God and His people. "Then the Lord said to Moses, 'Write these words, for according to the tenor of these words I have made a covenant with you and with Israel'" (Exodus 34:27).

A covenant of this sort was not strange to the people of Israel. It was actually known as a form of treaty between a conqueror and the conquered. It is in this form of a treaty that the Ten Commandments are presented. As such, they would have all been contained on one tablet for the conqueror's record, and again on another tablet for the conquered. In this case, God has conquered His people not for evil, but for good. Like a lover in pursuit of the object of His affection, God wins over the people who receive and honor His Being. He calls His people in Hebrew, *segulah*, a term of intense endearment which we translate as a "peculiar treasure." (See Exodus 19:5.) Once conquered by His love, the Lord of heaven goes to work (much like Dr. Henry Higgins did with the crude Eliza Doolittle in the musical comedy, *My Fair Lady*) transforming us from primitive barbarians into civilized human beings.

The two tablets of the Ten Commandments, then, are a relatively recent invention. The rabbis in Jesus' day used this device of breaking the Ten Commandments up into two listings to simplify their memorization. The first table contains what I call the "Vertical Commandments," that is, our duties and obligations to God. The second table contains the "Horizontal Commandments," which have to do with our duties and obligations to our fellow human beings. This simple division helps to organize the commandments in our minds, making them easier to remember. In some instances the first tablet contains Commandments I through IV, in others Commandments I through V. This depends upon whether the controlling rabbinic authority saw the commandment to honor parents as a responsibility to God or to man. I believe it fits into both categories, and therefore forms a bridge between the two tables.

It was to these two tables that Jesus alluded when He was asked by a religious lawyer, "Teacher, which is the great commandment in the law?" Jesus responded, 'You shall love the Lord your God with all your heart, with all your soul, and with all your mind.' This is the first and great commandment. And the second is like it: 'You shall love your neighbor as yourself.' On these two commandments hang all the Law and the Prophets'" (Matthew 22:36-40). (See also Mark 12:28-31.)

To both Jews and Christians, the Ten Commandments are not a double-edged blade, like the mystical sword of Damocles, waiting to drop on the necks of violators. Instead, they are an ideal code of human behavior that demonstrates the importance and sanctity of our obligations to God, to ourselves, and to others. Like the bar for a pole vault, God sets this standard high. He will not lower it simply because we don't make it on the first jump. His mercy is always there for us when we fail, but His expectations remain the same. He does not compromise to accommodate our shortcomings.

The Commandments form part of the *Torah,* which means instruction or command. The *Torah* comprises the first five books of the Old Testament written by Moses. In theological language, the Ten Commandments are called the *Decalogue,* which comes from the Greek translation of their title in Hebrew.[2] God himself refers to them as the "law and the commandments" in the book of Exodus. (See Exodus 24:12.) They are known as the "Torah" and "Mitzvah" in the Hebrew language.

Each one of the Commandment's brevity and clarity epitomize God's Law. They are not mere sayings, but are meant to translate into holy actions. Their literal translations show them to be "words," or "instructions" and "deeds," or "acts." So, the Commandments are not meant to be theoretical. They are to affect how human beings actually behave, and as such, form the crown of the moral law.

There are actually three dimensions to God's Law: The moral Law, the ceremonial law, and the civil law. The moral law, of which the Ten Words are a part, is different from other legal aspects in the Old Testament. It is universal in that it applies to all people at all times in all places. There are no exceptions, and the moral law never expires. It is preposterous to think that there would ever be a time when murder or stealing could be allowed, or that a group of people would be exempt from any such prohibition. If this is true of one of the commandments, then it is true of all of them.

But the same rule does not apply to the other aspects of the Old Testament law, that is the ceremonial and the civil dimensions. Ceremonial law had mostly to do with the Temple in Jerusalem and the sacrificial system, as well as the particular religious rituals of the Hebrew people. The civil law governed the affairs of the nation itself. Because the civil law is an extension of the moral law, it was theological in nature, yet secular in its application.

The civil law included statutes that controlled commercial, social, and domestic affairs. They regarded, for the most part, the order and protection of society in ancient Israel. Because we no longer live in the ancient Israelite state, we needn't hold to these laws any longer, though we may voluntarily decide to do so.

Our discussion of the Ten Commandments limits us to only the moral law, and even more specifically, only as it is expressed in the Ten Commandments themselves. This book is not meant to be an exhaustive exploration of God's Law, nor is it the last word on the Commandments. It is, however, a careful examination of what the Ten Commandments mean, how they apply to our individual lives, and especially how they apply to our American way of life.

A CRY FOR CHANGE

Our nation is currently starving for moral renewal. An astonishing 80 percent of Americans feel that the United States is in moral crisis and want politicians of both parties to address spiritual concerns. According to a poll conducted by the Luntz Research Corporation that was underwritten by the Christian Coalition in April of 1997, the vast majority of Americans agree that our nation's moral and religious well-being is of paramount importance.

These are not just idle concerns. The same people feel that we must do something about this crisis. One solution they suggest is the return of voluntary prayer to the public schools and the public posting of the Ten Commandments.[3] Yet, these sentiments are vigorously opposed by powerful minority interest groups like the ACLU, who launched a multimillion dollar fund-raising campaign in an attempt to frustrate such proposals. And a month before the Christian Coalition's poll was published, Dr. Bill Bright, the founder of Campus Crusade for Christ (one of the world's largest Christian missionary organizations), suffered serious criticism after he offered a prayer before the Florida legislature that included these words:

> You commanded us to "do unto others what we would have others do unto us"—to love You, our neighbors, even our enemies. We have ignored Your Word. You commanded us not to kill, yet we have murdered almost 40 million unborn babies. We are reaping a nation with an epidemic of drug addiction, an epidemic of alcoholism, an epidemic of crime, abortions, divorce, incurable diseases, racism—the list is endless.[4]

According to an Intercessors for America report on the incident, a storm of protest broke out. Dr. Bright was roundly criticized for his remarks by numerous Florida lawmakers and even chastised by a newspaper editorial.

Dr. Bright is not alone. In August of 1996, I was present at both major political party conventions where their respective presidential candidates would be selected. At the Republican National Convention in San Diego, I had joined in a special memorial service for aborted children held outside the Convention Hall. I challenged the so-called "moderates" who were agitating for the party to abandon the pro-life plank of its platform, appealing to them to remember that it had been a hard-line stance against another life issue, slavery, which led to the party's birth and success. The attendees gave me a mostly cordial response, and some were even enthusiastic about our presence.

The reaction at the Democratic Party Convention held in Chicago was quite different. I stood outside the United Center in my customary clerical collar at this political gathering, but this time I held two large stone tablets of the Ten Commandments in my arms. It was not just respect for human life that was at issue among the Democrats, but nearly every one of the moral absolutes embodied in the Ten Commandments.

Inside, as thousands of delegates were preparing to choose their candidates for President and Vice President, the homosexual political lobby was playing a decisive role in the process, pressing for recognition of their aberrant sexual practices and the social engineering required to get the public to approve of them. Abortion was also a major issue that year, so pro-life Democrats were shut out of any public venue. These included former Pennsylvania Governor Robert Casey, whose outstanding record of leadership should have placed him high on the roster of speakers. Ohio Congressman Tony Hall, another outspoken advocate for the pre-born, was reported to have been frustrated when he was given a small sideline spot after having initially been censored. And beneath the surface of it all another great scandal was brewing, compounding the Clinton Administration's reputation for prevarication, unethical behavior, and bawdiness.

Dick Morris, a trusted advisor and longtime confidant to President Clinton, would later confess to multiple liaisons with a high-priced Washington, D.C., call girl. She would tell the newspapers that Morris allowed her to listen to his telephone conversations with the President, and that she often knew about important campaign matters before the Chief Executive did. The story broke on the day President Clinton made his acceptance speech to the convention. Meanwhile, I was outside standing vigil communicating my message.

"Ladies and gentlemen, these are a reminder that there are moral absolutes," I said politely with a smile to the delegates on their way into the arena, directing their attention to the Commandments. I was stunned by what happened. Many of the delegates raised their middle fingers to me, or openly cursed me. Here are just a few of the remarks that I can remember:

"F*** your religion!"

"Shove it up your a**!"

"Take your commandments and go to hell!"

The vitriol came at me steadily for the several hours I stood there. At one point, two men holding hands and sporting delegates' credentials around their necks came up to me and sarcastically read the tablets out loud. Then one laid his middle finger along the length of my nose and said, "Go f*** the Pope."

I could not remember ever being treated with such vulgar contempt. But I'm convinced it wasn't me, but rather the words on those stone tablets that provoked such an angry response.

There is something about the Ten Commandments that demand something from us. They hold us accountable. They force us to face "the man in the mirror." So as long as these words can be read and understood, they will always cause conflict. In the infamous 1980 decision rendered by *Stone v. Graham*, six Justices of the United States Supreme Court ruled that posters of the Ten Commandments had to be removed from Kentucky public school classrooms, even though they were clearly identified as historical displays and were paid for by private contributions.

In that opinion, the majority wrote that the Commandments were unconstitutional, because if they were, "to have any effect at all, it would be to induce the schoolchildren to read, meditate upon, perhaps to venerate and obey, the Commandments."[5]

This is the crux of the matter. When the Commandments are ignored and kept invisible, when they are treated like nothing more than a quaint relic of the past, they trouble no one. But when they are taken seriously, held up as an immutable standard, and perchance, actually obeyed, they instantly bring conflict.

Why? Because God's Ten Words challenge the most passionate notions of moral autonomy.

"Don't you try to impose your morality on me!" goes the popular chant.

"I'll decide for myself what is right and wrong!"

What would a society look like in which each of its members decided for themselves what is right and wrong? It would be like living in a town where stopping at a stop sign was left up to the relative decision of each individual driver. What if the city council of that town decided that all street signs were considered nothing more than suggestions about one's conduct, and held no force of law and no criminal consequences? What if murdering your neighbor was a matter of choice? What if stealing was considered a bad thing for some people, but not for others? Is this the kind of community any of us would want to live in? This is the kind of community the "Don't impose your morality on me!" group would develop, on paper anyway.

The fact is, moral absolutes surround us. The stop sign is a moral statement: It says that it is wrong to endanger your life and the lives of others by sailing through an intersection without stopping. If it is a four-way stop, there are rules that govern who has the right-of-way. And if you violate these rules, chances are you will be punished by law enforcement, or at the very least, you will receive the reproach of other drivers.

So, the current debate is not really about right and wrong, but about whose standard of right and wrong is better for society. A quick look at the fruit of culturally forsaking God's absolutes will tell us immediately that it is the Judeo-Christian standard, epitomized in the Commandments, that our Founders had in mind.

In the thirty to forty years since our nation caved in to the "live and let live—anything that turns you on," attitude of cultural liberalism, every indicator of social well-being has plummeted, except for the good progress we have seen in racial integration. This decline has had an enormously negative impact on the physical and psychological state of Americans, as well as their economic status.

Out-of-wedlock births, abortion, substance abuse treatment, and psychiatric problems have caused health insurance premiums and taxes to skyrocket. The government now spends more on AIDS than they do on the number one health problem for Americans, heart disease. Divorce-on-demand has induced the feminization of poverty and has placed the welfare of millions of children at risk. Co-habitation, once rare in the U.S., now puts kids in serious jeopardy as boyfriends beat to death more and more of their girlfriends' children (we will discuss this at length in Chapter V).

Many businesses spend more today on security than they do on research and development of new products. And losses due to theft and fraud are higher than ever. Someone has to pick up the bill on all this, and it is mostly the consumer who ends up paying higher prices. Yet, the cure for this is still resisted.

A friend of mine from Louisiana, David, called me one day to tell me that he brought a small stone artwork set of the Ten Commandments to the bank branch that he manages and placed it on the wall near his desk. The next day a young woman whom he had recently hired indignantly walked up to his desk.

"I want you to take those down," she told him. "I don't have to be exposed to *that stuff* in the workplace."

David explained that the woman was not "required" to look at "that stuff." But she remained unsatisfied and threatened to call the corporate personnel office to file a formal complaint of religious harassment because, as it turned out, she was an atheist.

When David called me he was concerned that he would lose his job if he didn't comply with her demands, and that his bank could be sued. I assured him that neither was the case, and that our legal team would help him if it got to that point. As it turned out, the disgruntled employee, who did file a complaint, also quit that same week. So once it was moot, the company didn't pursue the matter.

Nevertheless, I advised David to explain to his boss why he placed the Ten Commandments on the wall. David was the top-producing manager in the entire bank and had built its most profitable branch operation. So I advised him to meet with his boss to explain that the reason he was so successful was that he adhered to these principles personally and that he looked for employees who did the same. A person who takes the Ten Commandments seriously will work hard, avoid wasting time and resources, give the business an honest day's labor, be much more conscientious, and be much less distracted by harmful personal behaviors. Not to mention the fact that they will be mindful of the God to whom we must all make account, who looks over our shoulders every hour of every day— even when the boss can't! So David set up the meeting; but, sad to say, his boss remained unconvinced.

Nonetheless, the facts remain that the Ten Commandments are good for individuals, good for families, good for business, and good for society. They make us happier, healthier, safer, and more productive. The prophet Isaiah echoed the voice of God when he wrote, "So shall My word be that goes forth from My mouth; it shall not return to Me void, but it shall accomplish what I please" (Isaiah 55:11). These words are tools that God has used for nearly four millennia to shape individuals and cultures. And while they will not get us into heaven (because they are essentially rules for living here on earth), they will change us individually and together as a people. As you apply them in your life you will be changed, permanently. And as you change, the people and things around you will change.

Those who will embrace the principles of the honorable lifestyle the Ten Commandments decree will align themselves with the integrity America so desperately needs today. That is why God is bringing these timeless truths to the forefront. We ignore them at our own peril.

Let the debate begin.

COME UP!

"Now all of the people were seeing the thunder-sounds, the flashing-torches, the shofar sound, and the mountain smoking; when the people saw, they faltered and stood far off."

EXODUS 20:15
THE FIVE BOOKS OF MOSES[1]

The old man carefully places a dark, weathered hand on his knee, pressing downward to heave himself over the rocky crag. His other hand grips the walking stick, carved from a knotty olive tree branch by years of wind and rain. At this height, much of the sagebrush has given way to crumbled rock. What little vegetation there is on this side of the mountain thins out to nearly nothing as his wiry form climbs higher. His chest heaves, straining for oxygen as his muscles demand more to complete the journey. A cool wind suddenly stirs, giving momentary reprieve to the hot stagnate air of the desert. As the early morning haze dissipates, the sun illuminates the golden-brown peak of Sinai.

His mind fixed on his destination, the old man climbs higher, undaunted by the increasingly difficult terrain. The straps of his sandals cut into his feet, but his objective is too important to allow his discomfort to slow his ascent. Finally, after he lifts himself for the last time to a rocky shelf, he crouches down, exhausted in body but invigorated in spirit.

A sudden peel of thunder breaks the silence, and he lifts his face toward the summit. There, heavy blue and orange-tinted clouds now loom, covering the mountaintop. Animated by lightning, their color flashes red. Twisting, the clouds coalesce around an invisible core. The air is charged with energy, causing the old man's heavy robe to cling tightly around his body. Thick smoke and fire swirl from out of the clouds. He gazes, petrified by both dread and reverence as the air boils around him.

Then the sky fills with words.

Instinctively, he attempts to speak back. He tries in vain to penetrate the seemingly solid air with his voice. In the end, his utterance is barely audible above the piercing wind. Suddenly, the command comes to descend the mountain and warn the people not to come near, lest they die. Attempting to reason with the divine presence, he explains that the people already know not to approach, but his plea is ignored and he finds himself descending the mountain.

When the old man returns to the mountaintop, he lifts an arm across his face to shield himself from the blazing light and over-whelming presence. The words come again and the mountain trembles:

> "I AM YAHWEH YOUR GOD, WHO LED YOU OUT OF THE LAND OF EGYPT, OUT OF THE HOUSE OF SLAVERY. YOU WILL PLACE NO OTHER GODS IN FRONT OF MY FACE!"
>
> AUTHOR'S TRANSLATION

The voice continues, uttering pronouncements that pierce the listener's heart, who feels them more than he hears them. Each phrase cuts deep and lodges in a place only God can touch. These are not idle words. They will mold the souls of men and women. They are permanent and lasting, words etched in stone by the finger of God himself:

> "YOU SHALL NOT MAKE FOR YOURSELF A GRAVEN IMAGE, OR ANY LIKENESS OF ANYTHING THAT IS IN THE HEAVEN ABOVE, OR

IN THE EARTH BENEATH, OR THAT IS IN THE WATER UNDER THE
EARTH: YOU SHALL NOT BOW DOWN TO THEM, NOR SERVE THEM:
FOR I THE LORD YOUR GOD AM A JEALOUS GOD, PUNISHING THE
INIQUITY OF THE FATHERS UPON THE CHILDREN UNTO THE THIRD
AND THE FOURTH GENERATION OF THOSE HATE ME; BUT
SHOWING MERCY TO THOUSANDS OF GENERATIONS OF THOSE
THAT LOVE ME AND KEEP MY COMMANDMENTS."

AUTHOR'S TRANSLATION

The wind now presses with constant force against the old man. His
face burns and his eyes tear. He steadies himself against the rock.

"YOU SHALL NOT TAKE THE NAME OF THE LORD YOUR GOD IN
VAIN; FOR THE LORD WILL NOT HOLD HIM GUILTLESS WHO
TAKES HIS NAME IN VAIN.

"REMEMBER THE SABBATH DAY, TO KEEP IT HOLY. SIX DAYS YOU
SHALL LABOR, AND DO ALL YOUR WORK: BUT THE SEVENTH DAY
IS A SABBATH TO THE LORD YOUR GOD: IN IT YOU SHALL NOT
DO ANY WORK, YOU, NOR YOUR SON, NOR YOUR DAUGHTER,
YOUR MANSERVANT, OR YOUR MAIDSERVANT, NOR YOUR
CATTLE, NOR THE STRANGER THAT IS WITHIN YOUR GATES: FOR
IN SIX DAYS THE LORD MADE HEAVEN AND EARTH, THE SEA,
AND ALL THAT IS IN THEM, AND RESTED ON THE SEVENTH DAY:
THEREFORE THE LORD BLESSED THE SEVENTH DAY, AND
HALLOWED IT."

AUTHOR'S TRANSLATION

Squinting through his tears, he can barely see a hand writing—
effortlessly carving each eternal word into the stone.

"HONOR YOUR FATHER AND YOUR MOTHER, THAT YOUR DAYS MAY BE LONG IN THE LAND WHICH THE LORD YOUR GOD GIVES YOU.

"YOU SHALL NOT TAKE THE LIFE OF THE INNOCENT.

"YOU SHALL NOT COMMIT ADULTERY.

"YOU SHALL NOT STEAL.

"YOU SHALL NOT MAKE A FALSE ACCUSATION AGAINST YOUR NEIGHBOR.

"YOU SHALL NOT COVET YOUR NEIGHBOR'S HOUSE, YOU SHALL NOT COVET YOUR NEIGHBOR'S WIFE, NOR HIS MANSERVANT, NOR HIS MAIDSERVANT, NOR HIS OX, NOR HIS DONKEY, NOR ANYTHING THAT IS YOUR NEIGHBOR'S."

AUTHOR'S TRANSLATION

Suddenly the wind disappears into the stillness of the desert. Silence lies heavily on his ears. The old man raises his shaken body to his full stature and slowly moves toward the tablets of stone. He stoops to pick them up and feels the weight of their purpose. He cradles them close to his heart and makes his way down the mountain.

The careless ones at the foot of the mountain will not hear the words until their idolatrous frolic is judged and peace restored. Even then, it will not be long before they forget. Their rebellious fists will shake again, divine wisdom will be lost, and conflict will rage among the human race for generations to come.

THE ONE AND ONLY

CHAPTER ONE

March 1997

The echo of Oxford shoes on the glazed stone floor in the United States Capitol makes an impressive sound. What might be a nuisance anywhere else seems to be an audible reminder that whatever takes place within these walls will be recorded in the echoes of time. A noisy walk through these stately corridors is, in itself, a signal act of citizenship.

On this particular day the clicking of shoe heels takes on an even more potent sound because they belong to Judge Roy S. Moore. The Judge, his wife, Kayla, Wyoming lawyer Steve Melchior, and I have just finished lunch in the elegant Members-Only Dining Room with Robert Aderholt, a youthful thirty-two-year-old first term congressman from the Judge's home district in Etowah County, Alabama. We are now weaving our way quickly but silently around clusters of Boy Scouts and Girl Scouts, parades of students in small, medium, and large sizes, and knots of tourists clad with cameras and dangling sunglasses around their necks.

I suppose it is our determined stride and dark business attire, together with the briefcases and poster tubes that we carry in our hands and under our arms, that suggest to these visitors that we are VIPs of some sort. A few ready their cameras, hopeful of a photo opportunity, while others crane their necks, scanning our faces for a familiar C-SPAN broadcast visage. But the group is disappointed by our appearance when they fail to recognize a single congressman or senator among us, and they quickly return their attention to the statues and artifacts.

Having cleared the crowds, we pick up our pace, dashing down a marble staircase to the lower level of the Capitol. We will assemble at the front of a small meeting room to celebrate a historic document just adopted by the United States House of Representatives. House Resolution Number 31 affirms the Ten Commandments as the foundation to a moral and just society and approves posting the Ten Commandments on all government buildings and courthouses.[1] It also commends Judge Moore for his brave stand in defending the display of the Ten Commandments in his small courtroom in rural Gadsden, Alabama. From the reactions of its many detractors, one would think that this resolution had sparked a new American revolution.

As we round a final corner, I can hear the din of busy conversation. Before seeing the crowd of attendees at our press conference, I know already that we have planned too small. Once the room is in view, I can see that there are as many people standing outside in the hallway as there are seated inside. I can feel the temperature rise as we approach.

"This is gonna be a hot one," complains a middle-aged reporter in khakis and a denim shirt.

"I wish they'd pick bigger rooms for this stuff," says a late-twenty-something woman with press credentials clipped to her shirt and a reporter's pad in her hand. I pause to survey the room and reflect on what has brought us to this moment.

A storm of protest had attended Representative Aderholt's proposal to declare the Ten Commandments as the building blocks for a just society. The measure was introduced into both the House and the Senate at the same time. The Senate, considered to be the more "august" chamber, pretended to hardly register it. But in the House, certain members of Congress ran the other way when they saw it. Antireligious secularists assailed it, and a homosexual activist took to the floor of the House chamber to decry it. Some thought that Mr. Aderholt had committed political suicide simply by presenting such a proposal. Even those of us who had worked tirelessly and hopefully to recruit support for it were worried that we would never succeed.

The week before the vote I had spent long days on the Hill visiting the offices of sympathetic members and staff. For weeks, numerous organizations such as the Family Research Council, Concerned Women for America, the Center for Christian Statesmanship, and the Traditional Values Coalition had been urging lawmakers to pass the measure. We argued that American culture needed to return to the strongest possible standards of right and wrong. And what better place to begin than the most enduring of all such standards, the Ten Commandments? When I wasn't actually on the Hill, I was back at my office, six blocks away on Pennsylvania Avenue, making phone calls, faxing letters, and sending e-mail notes, urging everyone I knew to do everything they could to help us achieve the two-thirds majority necessary for passage.

On the day of the vote, I was breathlessly making my way to the chamber through a basement tunnel in the Capitol when I spied, of all people, the late California Congressman Sonny Bono, who was using the ATM machine outside the federal credit union office. After retiring from his fame as Sonny of the 1960s music duo Sonny and Cher, he had become a restaurateur and, later, mayor of Palm Springs, California. He was now in his second term as Representative from that district. He seemed an unlikely candidate to help us win our resolution, but with only minutes left, I was ready to make my pitch to anyone.

"Congressman Bono," I called, presenting my business card with my left hand while extending my right for a handshake.

Startled, he examined the card and looked up at me, saying nothing.

"Congressman," I said, "in just a few moments a resolution will be presented affirming the Ten Commandments as the cornerstone to a just and moral society. If we are to return this nation to moral sanity, Sir, and solve the violence and crime that vex our culture, what better, more time-tested way to do it than with these?"

He looked at me as if I had just arrived from Mars. Then he pursed his lips, lifted his eyebrows and grinned.

"You know, Reverend," he began in his trademark pinched voice, "You make sense. We gotta do something."

Then he flashed two thumbs up and declared, "You got me, babe!"

It had been the only light moment in an otherwise sober affair. In the end, the vote was 295 to 125 in favor of the resolution. A framed copy of it awaited me next to the podium in the Capitol basement meeting room.

Snapping back into the present, I jostled for position at the podium and conspicuously cleared my throat. The camera lights snapped on with a glare, blinding my view of the audience. When finally cued I declared, "The Ten Commandments embody the highest of human ethics, and starting today, they will be back in view, where they belong."

What began as a tiny spark in Gadsden, Alabama, just three years previously, had burned its way to the steps of the world's greatest political and cultural superpower in 1997, and has now become a national firestorm. A new revolution is indeed underway, but it is not a revolution in the political sense. It is a revolution of the human heart.

WORD
ONE

"I AM THE LORD YOUR GOD,

WHO BROUGHT YOU OUT OF THE

LAND OF EGYPT, OUT OF THE

HOUSE OF BONDAGE. YOU

SHALL HAVE NO OTHER

GODS BEFORE ME."

EXODUS 20:2-3

"What if God had a name? What would it be, and would we call it to His face?" As I surfed the cable stations one bright summer afternoon, the nose-ringed alternative music diva, Joan Osborne, asked this question in her haunting lyrics while a faded home movie played in the video's background. It featured an elderly, bare-chested homely man, suggesting that if we could see God, He might have a potbelly or droopy pectorals. But it wasn't the bizarre imagery that caught my attention, it was Osborne's plaintive inquiry. She seemed sincere in her quandary.

What if God had a name?

What would it be?

Would we call it to His face?

The fact is that God does have a name, and it is a deeply personal one. We are introduced to it in the very first of His Ten Commandments, along with an address where we can always find Him. Why? So people like Joan can know that God invites us to call Him by this name and seek for Him.

It is not easy to see God's name in most translations of the Bible because our English versions follow a time-honored tradition to protect His name from abuse. The method that the ancient Jewish rabbis used for this was to substitute the Hebrew word *Adonai*, or Lord, for each instance in which the actual name of God appears in Holy Scripture. This custom continues today. Though the intention is laudable, wherever the generic title "Lord" replaces the more specific name of God, the harder it is for the uninitiated reader to understand exactly who the text is talking about. After all, many deities are called Lord; for example, the Hindu god Krishna. Like a theological game of *ad libs*, the generic terms, God and Lord, act as blank spaces to be filled in with whatever image or idea the reader associates with them. This fits in perfectly with the trendy religious pluralism that dominates modern American culture, but it violates the principle of the First Commandment.

"Pick a god, any god at all," say the proponents of this philosophy. "You may call God one thing and I may call God another. It doesn't matter who or what it is, so long as you sincerely believe in it." But nothing could be further from what the First Commandment teaches. In the original Hebrew in which it was delivered to Moses, this commandment says very specifically, "I am *Yahweh*, who led you out from slavery in Egypt. You are to place no other gods in front of Me."

The use of this specific name clearly indicates that there is only one, true God. And He makes it equally clear that we are not to claim any other besides Him. So, we are not left with the frustrating pursuit of an elusive and unknowable being who so many religions pursue and never catch. The Scripture tells us exactly who this one God is and how we can connect with Him. *Yahweh* is not a vague "higher power" who cannot be known and embraced. He is a personal being whose name reveals to us what He is like and how we are to relate to Him.

THE TETRAGRAMATAN

God's principal name, *Yahweh* is deeply personal and virtually unique. When He wrote it for Moses on the tablets of stone atop Mount Sinai, it most probably looked like this: YHWH. The four Hebrew letters that spell out His name are often referred to collectively as the *tetragramatan*, or the "four letters," because there are no other four letters that compare to them. No one really knows how this name was originally pronounced because the ancient Hebrew alphabet was made up only of consonant letters. Without vowels, each generation had to learn how to pronounce words by listening to their elders. Because this name was so rarely heard, the sound of it faded as the centuries went by. At one point, a Jewish philosopher named Maimonides (My-mon-neh-dees)[2] added long and short sounds to the four consonant letters by interspersing the vowels belonging to the alternate name, *Adonai,* in between them. This became "Jehovah." Though it is not actually God's name, Jehovah helped to preserve God's unique identity in our memory.

Knowing God's real name helps us to understand a lot about Him. In the ancient Near East, names were not only a means of identification, but also helped to record family histories, major events associated with a person's life, and even their character traits. Sometimes names were changed because the character or circumstances of a person's life changed. And often a person had more than one name so more information could be known about them. A good example of such a case is found in Jacob of the Old Testament. After an unusual encounter with God, God gave him the name of Israel. (See Genesis 35:9-10.) He is referred to by both names throughout the Bible.

God also has multiple names to reveal His character and will to people. His principal name, *Yahweh,* is often called *the name par excellence.* It is the most comprehensive of any of God's names and is probably related to a very old Semitic idiom meaning, "I will be all that is necessary as the occasion arises."[3] Reflecting the breadth of God's nature and authority, all of His other highly descriptive names fill in the details of how God can be all that is necessary in whatever situation. A sampling of these names include *El Shaddai* (God Almighty), *El Eyon* (Most High God), *Cur* (Rock), *Avhir* (The Strong One), *Eloheem Shawboth* (God of Hosts), *Yahweh-Shalom* (God our Peace), *Yahweh-Rophe* (God our Healer), *Yahweh-Tziskenu* (God our Righteousness), and *Yahweh-Yireh* (God our Provider).

God's description of himself is complete in His names. He gives every facet of His character, thinking, will, and behavior. If I were to be as thorough, I would say to someone I had never met before, "I am Rob Schenck. I own a house in Northern Virginia. Our home is a sanctuary, where love bonds together the people who live there. I am a minister, and I work in Washington, D.C., where I write books and articles and bring the Word of God to officials on Capitol Hill." Using such a comprehensive introduction would tell you a lot about me, most likely more than you would want to know! In fact, there probably wouldn't be much more you could ask after hearing my self-revealing presentation.

On the other hand, if I were to be superficial as are too many of our Bible translations when interpreting the First Commandment, I would say, "Hello, I am a man and I live in Virginia." This would get a very different reaction. People generally want to know more about me than this. Only then can they really be comfortable with me because missing facts leave room for suspicion and error. What do you think would happen if a man attempted to send an intimate note to his wife by addressing it, "To the woman I love on First Street"? Chances are that it would be returned, but it could also be delivered to the wrong person, causing much more serious problems!

This is true in relation to God. For this reason, the First Commandment is precise. It tells us exactly who we are to worship and obey. *Yahweh*, God Almighty who alone can be all things to all people, is the God of Israel. The Israelite nation was surrounded by tribes that worshipped all kinds of gods, but *Yahweh* demanded that they accord this status only to Him. (See Deuteronomy 4:35.) We will see in the next chapter that the Second Commandment describes *Yahweh* as a "jealous God," demonstrating that He will not share His status with anyone or anything else. (See Exodus 20:5.)

Such an exclusive claim will make some people angry and others nervous, particularly when "inclusiveness" is so popular in modern American culture: *How audacious that we should think that our God is the only God!* I suppose this isn't difficult to understand at a time when the notion of fidelity isn't in vogue. Sex has gone from being a sacred act of lifelong commitment to a weekend sport. The world's new divorce-on-demand generation has introduced what amounts to serial monogamy, which is becoming indistinguishable from the ancient practices of polygamy. Promises are routinely violated and oaths are disregarded. In a world of promiscuous relationships and meaningless words, why should we be exclusively devoted to anything, including God?

In contrast, *Yahweh* made an everlasting covenant, an unbreakable and exclusive agreement, with Israel (see 1 Chronicles 16:17). He pledged His love and care only to one people. He is the faithful God (see Psalm 18:25), married forever to His people. "'Return, faithless people,' declares the Lord, 'for I am your husband'" (Jeremiah 3:14 NIV).

Therefore, this First Commandment is about the virtue of fidelity as much as it is about God's identity. The Canaanites, who inhabited the land the Israelites were told to conquer and occupy, had a promiscuous worldview. Their gods were immoral and unfaithful. Consequently, so were those who worshipped them. Like gods—like people. A Canaanite would easily transfer his loyalty to a new divinity each time he moved to a new city. In contrast, the devotee to *Yahweh* is to be forever monotheistic.

Of course, most Americans wouldn't consider themselves polytheists. That is, they would grant you that there is only one God. In reality, though, many of these same people are for all practical purposes serving many gods. The German reformer, Martin Luther, once said, "Whatever you set your heart on and rely on, that is really your god."[4] So whenever we devote ourselves to those things that take precedence over what God wants of us, whether friends, lovers, jobs, careers, sports, education, ambitions, we violate this rule in spirit.[5]

Yahweh is to be number one in our lives, not only in the sense of being "the only," but also in terms of supremacy. He is to be the highest in rank, the chief, the boss. As such, our relationship to Him is to order all of our other affairs.

FINDING GOD

It used to be that in America when someone went looking for God, there were only two places to look: church or synagogue. But this is no longer true. As Terry Muck points out in his book, *Alien Gods on American Turf*, there are more than 1,500 religious groups in the United States, 600 of which have non-Christian roots. This is mostly due to the influx of Asian and Middle Eastern immigrants who bring with them varieties of Buddhism, Hinduism, Shintoism, and Islam.[6] When you add to these the smaller influences of Native North and South American, African, and Oceanic religions, along with the growing phenomenon of New Age spirituality and even resurgent paganism and witchcraft, the cacophony of spiritual claims in contemporary America is staggering. Growing numbers of New Age seminars, bookstores, and websites, along with the increased visibility of neo-pagan personalities and events (for example the Burning Man who now draws thousands of participants) is testimony to this fascination with "alternative" religious belief.

While many of these religions have enriched American culture, as the addition of immigrants have since the nation's inception, the result has been spiritual confusion. Although the vast majority of Americans still claim affiliation with a Christian denomination,[7] for the most part such claims don't translate into vigorous faith. Practical Atheism (the disavowal of God altogether) or Agnosticism (the confessed "ignorance" of religious belief which makes no demands on its adherents) seem to be the rule of the day.

How can we then cut through this modern-day pantheon to find the One True God? By working our way through the Bible, we discover who God is. We learn that He is alive. (See Jeremiah 10:10.) He is personal (see Exodus 3:14 and Psalm 139:1-4). And we can know Him (see John 17:3). We also learn that God needs nothing outside of Himself in order to exist (see Exodus 3:14, 6:3).

God is unchanging (see Psalm 102:27; Malachi 3:6; and James 1:17). He embodies truth (see Deuteronomy 32:4; John 17:3; and 1 John 5:20), love (see Deuteronomy 7:13; John 3:16, 17:24; Romans 15:30; and 1 John 3:16, 4:8), moral excellence and holiness (see Exodus 15:11, 19:10-16; Isaiah 6:3; and Hebrews 12:10).

God is merciful (see Deuteronomy 13:17; 2 Samuel 24:14; 1 Chronicles 21:13; Nehemiah 9:31; and Psalm 25:6), faithful (see Psalm 84:11, 91:4; Matthew 6:33; and 1 Corinthains 2:9), and just (see Genesis 18:25-26; Deuteronomy 32:4; Psalm 5:5, 7:9-12, 18:24-26; and Matthew 5:48).

In terms of age, God is eternal, without beginning or end (see Genesis 21:33; Deuteronomy 32:40; Psalm 90:2, 102:27; Romans 1:20; and 1 Timothy 1:17). Regarding presence, He is everywhere at once, what is called omnipresent in theology (see Psalm 139:7-10; Jeremiah 23:23-24; and Acts 17:27-28). And He is omniscient, knowing everything—past, present, and future—at the same time (see Genesis 16:13; Psalm 4:5; and Isaiah 48:18).

We can also locate Him by using the address He gives for himself in the second clause of the First Commandment: "I am the Lord your God, *who brought you out of the land of Egypt.*" To find *Yahweh*, we must go there, to that awesome moment sometime around 1300 B.C., when God rescued His people from Pharaoh's cruel domination. (See Exodus 1-12.)

When God delivered Israel from Egypt, He also established one of the most important Jewish holidays, the Passover. Passover, from the Hebrew word *pesach*, means to pass, spring over, or spare. It refers to the events recorded in Exodus 12-13, when the death angel, sent by God to destroy the firstborn of Egypt, passed over the houses of the Hebrews which were marked by lamb's blood on the lintels and doorposts.

Today, this holiday is so significant that each spring, many religious Jewish mothers may zealously purge their houses of any leavened bread and even sweep, vacuum, and pick up the crumbs. They may have the carpets professionally cleaned, the basement and garage straightened, and even paint, wallpaper, or build an addition, all in preparation for the sacred week-long festival. In Israel, the Passover is celebrated over seven days, while in the rest of the world it is observed for eight days, but Jews all over the world remember how God supernaturally freed them from cruel slavery.

The *seder*, or program, that surrounds the Passover meal eaten on the eve of the holiday, is an elaborate banquet presided over by the father of the family, who stands at the dinner table wrapped in a special white robe called a *kittle*, which represents the garment of the ancient high priest. The evening will feature symbolic foods, prayers, readings, songs, and tableware that reveal God's nature through rehearsing His behavior towards His people and His enemies.[8] The entire story of the Exodus—the enslavement of the Hebrew people by Pharaoh, the brave leadership of Moses, the miraculous signs of God's power, and the successful emancipation of the Hebrew nation—are all told in one sitting.

The recounting of the Exodus story at the Passover seder demonstrates that *Yahweh* is a *saving God*. He saves those in peril, as the Israelites were saved out of their enslavement in Egypt. In the New Testament, the sinful state of humankind is often made analogous to slavery. (See Romans 6:19; Galatians 4:3.) The saving *Yahweh* is embodied in Jesus (see John 1:18), whose real birth name is *Yeshua*, which means *Yahweh Saves*. The *Jewish New Testament* translation of Matthew 1:21 by David Stern makes this very clear, "'Yosef, son of David, do not be afraid to take Miriyam home with you as your wife; for what has been conceived in her is from the *Ruach-HaKodesh*. She will give birth to a son, and you are to name him *Yeshua*, [which means 'Adonai saves,'] because he will save his people from their sins.'" It is Jesus who saves His people from their sins. (See Matthew 1:21.)

Passover should be celebrated by Jews and Christians alike because it instructs us, in a dramatic and entertaining way, about the One True God and His redemptive nature. The Passover ritual also teaches that God is a moral being. He is the God of right and wrong. What Pharaoh did to the Israelites by enslaving them and abusing them was morally wrong. God intervened to stop suffering and punished Pharaoh severely for his actions. This again demonstrates that He is righteous and just. *Yahweh* is the only and absolute moral authority in the universe. He is the standard by which we are to measure all things. As such, He imposes certain claims on human behavior.

Until we realize and accept this truth of God's supreme moral authority, we are doomed to live in an insecure world of moral relativism where there is no absolute right or wrong. If this is true, then there is really nothing that we are forbidden from doing. The implications of this are far reaching. Associate Professor of Philosophy Christina Hoff Sommers of Clark University tells the story of a teacher in Newton, Massachusetts, who had attended numerous "values clarification workshops." This is a method of moral education that maintains the teacher should never directly tell her students what is right and wrong, but rather apply techniques that help students come to their own conclusions.

The teacher was assiduously applying what she had been taught in these seminars when her sixth graders announced that they valued cheating and wanted to be free to do it on their upcoming test. The teacher was uncomfortable with her dilemma. So she told the students that since *she* was opposed to cheating, they couldn't do it in her class. "In my class you must be honest. In other areas of your life you may be free to cheat," she said.[9]

This story explains the moral dilemma in America. Without a moral standard, we are free to do whatever we please and powerless to correct bad behavior. Nearly three-quarters of today's high school students and almost half of college students admit that they routinely cheat. Thirty-four percent of young people surveyed by *U.S. News and World Report* magazine said that they would steal from an employer if given the opportunity.[10] An entire generation of youth in the inner cities embrace music and lifestyles that glorify murder, assault, rape, and robbery. Younger and younger offenders are being arrested for gruesome crimes.

Kids put two and two together. If the adults in their lives are telling them that there is no such thing as a moral authority, the only thing preventing them from acting the way they please is the threat of punishment. And if they can get around that or learn to live with it (as more and more repeat criminals are doing), they can literally get away with murder—and have.

RECOGNIZING GOD'S AUTHORITY

For anything to be orderly, someone must be in charge and have the last say. This is especially true when it comes to morality. This is the basis upon which the Founders of our country crafted our theory of self-government. Back in the eighteenth century, most civic leaders were well educated in the Bible and religious things in general. Most were active churchgoers, and some were even clergy. For example, two famous ministers of the Gospel were John Jay, first Chief Justice of the United States, and John Witherspoon, a signer of the Declaration of Independence. They knew exactly which God they were duty bound to acknowledge, and they believed if they did not do so, their new democratic republic would become a nightmare of moral anarchy.

In his famous address to the Delaware Chiefs on May 12, 1797, George Washington said, "You do well to wish to learn our arts and ways of life, and above all, the religion of Jesus Christ."[11] Others among the Founders were equally clear. Benjamin Rush, a signer of the Declaration of Independence and a philosopher of the Revolution, wrote: "The only means of establishing and perpetuating our republican forms of government (is) the universal education of our youth in the principles of Christianity by the means of the Bible."[12]

Jedediah Morse, a patriot who was called the "Father of American Geography," said in a sermon delivered at Charleston, Massachusetts, in 1799: "Whenever the pillars of Christianity shall be overthrown, our present republican forms of government, and all blessings which flow from them, must fall with them."[13]

James McHenry, who signed the Constitution, said, "The Holy Scriptures . . . can alone secure to society order and peace, and to our courts of justice and constitutions of government, purity, stability, and usefulness."[14]

When George Washington and his contemporaries referred to God, they had a specific idea of whom they were talking about. Their understanding of God was principally a New Testament understanding, which necessarily incorporates Old Testament moral law. T. Rees states, "Jesus Christ and His disciples inherited the idea of God revealed in the Old Testament, as it survived in the purer strata of Jewish religion."[15] Jesus himself quoted from the keystone of the Jewish Torah when He was asked about the greatest of the commandments: "Hear O Israel, the Lord our God, the Lord is one" (Mark 12:29). In referring to "the religion of Jesus Christ," Washington directly connected with the God of the Bible. His was the same God of whom Moses and Jesus spoke.

It was John Quincy Adams, however, who best summarized how critical a role the recognition of God and His laws must play in our national life when he said, "Human legislators can undertake only to prescribe the actions of men; they acknowledge their inability to govern and direct sentiments of the heart. . . . It is one of the greatest marks of Divine favor bestowed upon the children of Israel that the legislator gave them rules not only of action, but for the government of the heart."[16]

It is this issue of governance that is at the center of the controversy over the posting of the Ten Commandments in Alabama. What Judge Moore did in his courtroom was to acknowledge the absolute moral authority of the One True God. His attorney argued before the Alabama Supreme Court: "American history abounds with evidence that the mere acknowledgment of God by government is not a violation of the establishment clauses of the United States or Alabama Constitutions. It is axiomatic that our nation and its laws . . . were founded on a belief in and dependence upon God."[17] His legal case is so compelling that I have included Judge Moore's law review article, *Religion in the Public Square*, in the back of this book.

This dependence on God is axiomatic, or self-evident, because there would never have been a break with England if the colonists had not asserted their God-given rights of life, liberty, and the pursuit of happiness. These rights are not given by any human agency, including government. They are given by God who is the supreme moral authority. Therefore, no man has the right to abridge them or take them away.

If, on the other hand, a nation and its people turn away from any acknowledgment of the One True God and His moral laws, then these freedoms can and will be taken away. Either directly by the governing authority, or by the moral degeneration of the people themselves, liberty will disappear from those who reject liberty's Giver. In a society where I am not duty-bound to respect my neighbor's God-given rights, I cannot expect my neighbor to respect mine.

In an 1852 speech, Robert Winthrop, Speaker of the House for the Thirtieth Congress, said, "Men, in a word, must necessarily be controlled either by a power within them or by a power without them; either by the Word of God or the strong arm of man; either by the Bible or by the bayonet."[18]

No Others Allowed

The last clause of the First Commandment, *"You shall have no other gods before me,"* is surely its most politically incorrect assertion. We have already established that God requires an exclusive relationship with humankind, but here He makes it emphatic. To the original listeners this part of the commandment was quite forceful. It said very curtly, "Don't put any gods in front of my face!" The phrase here literally reads, *"Lo yeyeh le-ach elohim acherim al panai!—No gods to be in my face!"* This was a pretty effective way for God to get His point across. Quite accidentally, my children once did something to illustrate God's point.

When my children were small and I was serving as a minister in a large church, they would often complain that they had to stand around bored and hungry after service because the people wanted to talk too long with me. One time they came up with what they thought was an ingenious plan. My daughter begged to be lifted up on my shoulder while someone was asking me a question. Then my son, who was the younger and smaller, passed her a drawing from a Sunday school lesson. *Voile!* The paper was suddenly in front of my face, cutting off my conversation. This is a perfect illustration of what happens when we place other gods in front of *Yahweh.* Once the drawing was between me and the person talking to me, it effectively cut off communication. In the same way, those things we deem more important than God cut off our communication with Him.

If we are to return to spiritual health and moral sanity, whether as individuals, families, communities, or as a nation, we must put away all the things that get in the way of our communication with God. Whether it is our ignorance, our arrogant self-reliance, our lust for power and pleasure, or our outright defiance and rebellion, it must be put aside in repentance.

The First Commandment is the first step on a long road to healing America spiritually as individuals and families. Recognition of the One True God will lead us back to moral rectitude, proper social intercourse, and civility. Only *Yahweh* can take us out of slavery and into the Promised Land!

The following words from the Old Testament book of Chronicles have been quoted often in recent years, and that is no accident because there is no better way to summarize what we have learned from this First Word from Sinai: "If My people who are called by My name will humble themselves, and pray and seek My face, and turn from their wicked ways, then I will hear from heaven, and will forgive their sin and heal their land" (2 Chronicles 7:14). When a nation turns back to God and repents, He heals them and moral prosperity returns to their land. He will never turn away from those who seek Him:

> **And those who know Your name will put their trust in You; for You, Lord, have not forsaken those who seek You.**
>
> PSALM 9:10

MORTAL AND PECEL:
MAKING POISON WORSHIP

CHAPTER TWO

The title of this chapter is a play on words. It is with "mortar and pestle" that the pharmacist mixes his potion. Here I've used the term "mortal," referring to man, and *pecel* (prounounced peh-sel), the Hebrew word used in the Bible for a carved image, or idol. It is the mixing of these two, human beings and idols, that makes for a deadly spiritual elixir. The Second Commandment may surprise you, however. It is not just about idols. It is about something far more serious.

◢

It is a gray day in October, and it is raining in New York City. Harley Belew and I cross Pearl Street to climb the long ascent of stairs leading up to the majestic Greek Revival Courthouse for the Southern District of Manhattan. The closer we get, the more our conversation is drowned out by the chanting mob that surges threateningly towards us from behind a long stretch of police barricades.

Harley is a producer for a religious radio station in Fort Worth, Texas. We are appearing in federal court after being sued for organizing pro-life activity during the 1992 Democratic National Convention. Abortion is a major theme during this nomination process as Governor Bill Clinton of Arkansas reverses his previous pro-life position to become the "pro-choice" candidate.

A gaggle of bare-breasted lesbian activists, their faces and chests spattered with fake blood, angrily shake their fists at us while whirling rubber snakes above their heads as they chant: "Not the church, not the state, women will decide their fate!"

"Reverend Schenck, Reverend Schenck," one young woman calls to me. "Want to kiss my fetus?" She holds up what appears to be a urine-filled jar with a Barbie doll suspended inside. Their bizarre street theater reminds me of a scene from a B-rated horror movie.

"Don't you shove your morality down our throats!" a goateed young man shouts, spraying his saliva on my face as I pass by him to go into the building. Amazingly, once behind the thick brass doors and marble walls, I can still hear the pandemonium outside.

The brouhaha on the courthouse steps that day has actually been going on for a terribly long time. It is a continuation of a moral rebellion that began thousands of years before. It was happening when Moses came down from Sinai. Ever since Adam and Eve disobeyed God's order not to eat from the Tree of the Knowledge of Good and Evil (see Genesis 2-3, especially 2:16-17), the human race has made continuous bids for moral autonomy. Every generation since humankind's progenitors fell in the Garden of Eden has attempted to fashion for themselves their own code of right and wrong. Like new lines of designer jeans, the lists of do's and don'ts have alternately shrunk and lengthened over the years, depending on what's hot and what's not—and appropriate idols have been fashioned to accommodate the hot.

W O R D
TWO

"YOU SHALL NOT MAKE FOR YOURSELF
A CARVED IMAGE—ANY LIKENESS OF
ANYTHING THAT IS IN HEAVEN ABOVE,
OR THAT IS IN THE EARTH BENEATH, OR
THAT IS IN THE WATER UNDER THE EARTH;
YOU SHALL NOT BOW DOWN TO THEM NOR
SERVE THEM. FOR I, THE LORD YOUR GOD,
AM A JEALOUS GOD, VISITING THE INIQUITY
OF THE FATHERS UPON THE CHILDREN TO
THE THIRD AND FOURTH GENERATIONS OF
THOSE WHO HATE ME, BUT SHOWING MERCY
TO THOUSANDS, TO THOSE WHO LOVE ME
AND KEEP MY COMMANDMENTS."

EXODUS 20:4-6

WHAT IS IDOLATRY?

What do you think of when you hear the word "idolatry"? Perhaps, like many, you imagine a primitive tribesman bowing his head to the ground in front of a carved statue. If you do, you are partly right, but only in a technical sense. Bowing to a statue is an expression of idolatry, but it is only an expression. Idolatry itself is not about statues at all, but rather about the motivation for making them.

Contrary to popular misunderstanding, this commandment is not a prohibition of religious art. This is not a law against stained glass windows, crucifixes, pictures of Jesus, or other renderings of God and His heavenly angelic beings. If it were, then we would have to draw the impossible conclusion that God contradicted himself when He ordered the Israelites to decorate the Tabernacle with images of heavenly beings made out of gold.[1] (See Exodus 25:18.)

Idolatry is, more than anything else, a projection of the human will upon a god-like subject. In other words, it is the usurpation of ultimate authority by a human agency. It reduces "God" to something that can be controlled, bullied, or deceived by man. In America, the actual worship of physical images has always been a rare practice, though it can be found. It is more common to find those who worship ideas or ideologies that set themselves against the God of the Old and New Testaments. This practice is as much idolatry as statue worship.

Idolatry is the purest act of human pride. It seeks to control and manipulate God. It was for this sin that Isaiah the prophet denounced the King of Babylon:

> **How you are fallen from heaven,**
> **O Day Star, son of the morning!**
> **How you are cut down to the ground,**
> **You who weakened the nations!**

> For you have said in your heart:
> "I will ascend into heaven,
> I will exalt my throne above the stars of God;
> I will also sit on the mount of the congregation
> On the farthest sides of the north;
> I will ascend above the heights of the clouds,
> I will be like the Most High!"
>
> ISAIAH 14:12-14

Exalting oneself to Godhood, if you will, suggests that there is no higher moral authority to which one must make account than oneself. This was common among ancient monarchs who often referred to themselves as gods. The story of the Jewish Holiday of Chanukah (Hanukkah) revolves around the pompous and grandiose Antiochus, the Syrian despot who called himself Epiphanes, "the revealed one." Antiochus decreed that the Jews could follow their religion, provided that their God was subordinated to the Emperor. The Jews knew that the One True God would bow to no human being, so they fought back in His name and miraculously reclaimed the Holy Temple that had been polluted by a statue of the tyrant.[2]

Emperors are not the only ones who play God, however. Ordinary people play God when they decide for themselves what is right and what is wrong. It is in making moral judgments that the highest expression of power is exercised. The course of our very lives stems from our presuppositions of right and wrong. In a society that makes its own judgments about the ultimate questions of life, including who lives or dies, one's own existence is never secure.

THE MEANING OF THE SECOND COMMANDMENT

This commandment, prohibiting the making of idols or "graven images," is aimed directly at this human predisposition for taking matters of right and wrong, or ultimate moral authority, into our own hands. This is idolatry in its purest form. When a person chooses a lifestyle that violates the moral will of God, such as the homosexual activists who harassed me outside of the courthouse, they erect an image that reflects their own nature rather than the nature of the One True God.

Properly understood, the Second Commandment is simply a reiteration of the directive God gave to Adam and Eve in the Garden, "And the Lord God commanded the man, saying, 'You are free to eat from any tree in the garden; but you must not eat from the tree of the knowledge of good and evil, for when you eat of it you will surely die'" (Genesis 2:16-17 NIV). By instructing the newly formed humans not to partake of the tree, God was prohibiting them from putting their hands to "the knowledge of good and evil" and meddling with morality. They were not to change in any way what God had declared to be right and wrong. They were endowed with no right to take possession of humankind's moral code. It was off-limits. They were allowed to put their hand to other things, but not to this one.

Notice, though, that God first gave *permission* before He a gave *prohibition* to Adam and Eve. So many take this passage to be a blanket decree against having fun and enjoying life, but nothing could be further from God's original intent! When God said, "Of every tree of the garden *you may eat freely*," He was actually saying, "Go ahead, Adam and Eve, enjoy what I have given you. Live life to its fullest. Enjoy the beauty of My creation, the scents, the tastes, the sensations, they're all for your pleasure. The only thing you must not do is usurp My moral authority. Only I possess the right to decide what is good and what is evil."

The lesbian activists I encountered outside the courthouse in Manhattan were sure that if the Bible restricts us from one sort of pleasure, then it must restrict all pleasures. But this is not so. One of the Old Testament poetical books, Song of Solomon (also called Song of Songs), celebrates sexual pleasure, but only inside the moral parameters for which its Creator designed it to function, which is marriage between a man and a woman. (See Genesis 2; Leviticus 18:22; 20:13; 1 Corinthians 6:9; 1 Timothy 1:9-10; Romans 1:20-32.)

Shortly before my trial in New York City, I participated in a pro-life prayer walk through the city with other religious leaders. Along the way, a young man appeared on the sidelines, screaming to us that he was HIV positive. He asked us why we hated him so much. I turned and asked, "Whatever gave you that idea?"

"You wouldn't ever let me in your church!" he shouted.

"Oh, you're wrong," I said, pausing and stepping away from the parade of ministers and priests. "I wouldn't only allow you into my church, I would welcome you with a holy kiss."

With that, I gently embraced the young man and kissed him on his neck in typical Christian fashion. He was stunned. I said to him, "That may have been the first nonsexual kiss you've received from a man. You see, God allows men to love men; in fact, He commands men to love men, but never sexually. If you play by His rules, the Lord will show you the joy of living." He began weeping and I prayed with him.

Eve was beguiled by the serpent's suggestion that if she were to take of the forbidden fruit, she would become just like God. (See Genesis 3:1-3.) In other words, once she was "just like God," Eve wouldn't have to listen to the rules anymore. She would now be able to make them herself. The Second Commandment stands in stark contrast to this wrong-headed assumption. The key to understanding this is the Hebrew word that we translate "idol" or "graven image."

Pecel (peh' sel) is the Hebrew word for "graven image." This refers to a physical object that is "graven" or "tooled" by a human hand but asserted to have divine powers. This could be a statue, a painting, or anything that has its origin in human artistic prowess or ingenuity. "Graven" stresses the human crafting of the image and the worship of it, not the image itself. The idol can also be something intangible, like the ideas I spoke of earlier in this chapter. For most people still clinging to the ideology in the former Soviet Union, Communist China, or Castro's Cuba, communism is more than a philosophy; it is an object of worship.

It is not a thing or idea that constitutes the violation of the Second Commandment. No physical object or humanly contrived philosophy is, in and of itself, inherently evil. The emphasis here is not on the object or idea, but rather on the making of it into a deity or an object of worship. This is why I prefer the translation, "graven image," as it is in the *Authorized Version*, or even "carved image," as it is in the *New King James Version*. Whenever I use my hand or my mind to shape or craft something into a god that isn't God, I violate the Second Commandment.

"I the Lord your God am a jealous God" (Exodus 20:5), *Yahweh* declares. He will allow no substitutes for Himself. He loves His creation too much to give any member of it up to unfit surrogates. Godly jealousy is not the insecure, insane, and possessive human jealousy that we often interpret this word to mean. Rather, it is an intensely caring devotion to the objects of His love, like a mother's jealous protection of her children, a father's jealous guarding of his home, or a professional's jealous defense of their reputation.

Idolatry subverts this protective relationship. If God were to allow His people to engage in idol worship, He would be willfully abandoning us to the numerous harmful counterfeits who seek to inflict cruel disappointment and disillusionment on humanity every day.

THE NEW AMERICAN IDOLATRY

Return with me for a moment to that gray day in Manhattan. The pro-abortion demonstrators were essentially saying, "We're not playing by God's rules anymore. We don't like the way He does things. We don't like His rules about sex and babies. We're going to have sex with anyone we please, and if we want to, we'll get rid of any babies we conceive by aborting them. We're making our own rules now!"

These activists are an echo of those who have rejected God and His commands throughout history. Instead of the young MTV generation, they could be the Hebrews who dressed themselves in the finery of their pagan Egyptian captors and then indulged in sexual revelry at the foot of Mount Sinai while Moses was receiving the Ten Commandments.

When I think of those lost souls on the courthouse steps, my heart goes out to them. I can only imagine how the Lord weeps for them, as He must have for the Samaritan woman at the well (see John 4) or the rich young ruler (see Luke 18:18). As I stood among them and they hissed at me, spit at me, and even urinated on me, my impulse was to somehow communicate to them the enormous love of God who cares enough to enforce the rules that are meant only for their protection and happiness.

Unfortunately, cheering these wayward souls on toward misery and death are major forces within American culture. Among these cultural cheerleaders are the arts and entertainment industry (especially Hollywood) and cultural and professional groups like the National Education Association and the American Psychological Association—all of which expressly endorse sinful human behavior. To add to these influences, the Republican Party, often seen as the conservative counterbalance in American politics, is being influenced more and more by so-called moderates who embrace the very same patterns of immoral behavior the Democrats promote and approve. As is often the case in human history, money talks.

Several large, multinational corporations, including Disney, MCI, Sprint, McDonalds, and Microsoft, have all jumped on the diversity bandwagon by offering full company benefits to the unmarried partners of their employees. These modern-day idolaters think they are sending their constituents a message of personal liberation and self-actualization, when they are actually feeding them to the lions. This organized rebellion against God extends to the most powerful places in American society: At this writing, the White House and the Federal Judiciary. Nowhere is it better illustrated than in recent government efforts to elevate homosexual eroticism to the equivalent of heterosexual love.

Shortly after President Bill Clinton took office in 1993, a major campaign to boost the image of those who practice homosexual behavior began in nearly every department of the federal government. The ban on homosexual behavior in the military was lifted. Organizations calling themselves Gay, Lesbian, or Bisexual Employees (G.L.O.B.E.) had the official imprimatur and support of the Executive Branch. Representatives of G.L.O.B.E. were directed to conduct special events tied to Gay, Lesbian, or Bisexual Awareness Months.

The most blatant endorsement of immorality on the part of a high-profile federal official came when the President himself (arguably the most powerful agent for advancing the sexual counter-culture movement) addressed the annual dinner of the self-styled Human Rights Campaign (HRC) in November of 1997. This homosexual and lesbian political action group has been a major force throughout the Clinton Administration.

Mr. Clinton's speech was the first ever delivered by a sitting president in person to a gathering of homosexual activists. Joining him that night in the ballroom of the Grand Hyatt Hotel in downtown

Washington, D.C., were a number of White House officials, including his chief of staff, deputy chief of staff for policy and political affairs, press secretary, AIDS czar, communications director, and his full-time special assistant/liaison to the gay and lesbian community. Mr. Clinton began his remarks that night by recognizing the large number of his homosexual political appointees who were present.

The President then focused on his vision of an America where homosexuals would be fully affirmed in their behavioral disorders. He encouraged them to expect a new "liberated" America in which they would be free to talk about it, exhibit it, and even be applauded for it. "I want this country to embrace the wider world . . . and I want us to come together across all our lines of difference into one America . . . I think if we . . . believed in a community of all Americans, we could truly meet every problem we have."[3] Incredibly, President Clinton proposed that realizing such a vision (which included recognizing homosexuality and heterosexuality as compatible equals) would lead to solving every human problem!

At the end of the evening, Elizabeth Birch, executive director of the HRC, took to the podium to declare that there could only be one explanation for the historic visit of the president: "Divine intervention!" According to her, God had to have approved of the machinations of her group. If a president had kowtowed to her group's demands, what right did God have in doing any differently? The HRC is on a roll. Vice President Al Gore, the leading Democratic contender for the presidency in 2000, also addressed the group, pledging the full support of his office in helping homosexuals achieve their goals of legal marriage.

It bears mentioning here that homosexual political and social activism is not the same thing as the private sin of homosexual desire.[4] Those who struggle with homosexual desire as a private sin are no different from any other person. We are all sinners and we all struggle against temptations that fall into one of three categories: the lust of the flesh, the lust of the eyes, or the pride of life. (See 1 John 2:16.) At one time or another, we are all tempted in one of these areas. Some of us succeed in resisting these temptations; others of us do not. The Bible has promises for both:

> **Blessed is the man who endures temptation; for when he has been approved, he will receive the crown of life which the Lord has promised to those who love Him.**
>
> JAMES 1:12

> **God is faithful, who will not allow you to be tempted beyond what you are able, but with the temptation will also make a way of escape, that you may be able to bear it.**
>
> 1 CORINTHIANS 10:13

Let there be no mistake about the fact that the homosexual political and social activist movement is something different from homosexual sin. This movement, better known as The Gay Agenda, is an attempt to morally legitimize sin and to institutionalize it in the culture. This waving of the fist at God is almost always a corporate act rather than a private one, and it has far greater consequences. For this, the Bible has an ominous warning:

> **But whoever causes one of these little ones who believe in Me to sin, it would be better for him if a millstone were hung around his neck, and he were drowned in the depth of the sea.**
>
> MATTHEW 18:6

THE LONG MARCH OF CAESAR

The federal courts are the most serious offenders when it comes to this kind of corporate violation of the Second Commandment. The last fifty years have seen a string of enormously consequential decisions by district and appeals courts, as well as the United States Supreme

Court, that have limited religious expression and placed religious believers, particularly Jews and Christians, on the margins of society. By doing so, they have removed God from many corners of American life and have replaced Him with an idol of the secular state.

It is the Supreme Court that is most to blame for this war waged against God during the last half-century. Under the banner of "separation of church and state," the Court has marched in a veritable Roman cavalcade toward the same sort of idolatrous civil religion that brought down that great empire.

The assault began in 1947 with a decision dubbed, "The New Jersey School Bus Case." Officially argued as *Everson* v. *Board of Education of Ewing Township*, this case concerned the reimbursement of parents for bus fare necessary to send their children to independent schools. The plaintiff argued that these reimbursements amounted to a government subsidy, and that doing so for the parents of children at religious schools resulted in government support of religion. They further contended that this was strictly prohibited by the Constitution. Ironically, the plaintiffs lost their case. The justices ruled that the fare reimbursements constituted aid to the families and not a subsidy for the schools. However, the majority opinion included a strong statement that maintained "the separation between church and state is a wall that must be kept high and impenetrable."[5]

The *Everson* case was followed by the *Torqueson* decision of 1961, in which the Supreme Court struck down an oath to God required of all notaries public in the Commonwealth of Pennsylvania. On top of this came *Engle* v. *Vitale*, which removed prayer from public schools in 1962, and a similar case called *School District of Abington* v. *Schempp* the year following, which did away with Scripture readings over school public address systems.

In 1980, an appeal from Kentucky known as *Stone* v. *Graham* banned the Ten Commandments from display in public schools, even if they are used strictly for historical purposes. A later 1985 decision, *Wallace* v. *Jaffee*, struck down the modification of a 1978 Alabama law that allowed for a moment of silence at the beginning of each school day. The legislature had added a clause that would include "voluntary prayer" during that silent moment. But the new language of the law was challenged and the court eliminated that option from the students' day.

Then, in *Edwards* v. *Aguilard*, a 1987 case from Louisiana, public school teachers were restricted from servicing students in parochial schools. This was later overturned in part, but nevertheless created an atmosphere of hostility and fear between public and parochial schools. Public school personnel were left with the impression that parochial schools were outside the mainstream and perhaps even unconstitutional. Parochial school personnel, on the other hand, sensed the tension and suspicion of their secular counterparts and withdrew from interaction with them.

The most spiritually damaging of any of these types of decisions, however, is the infamous 1973 ruling of the High Court in *Roe* v. *Wade*, which constructed a whole new definition of human life based on an entirely secular, humanistic theory of life's origin. It also struck down foundational rights enunciated in the Declaration of Independence which are secured to every American citizen in the Constitution. Prior to 1973, every American was guaranteed the right to life, liberty, and the pursuit of happiness. This guarantee was based on the presupposition that our most sacred rights come from God:

> When in the Course of human events, it becomes necessary for one people to dissolve the political bands which have connected them with another, and to assume among the powers of the earth, the separate and equal station to which the Laws of Nature and of Nature's God entitle them, a decent respect to the opinions of mankind requires that they should declare the causes which impel them to the separation.

> We hold these truths to be self-evident, that all men are
> created equal, that they are endowed by their Creator with
> certain unalienable Rights, that among these are Life,
> Liberty, and the pursuit of Happiness.

I believe Thomas Jefferson's listing of "life" as the first right in our nation's Declaration of Independence was not a random choice. Without the right to life, liberty and happiness have no meaning.

My generation has a constitutionally protected right to be here based on the presupposition that only the Creator is the giver of life. In contrast, however, my children, because they were born after the *Roe* decision, do not have such a right. They are only here by someone else's permission, namely my wife's, and that only because the U.S. Supreme Court took the power over life away from the "Creator" and gave it, in this instance, to her. Had my wife decided that we were not ready to receive our children when they were conceived (what Justice Harry Blackmun called in *Roe*, "the problem of the unwanted child"[6]) we could have eliminated them without penalty!

This arrogant usurpation of the power over life itself, epitomized in *Roe*, continues apace. In early March 1996, Judge Stephen Reinhardt of the United States Court of Appeals for the Ninth Circuit wrote for a majority of the justices in a case called *Compassion v. State of Washington*. In it, seven of the eleven justices on the appeals panel decided that human beings have an inherent right to kill themselves in whatever manner they wish, including soliciting the assistance of doctors and even strangers to help them do it. In a further offense to the Sixth Commandment, Judge Reinhardt seemed to imply that murdering oneself may, in fact, be a noble act. He suggested that the elderly and infirm may have a duty to commit suicide if their medical care threatens to leave behind excessive bills for their loved ones to pay!

In justifying these claims, Judge Reinhardt cavalierly dismissed five thousand years of Jewish and Christian moral reform and chose instead to base the most important part of his reasoning on pre-Christian and non-Jewish pagan notions about death. He writes in part: "In Greek and Roman times, far from being universally prohibited, suicide was often considered commendable in literature, mythology, and practice."[7]

Judge Reinhardt, like the hecklers outside the courthouse, repeats the sin of Adam and Eve in the Garden. When you don't like what God says, jettison Him and take something else as your final moral authority! Judge Reinhardt exchanges *Yahweh* God for the immoral humanistic pagan notions of ancient Greece and Rome because they conform to his personal will.

What the Judge does not bother to mention in his ruling is that infanticide, certain forms of homicide, and pederasty (adult men having sex with young boys) were also allowed at various times and places in ancient Rome and Greece, and that they were even celebrated as human rights! Nevertheless, he goes on to quote Athenian law: "If you are bowed with grief, abandon life. Let the unhappy man recount his misfortune, let the magistrate supply him with the remedy (usually hemlock poison) and his wretchedness will come to an end."[8]

In rationalizing self-murder, Judge Reinhardt says, "When religious superstitions faded, (the misery of the sufferer) was justification enough."[9]

GRAVEN IMAGES IN GRAVE ROBES

Thanks to the likes of Judge Reinhardt and others, the Federal Judiciary in America has metamorphosed from a simple arbiter of human law into an imperial council of demigods who have hijacked the moral prerogatives that rightly belong only to the One True God. This is what is meant by making a graven image. Once again, it is remaking God in our own image.

This egregious offense to the creator status of God is the emphasis of the Second Commandment. It is the fact that the idol, the graven image, the *pecel*, is the work of our own minds and hands. It comes from us; therefore, it is subject to us. By offering it money, incense, or meat, it changes its disposition toward us and gives us what we want. It does our will; we do not do its will. This is an inversion of a proper relationship to God. The Second Commandment does not allow us to bend and twist God into such a desired shape. On the contrary, it mandates that we conform ourselves to His will. The Old Testament prophet, Isaiah, wrote:

> **You turn things upside down, as if the potter were thought to be like the clay! Shall what is formed say to him who formed it, "He did not make me?" Can the pot say of the potter, "He knows nothing"?**

> ISAIAH 29:16 NIV

Human beings are not to decide who will be their god, what he will be like, and what he will require of them. That has been decided already and is immutably enshrined in the First Commandment.

There are, of course, those who persist in attempting to fashion God in the image they would like. It is being played out vividly in the crusade to legitimize so-called same-sex marriage. We will look at this again in our chapter on adultery, but suffice it to say here that these activists, discontent with God's rule for male with female marriage only (see Genesis 2:24), invent their own criteria for sexual union based on purely subjective and selfish notions.

Of course, in a democratic republic, the government ultimately reflects the will of the people. Political, judicial, and cultural institutions will always reflect, in some part, the people who elect and appoint their leaders. The Second Commandment informs us that we must personally, in each of our hearts, accept God for who He is and what He demands of us, regardless of how we feel about Him.

Furthermore, based on a long history of national homage to the God of the Old and New Testaments, America is obligated to continue in this allegiance. Though our population may change its religious makeup, this does not mean that God changes, nor must our trust in Him. "I am the Lord," He declares in the Bible upon which every President takes his oath of office. "I change not" (Malachi 3:6). And on every minted coin or American dollar bill you will read, "In God We Trust."

The idea that Americans must accommodate every religious and moral idea is disingenuous. The United States was not founded on the sacred writings of Hinduism, the Koran, nor the Communist or Humanist manifestos. Had our nation been founded on such philosophies, we would be a very different country. Witness, for example, Iran, India, the former Soviet Union, or the People's Republic of China. These cultures are quite different, and the majority of Americans would prefer not to be like them because they each limit religious freedom. It is not the Jewish or Christian cultures that quell personal freedoms, as today's false prophets of political correctness so often accuse us of doing. In fact, it can be effectively argued that America has afforded all faiths the greatest religious liberties precisely because it was established on a Jewish and Christian ethic.[10]

In the People's Republic of China or Cuba, which are both purely secular states, there is no guarantee for human rights such as the right to practice one's religion because the state is atheistic and doesn't believe anything comes from God. This being the case, all rights are seen as being granted from the state, so the state is therefore seen as authoritatively endowed to take them away at will.

When I was on a preaching tour of the then newly freed Russian Republic, I visited a government school where I explained to the students what it means for me, personally, to be a Christian. I talked about God's Law and its implications for our lives. Afterwards, the school administrator came up to me with tears in her eyes.

"Please," she implored, "go back to your country and tell the American people not to forget God. We are like those lost in the forest without a compass. For 74 long and terrible years the government would not allow us to hear about God. Now our young people do not know what is right or wrong, good or bad, truth or a lie."

Human beings are the most happy when they are the most free. To be free, one must live in truth. Truth must be grounded in that which is unchanging. Only the One True God is unchanging. And this God, whom the Bible defines as love (see 1 John 4:8), reaches out to draw back to Himself all those who have come under the spell of any pretentious idol.

Norma Finds Home

My dear friend and sister in Christ, Norma McCorvey, was once known as Jane Roe of the *Roe* v. *Wade* case. At the suggestion of her pro-abortion attorneys (to ensure the Justices' sympathetic ruling in her favor), Norma had lied to the Supreme Court by claiming that she had been raped. After the decision was filed, she bore the terrible guilt of that act as well as the pain of the countless abortions that would follow. Each year on the anniversary of the decision, while pro-choice activists around the nation were throwing parties, Norma and her lesbian lover would lock themselves in their house outside Dallas, Texas, and begin a week-long drinking binge that would sometimes include other powerful drugs. She was so high during those times that she can't remember a single anniversary week between 1973 and 1994, the year she was set free.

Flip Benham, a fiery holiness preacher and leader of the controversial pro-life group, Operation Rescue, had moved his offices next door to the Dallas abortion clinic where Norma was marketing director. They struck up a strange friendship. Then one day, little seven-year old Emily MacKey, the daughter of Rev. Benham's office manager, invited Norma to church. She didn't want to go. Actually, Norma thought she couldn't go because she was an alcoholic, drug-addicted lesbian who was deeply into the occult. But little "Miss Emily's" pleading was just too much for Norma, so she finally went to church with the MacKey family.

"I thought the roof would come down on me," she would say later. But as Norma heard the congregation sing of God's love, she felt a warmth envelope her. She dropped to her knees and cried out to Jesus Christ, and Norma McCorvey's terrible burden of guilt was lifted. Today she is a new creature in Christ, old things have passed away, and all has become new. (See 2 Corinthains 5:17.)

What a wonderful testimony! If Miss Norma McCorvey could find her way home from the empty world of idols to the fullness of the one true and living God, so can you or anyone you know who is waving a rebellious fist at God and His Word—or experiencing the bitter, tormenting fruit of that rebellion. The same joy awaits those young men and women who gathered on the sidewalk outside the court-house in Manhattan. May they soon discover that the idol they have created cannot help or satisfy them. Only One can truly satisfy the deepest human needs, and He bids them to come to Him.

> "[R]eturn to me," declares the Lord. "If you put your detestable idols out of my sight and no longer go astray,
>
> and if in a truthful, just and righteous way you swear, 'As surely as the Lord lives,' then the nations will be blessed by him and in him they will glory."
>
> JEREMIAH 4:1-2 NIV

HIS NAME IS WONDERFUL

CHAPTER THREE

In the name of God, Amen. We, whose names are underwritten, the Loyal Subjects of our dread Sovereign Lord, King James, by the Grace of God, of England, France and Ireland, King, Defender of the Faith, e&. Having undertaken for the Glory of God, and Advancement of the Christian Faith, and the Honour of our King and Country, a voyage to plant the first colony in the northern parts of Virginia; do by these presents, solemnly and mutually in the Presence of God and one of another, covenant and combine ourselves together into a civil Body Politick, for our better Ordering and Preservation, and Furtherance of the Ends aforesaid; And by Virtue hereof to enact, constitute, and frame, such just and equal Laws, Ordinances, Acts, Constitutions and Offices, from time to time, as shall be thought most meet and convenient for the General good of the Colony; unto which we promise all due submission and obedience. In Witness whereof we have hereunto subscribed our names at Cape Cod the eleventh of November, in the Reign of our Sovereign Lord, King James of England, France and Ireland, the eighteenth, and of Scotland the fifty-fourth. Anno Domini, 1620.

—The Mayflower Compact

It is January 16, 1999. The Sacramento Community Theater echoes
with the vibrant sound of more than one thousand voices as clergy
members from several denominations, each in their traditional
regalia, make their way down two side aisles, converging on the
stage. A woman reads a poem entitled, "A New Covenant," followed
by a beautiful duet from the musical, *Phantom of the Opera,* sung by
two pretty young girls. Mutual pledges of fidelity are exchanged and
a blessing is pronounced:

> "O God, our Creator, Redeemer, and Sustainer, we bow
> before You to ask Your blessing upon Ellie and Jeanne, whom
> we now bless in Your name. Their commitment to one
> another grows out of their commitment to You, whose love
> is revealed through Jesus Christ."

Ellie Charlton and Jeanne Barnett have lived together for thirteen
years. Standing on stage in their matching purple jackets with
embroidered violets, they look like two retired grammar school
teachers about to receive a PTA award. But Ellie, 63, a great-grand-
mother, and Jeanne, 68, a state government retiree, are not receiving
awards. They are, in fact, joining in a "Holy Union." Presiding over
the ceremony are 75 defiant United Methodist ministers and some
20 clergy of other traditions. Hundreds of witnesses sit in the
audience. This "Service of Celebration" is in protest of a recent
ruling by the denomination's Judicial Council declaring it impermis-
sible for United Methodist clergy to solemnize same-sex marriages.

A solo offered by a man named Jim begins the festivities:

"Same sex and different, straight folks and gays,
We share in God's love that finds many ways . . .
Women loving women and men loving men—
The key is commitment, the blessing comes when,
We renew our devotion again and again . . . ."

This wedding-like ritual is no longer rare. "Partners," a homosexual political activist organization based in Seattle, Washington, reports that 15 percent of homosexual couples have exchanged vows in wedding-like ceremonies, while upwards of 50 percent of all homosexual partners wear a wedding-like ring or other symbol of mutual devotion.[1]

This caricature of holy matrimony is currently at the epicenter of a furious American rebellion against God's authority and moral order. Each one of these rituals flies in the face of the Lord's decree that it shall be exclusively a man that shall "leave his father and mother and be joined to his wife" (Genesis 2:24). To add insult to injury, these unholy unions invoke the name of God in order to lend a corrupt facade of the sacred to that which is profane.

When we think of taking God's name in vain, we generally think of using it as a curse word. This is the most obvious and common way of abusing God' name. But the Third Commandment goes much deeper than this. In this chapter we shall see that this is really what the Third Commandment is all about.

◢

WORD
THREE

"You shall not take the
name of the Lord your God
in vain, for the Lord will
not hold him guiltless who
takes His name in vain."

■

Exodus 20:7

On my son Matthew's sixteenth birthday, my wife and I decided to indulge him in his longing for a pager. All the kids were wearing them and, after all, my wife and I figured that we may even like to use it from time to time to call him home from a friend's house. Standing at the counter of a local retail store, I picked out the unit I knew he would enjoy. It had a translucent case with a switch you could set to play one of several sounds or even lines of songs when it rang. I knew Matthew would love it.

Michelle, the young lady who waited on me, was quite courteous and professional. But when she could not open the battery compartment to reset the program chip, she became flustered and exclaimed, "Jesus Christ! God, they make these things hard!"

Her words hit me like a slap in the face. I was offended by the way she so thoughtlessly referred to the Creator of the world and the Redeemer of mankind. I could not let it go by without helping her to understand what she had done.

"You know, Michelle, you have been so helpful to me," I said, careful to whisper so that I didn't embarrass her in front of her coworkers and the other customers in the store. "And, you've been a real compliment to your company. But when you misuse the name of the Lord, you offend those of us who love and serve Him. We reserve that name for worship."

"What name?" she asked.

"Jesus Christ and God," I answered.

"Did I say that?" she responded with credible denial.

"You did indeed," I assured her.

Michelle turned to another saleswoman standing nearby and asked sincerely, "Did I say Jesus Christ?" The young woman nodded her head, rolled her eyes, and walked into the back room.

As I paid for the pager, I explained to her why the Lord's name is so important to me. "You learn to treasure the names of the ones who love you," I explained. Then, in a few brief moments, I tried to convey how the name of God represents who and what He is, and most importantly, the fact that Jesus is our Savior.

The Third Commandment is more than a prohibition. It is a positive mandate to highly esteem the name of God which the Bible declares to be majestic and exalted. (See Psalm 8:1; 148:13.) God's name, or more accurately His *names*, represent His very nature. When this Commandment refers to the name of the Lord, it means more than simply a proper noun used to identify a subject. It is something called *synecdoche*, or one part of something used to represent the whole of it. In this case, God's name really represents everything about Him: His nature and character, and most notably, His power and authority.

The Third Commandment tells us that respect for the Lord's name is the same as respect for God himself. The Bible says, "The fear of the Lord is the beginning of knowledge" (Proverbs 1:7). Of course, this verse is not talking about being frightened of God. Fear, in the biblical sense, coming from the Old Testament Hebrew word *yiraw* (see Proverbs 1:7) and the New Testament Greek word *phobeho*, means to give awesome respect and reverence.

The Third Commandment, "You shall not take the name of the Lord your God in vain," therefore indicates that our human temptation, maybe even our predisposition, is to disrespect the Lord. The *New International Version* interprets this commandment to read, "You shall not misuse the name of the Lord your God." To misuse God's name is to disrespect His authority. How do we misuse God's name? There are a myriad of ways, but they boil down to two categories: Profanation, which is swearing and cursing; and misappropriation, which is illegitimately applying God's name to something He does not approve.

THE SPLENDOR OF GOD'S NAME

In Bible times, much more so than today, names had great meaning. They often reflected something important about a person's character or personal history. Hannah named her son Samuel, from the Hebrew, *Sh'muel*, "Heard by God," because she had prayed that the Lord would give her a child in spite of her infertility. (See 1 Samuel 1.) Sometimes names changed to memorialize a great moment with which the bearer was associated. For example, Jacob's name was changed to Israel because he had wrestled with God. (See Genesis 32:28.) And still others had more than one name because, like organizational titles, these names often indicated different roles or periods in a person's life. Peter had been called Simon (a common Hebrew name) before his confession of Jesus as Messiah became one of the "rocks" in the foundation of the Church, earning him the name "a piece of rock." (See Matthew 16:18.)

This use of meaningful and multiple names is true for God himself, whose innumerable roles and limitless nature demand many names. In addition to His very special name, *Yahweh*, to which we were introduced in the first chapter, there are actually eight other personal names for God in the Old Testament and nine descriptive names. His personal names, or the ones by which God calls himself, are *Elohim*, *El*, and *Eloah*, each of which refers to His strength and majesty. Elohim (see Genesis 1:1) appears more than 200 times in the book of Genesis alone. El and Eloah are primarily found in the poetical books, with the greatest number of uses occurring in Job.

El Shaddai (see Exodus 6:3; Numbers 24:4,16), a name which we will look at later, suggests might and is often translated as "Almighty." *Adohn* and *Adonai* (see Judges 6:15; 13:8; Psalm 2:4; Isaiah 7:7), or "Lord," represents His authority and superiority. *T'sur* (see Deuteronomy 32:4,15,18,31), or "Rock," speaks of certainty and security. And *Kahdosh* means "Holy One," signifying God's transcendence and separateness from all other things. "Holy" or "Holy One" is found 32 times in Isaiah (see 40:25; 43:3; and 48:17 for examples) as well as elsewhere in the Old Testament.

The descriptive names given to God by others include:

Avhir, "Mighty One," (see Genesis 49:24; Psalm 132:2-5);

Elyon, "Most High," (see Deuteronomy 32:8; Psalm 18:13);

Gibbor, "The Great One," (Psalm 24:8);

Tzaddik, "Righteous," (see Isaiah 41:10; Hosea 2:19; Psalm 34:17);

Khanna, "The Zealous One"[2] (see Exodus 34:14);

Tzevaoht, "Master of Everything," (see Psalm 46:7-11); and

Eyeh-Asher-Eyeh, "I-Am-that-I-Am," (see Exodus 3:14 KJV).

Eyeh-Asher-Eyeh, "I-Am-that-I-Am," is the name God used to introduce himself to Moses and is also a Hebrew idiom meaning, "When you get there, I will be there." God encouraged Moses that, "I will always be what you need Me to be, and I will always be there before you get there." Putting it in colloquial American language, as one country preacher put it, "I-Am-that-I-Am" means "God ain't ever short, and He ain't ever late!"

In the New Testament, the Greek titles *Theos* and *Kurios* are used most frequently, meaning God in its broadest sense. Jesus is the English rendering of the Greek *Iyeasuz,* itself a translation of the Savior's Hebrew name, *Yeshua,* meaning *Yahweh*-Saves. "Lord" or "Master" are other designations for God. In John 10:30, the Holy Spirit added a particularly endearing name for our loving God, *Abba* or "Daddy."

All of these names reveal the beauty and fullness of God's personality and character. He is powerful, yet intimate. He is above all things, yet is as immediately present in our lives as a doting daddy. God is righteous, but He is still so zealously possessive of His people that He will not let our sins hopelessly separate us from Him. He is the Lord over all, yet He comes to serve those in His charge as Savior. The totality of God's being can never be fully comprehended by the human mind.

PROFANING THE NAME OF GOD

You shall not use the name of the Eternal, your God, profanely; for the Eternal will never acquit anyone who uses his name profanely.

EXODUS 20:7 MOFFATT

When we profane the name of God, we belittle and demean His majesty in the minds of others. Not that our words can ever have any real effect on God's nature, but the way others perceive Him can be gravely affected by our attitude toward Him. This is why the commandment charges us with guarding ourselves, and by implication, charges us with guarding others from abusing God's name.

Like most Americans, the young woman helping me with my son's pager did not know what offense she was committing. I am sure you have had the experience of hearing someone revile or degrade God by name. Maybe you've even done so yourself. Sometimes it is done unconsciously. Language that was once reserved for pool halls, army barracks, and repair shops is now heard in everyday conversation, on radio, and is a staple in every grade of movie.

Some years ago, after a long speaking itinerary in the midwest, I boarded a late-night flight to return home. I was tired and looking forward to a rest. Sitting behind me in the airplane were two salesmen whose conversation was peppered with profanity. I had finally had it when they began running the Lord's name into the gutter. I raised myself up from my seat and turned around so that I was looking down on them from my perch. Then I asked, "Are either of you in the ministry?"

The one in the aisle seat raised his eyebrows incredulously and said, "What the h*** would ever make you think that?"

"Well, I am in the ministry," I said with a smile. "And I am amazed at your communication skills. You just said God, damn, hell, and Jesus Christ in one sentence. I can't get all of that into a whole sermon!" They both blushed, and I didn't hear another word from them for the remainder of the flight!

While my two traveling partners chose to use the crudest form of profanity, some of us choose milder versions. Expressions like, "Oh God!" and "I swear to God!" do no better in promoting a high regard for the position that God is to occupy in our lives and in our culture. I'm not a legalist when it comes to this kind of language, but I do believe that we need to be far more careful about the phrases we use, especially when we are referring to the One whom Isaiah saw "high and lifted up" (Isaiah 6:1).

MISAPPROPRIATION

While swearing and cursing in God's name are serious offenses against the Third Commandment, they are not at the heart of its meaning. These transgressions, notwithstanding their gravity, pale into misdemeanors when compared to the first-class felony of misappropriating God's name. To understand what I mean by misappropriating God's name, we need to return to the original sense of the Third Commandment.

The literal translation of this commandment from its original Hebrew is, "No *lifting up* of the Lord's name!" Everett Fox, in his *The Five Books of Moses* translation, captured the essence of this phrase, "You are not to take up the name of YHWH your God for emptiness."[3] One way of interpreting this peculiar idiom is to say, "No *stealing* the Lord's name."

How do we steal God's name? By applying it to places it doesn't belong. For example, when we claim God's approval on something that clearly is not His will, or when we claim His direction for something that is of our own making, we misrepresent Him and take His name in vain. In these ways we illegitimately lend the imprimatur of God's good name to something that is not good, which is tantamount to a fraudulent claim endorsement.

In the ancient Near Eastern world at the time the Ten Commandments were delivered to Moses, this sort of religious fraud was commonly carried out in the form of an oath. The Babylonians, for example, often used oaths to bolster otherwise suspicious business deals. By invoking the name of one of their many gods, they could often relieve the anxiety of a suspicious buyer.

"In the name of Hadad," a merchant from Babylon might say, "this is the best price in town!" And so the superstitious Babylonian consumer was easily duped by the bogus endorsement of the famous weather-god, which was roughly the equivalent of our modern sports star or Hollywood celebrity today. If someone famous lends their name to a commercial in America today, it is assumed to be credible. In the ancient world, no one was more famous or believable than the local deity.

Because of their previous contact with the pagan peoples of Egypt and the prospect of moral contamination from the Canaanites, the Israelites were vulnerable to picking up this bad habit of co-opting God's name for self-serving ends. Therefore, God said, "You shall not lift My name (as an endorsement)!" Some biblical scholars also see the Third Commandment as exclusively a prohibition against false swearing, as in a false or pagan oath. This is reflected in The Jewish

Publication Society's Translation of Exodus 20:7, "You shall not swear falsely by the name of the Lord."[4]

PLAYING THE "GOD CARD"

During the early 1980s, my family and I lived in New York City where I served as an assistant pastor in a large evangelical church. One day a young man who was known to our congregation decided to parachute from the top of one of the one hundred-story twin Trade Towers in lower Manhattan. Bouncing gently on the updrafts generated by a labyrinth of streets, tunnels, and alleys, the surprise visitor caused a world class traffic jam below as rubberneckers looked up to see his multicolored chute and gear. Touching down in a flawless landing, he was promptly arrested by New York City police officers who were not amused by his antics. When asked on camera why he made the jump, the born-again acrobat said, "The Lord told me to do it."

While this story brings an exasperated chuckle each time I tell it, imagine it in another way. Imagine if someone had been injured or even killed had something gone awry with his stunt. The implications would be far more grave. The sad lesson of American history is that there have been many tragic instances when God's leading and approval were claimed in situations that led to enormous human suffering. Jonestown and Waco are only two on a terribly long list. But you don't have to go to the history books to find pain inflicted in the name of God. There are plenty of smaller, more private abuses of God's name as spouses, parents, children, and fellow church members bludgeon one another with an illicit, "Thus saith the Lord!"

This declaration is used by some to control others. After all, who can trump a claim on the will of God? I've even seen this technique used in churches and Christian ministry organizations by individuals who feel that their ideas or recommendations are not being heeded. In an effort to shortcut their way to getting what they desire, they simply play the "God card."

"Well, you pray about it," they say benignly, "and you'll see that it's God's will."

What do you do with that? There's not much you can do, but one thing I often say is, "I do pray, and I haven't heard anything like that from heaven. I wonder why God would talk to you about that and not to me?" Of course, you must beware. There is always a risk that you may get an answer to your question!

We may also use this device to insulate ourselves from blame by claiming "the Lord's leading." Or, worse yet, "God told me to do it." I'm not suggesting that this is never the case. God does lead in our lives, sometimes in very detailed and unique ways. Nevertheless, the Third Commandment should be a sober warning against claiming divine direction too quickly. Borrowing God's name to manipulate others or as a cover for our actions, as sincere as they may be, could be committing a deep offense against His integrity.

ACCOUNTABILITY

For the most part, the Third Commandment is about accountability. It says, "Enough! You are to take responsibility for yourself. You are accountable for your own actions. No blaming God! No shirking of your responsibility! No wiggling out of it!" Keeping God's name pure and holy enforces personal responsibility by not allowing us to place anything between ourselves and our actions, least of all the cover of false spirituality.

Many people who call themselves Christians today have twisted the Bible to fit their own ideas and lifestyles. Refusing to be accountable to the commands and truths of God's Word, they misinterpret and even rewrite Scripture. Their false spirituality then claims that they are in God's will, which means true accountability to God is lost. We are now seeing whole groups who lay false claim to God's will, primarily in so-called mainline denominations and in the nation as a whole.

The story of Ellie Charlton and Jeanne Barnett's "marriage" related in the opening of this chapter is the story of a great sin in the Church. The vacuum created in the historic churches when they turned their backs on the authority of Holy Scripture is currently being filled with a new paganism. Abandoning the One True God for lesser gods of their own making, many mainline denominational leaders are returning to Ur, to the time before Abraham was commanded to leave his idols behind and give his full devotion to *Yahweh*. Ur was the ancient Mesopotamian city where Abraham grew up. It was inhabited by the Chaldees and was the seat of worship of the pagan moon god. Abraham's father, Tera, was an idol maker there. Today, goddess worship, reincarnation, and sexual license are once again the touchstones of this ancient earth-bound religion, which today have found a new disguise in many "updated" versions of Christianity.

CO-OPTING THE NAME OF GOD

The Foundry United Methodist Church in Washington, D.C., became famous when First Lady Hillary Rodham Clinton chose it to be the First Family's Washington church home. Boasting that they are a "reconciling congregation," Pastor J. Phillip Wogaman welcomes practicing homosexuals into all aspects of the church's life without offering them any help in forsaking their sin. P.F.L.A.G. (Parents and Friends of Lesbians and Gays), an organization that promotes the acceptance of homosexual behavior, has a chapter that meets there. The infamous Bishop of the Newark, New Jersey, Diocese of the Episcopal Church once spoke at Foundry, suggesting that Jesus could have been a drag queen, that the apostle Paul may have been a "self-loathing gay man," and that the Ten Commandments are immoral because they treat women as property.[5] On "Reconciling Sundays," banners incorporating symbols of militant homosexual political movements blended with crosses and doves hang in front of the altar area.

This attempt to co-opt God's blessing and apply it to behavior clearly condemned in both the Old and New Testaments is an abuse of His name and His nature. God is holy and the unrepented sin of homosexual intercourse of any kind is an abomination to Him. (See Leviticus 18:22; Romans 1:24-27; 1 Corinthians 6:9-10.) To suggest otherwise is to slander God and to defraud His people.

It is not only the apostate church, however, that is guilty of such divine character assassination. During the last 30 years, one of the most powerful forces in our culture has joined in the crusade to defame God. It began when the Federal Judiciary took prayer out of the schools, then progressed when succeeding liberal congresses were elected, and fully bloomed when the Clinton White House, the most blatantly immoral administration in American history, began a full-bore attack on biblical truth and morality.

Ironically, Mr. Clinton was known as a religious man before he ran for President. He had attended a Catholic parochial school as a boy, joined a Southern Baptist Church, where he sang in the choir, and frequented camp meeting revivals in his native Arkansas while he served as governor. Liberal Democratic political activist Rabbi David Saperstien called President Clinton "the most religious of any of our presidents." Indeed, Mr. Clinton himself was quoted as saying, "If I weren't, in my view, a Christian . . . my life would have been much more difficult."[6]

This unusually strong mixture of religion with politics in the Clinton Administration brought it under extraordinary scrutiny by various religious groups. The National Clergy Council (of which I have had the privilege of serving as chief executive officer), an association of church leaders from virtually every tradition, including African-American, Catholic, Evangelical, and Protestant, undertook an exhaustive examination of Clinton Administration policies. We appointed a panel of distinguished moral philosophers, theologians, and church historians who compared Mr. Clinton's positions on the two principal moral issues of homosexuality and abortion with what the Bible clearly teaches on these subjects. Our panel concluded, "[Mr. Clinton] has continued to claim the name of Christ while advancing policies and actions that are contrary to Holy Scripture."[7]

That a government should take stands that are contrary to the Word of God is not strange. It has been true throughout the history of the Church. But Mr. Clinton's use of religious imagery, personalities, and language in the advancement of his policies, programs, and even high-level personnel who are known to be hostile to all forms of traditional Christianity has been extraordinary. His audacity reached an all-time high in January 1995 when, during his annual State of the Union speech to Congress, he took the very words of Jesus Christ to dub his own political ideas as, "The New Covenant."[8]

THE ANTIDOTE: HALLOWING GOD'S NAME

With so many ways to dishonor God and abuse His name, how then are we to keep the Third Commandment? How may we honor the name that is above every name? (See Philippians 2:9.) I have a good friend who is an orthodox Jewish rabbi in Brooklyn, New York. He is a rotund man with a permanent smile in his eyes. His long black beard cascades over his regulation white shirt and black tie and even fans out across the lapels of his always dark suits. He thinks like a scholar, waddles like a sage, and cracks jokes like a stand-up comedian. He is one of the most delightful people I have ever met.

One day, my friend was visiting with me during the annual March for Life, when tens of thousands of Christians from around the country walked the length of Constitution Avenue from the White House to the Supreme Court to pray for an end to the abortion holocaust in America. He was there to blow the *shofar*, a ram's horn used in Bible times to call sacred assemblies for prayer and repentance. (See 2 Chronicles 15:9-15.)

On this particular day, I was hosting a reception at the Hyatt Regency Hotel on Capitol Hill, where I was introducing Christian leaders from across the country to the Ten Commandments Project, our effort to promote the display of beautiful stone artwork tablets of the Ten Commandments in the offices of public officials. To draw attention to our presence, we had set up a table at the entrance to the room. On it were several sets of the stone plaques that we hand out to members of Congress, federal judges, and others in government. One such set was in the original Hebrew, etched in gold lettering on an exquisitely polished blue marble surface.

The Rabbi's eyes fell immediately on it and he remained transfixed. I thought at first he was impressed, but when I looked again, I could see that he was disturbed about something. "Rabbi, what's on your mind?" I asked.

He pulled me aside. "That first tablet," he whispered, waving his finger towards it. "It should not have the *Name* spelled out."

I glanced over at the table. It never occurred to me that the First Commandment on the Hebrew tablet used the actual four-letter name of God, YHWH. The Rabbi was more concerned than offended by our insensitivity. (Devout Jews never openly display God's name, particularly on pieces of art.)

"What would happen if someone inadvertently placed the tablet on the chair over there, and someone sat on it?" he asked rhetorically. "Would you want someone's fanny on top of God's name?"

While you may be tempted to dismiss the rabbinic zeal for protecting God's name as legalistic, think about how careful most of us are with the things we value. My wife and I are always careful to place our keepsakes on high shelves when our toddler nieces and nephews visit. And who would place their Armanni sunglasses on a car seat, or an antique watch on the pool railing? Is the name of God any less important? I am not necessarily suggesting that we follow the Rabbi's strict code, but it does help us to think about how we treat references to the Holy One of Israel. (See Psalm 71:22.)

When asked by His disciples how to pray, Jesus began, "In this manner, therefore, pray: 'Our Father in heaven, Hallowed be Your name,'" (Matthew 6:9). The *Oxford Dictionary* says "to hallow" means "to consecrate, set apart for an exclusive use, dedicate." The Greek word used in the New Testament is *hagiodzo*, which has its origin in the word for purity. Jesus likely spoke these words in the religious language of the Jews and would have therefore used the Hebrew *yit'kadosh shimcha*, which has the added meaning of keeping God's name morally or ceremonially clean.

In other words, we are to set apart references to God and treat our conversation about the Lord in a different way than we talk about normal, mundane things. I don't mean we are to speak about God only in hushed tones or celestial accents. I merely recommend that we frame our discussions about God in the reverential context that even the angels understand.

> **Then I looked, and I heard the voice of many angels around the throne, the living creatures, and the elders; and the number of them was ten thousand times ten thousand, and thousands of thousands,**
>
> **saying with a loud voice: "Worthy is the Lamb who was slain, to receive power and riches and wisdom, and strength and honor and glory and blessing!"**
>
> REVELATION 5:11-12

Ambassadors of the Name

When we consider the name of God, we must always consider the task of guardianship. We are stewards of the great name of God, having been given the privilege of bearing it upon our lips. Like a trusted heirloom, His name has been bequeathed to us, and it is up to us to protect it, keep it clean, and present its beauty to others. Like the envoy of a king, we conduct our affairs in the Lord's name. "[W]e are ambassadors for Christ, as though God were pleading through us" (2 Corinthians 5:20). Therefore, even our behavior, what we do and say, as much as what we refrain from doing and saying, is a part of faithfully discharging this sacred trust.

Finally, we can honor God's name by drawing attention to its holiness. We must "contend earnestly for the faith that was once for all delivered to the saints" (Jude 3). Whether in private, in the pulpit, or in the public square, we must herald the truth, lifting up the name of our God in worship and adoration.

The ministers who witnessed the two women pledging themselves to one another in violation of God's holy law that day in Sacramento did much more than simply profane God's name. They cheapened His grace by lowering His high position. When the law of God is set high as it is in His Word, and our sins set us low, the difference between the two is the depth of God's forgiving love. But when we bring His name down to where we are in our failings, we can no longer appreciate the magnitude of His mercy.

In the prophet Micah's great announcement of the coming Messiah, he promised a day when the Redeemer will "stand and feed His flock in the strength of the Lord in the majesty of the name of the Lord His God" (Micah 5:4). To this, the Psalmist adds:

> **I will praise thy name, O Lord; for it is good.**
>
> PSALM 54:6 KJV

HOLY R&R!

CHAPTER FOUR

"Bill Gates is Satan."

What a strange title for a home
page, I think to myself as the title scrolls across my screen. I look at
a few of the Internet articles on the software mogul. As I read the
following quote, I understand why the author of this site has dubbed
the geeky multibillionaire this way.

> I don't have any evidence of that . . . Just in terms of alloca-
> tion of time resources, religion is not very efficient. There's a
> lot more I could be doing on a Sunday morning.
>
> — Bill Gates, when asked about religion
> and God's existence, *Time* magazine[1]

◪

The world's most wealthy computer nerd is not known for his
likeability. In fact, he is described as ruthless, fiercely competitive,
and arrogant. Employees say that he can be condescending and rude,
openly chastising subordinates in humiliating ways. Bill Gates grew

up in Seattle, where he attended Lakeside High School. That's where he met Paul Allen, who would become his partner in founding Microsoft, now the world's largest software producer. By the time Gates had reached the eighth grade, he and Allen were already in business together. That year they started the Traf-O-Data company and manufactured a crude computerized device for monitoring automobile traffic at busy intersections.

Since then, Gates' rise to the top has been breathless. After a stint at Harvard, he dropped out to pursue his dream. In 1990 his company came out with Windows 3.1. Five years later he would virtually corner the software market with Windows 95. These two products gave Microsoft the commanding lead over all its competition.

Let there be no mistake about the fact that Bill Gates is brilliant and knowledgeable. He is an insatiable reader. And it goes without saying, he is an excellent businessman. But when it comes to those invisible assets that have so much to do with a person's inner success, Bill Gates, from all reports, is ignorant of them. As we will see, religion and worship are, in fact, the most efficient, cost effective ways to deal with the impediments to social progress. It is also, no doubt to Mr. Gates' surprise, the best way for Americans to spend a Sunday morning.

◪

WORD
FOUR

"REMEMBER THE SABBATH DAY, TO KEEP IT
HOLY. SIX DAYS YOU SHALL LABOR AND DO ALL
YOUR WORK, BUT THE SEVENTH DAY IS THE
SABBATH OF THE LORD YOUR GOD. IN IT YOU
SHALL DO NO WORK: YOU, NOR YOUR SON, NOR
YOUR DAUGHTER, NOR YOUR MALE SERVANT,
NOR YOUR FEMALE SERVANT, NOR YOUR CATTLE,
NOR YOUR STRANGER WHO IS WITHIN YOUR
GATES. FOR IN SIX DAYS THE LORD MADE THE
HEAVENS AND THE EARTH, THE SEA, AND
ALL THAT IS IN THEM, AND RESTED THE
SEVENTH DAY. THEREFORE THE LORD
BLESSED THE SABBATH DAY AND HALLOWED IT."

EXODUS 20:8-11

Christ (pronounced Chris) and Dolly Lapp are the proprietors of the bustling Good n' Plenty restaurant in Lancaster, Pennsylvania. Six days a week, long lines of diesel buses drop off hundreds of tourists from Toronto, Akron, Poughkeepsie, Paterson, and scores of other cities and towns to enjoy the Lapps' sumptuous Lancaster County fare. Dolly, who has been married to Christ for 52 years, supervises the kitchen/bakery staff of 35 who cook from scratch and serve up 650 homestyle meals at a single sitting in their expansive dining room. The success of the Good n' Plenty has afforded Christ and Dolly a comfortable lifestyle that includes beautifully decorated homes in Pennsylvania and Florida[14]. Most importantly, they have achieved a life-long security for their children who now operate the business.

The Lapps are known as faithful givers in their church, generous benefactors to charities and other causes in their summer and winter communities, and they have been extremely kind to the work that I do in Washington, D.C. Ask Christ and Dolly what has been the secret to their success, and they will instantly tell you that it is because they have honored the Lord in all their enterprises. One outstanding way in which they have done that is to never open on a Sunday.

When the Lapps opened their restaurant in 1969, many people told them that they would have to open on Sundays if they were to be profitable. Next came the pressure from the competition who siphoned off regular Good n' Plenty customers who "wandered" to other establishments on Sundays. The Lapps have also had to deal with the lobbying efforts of the loyal customers who often try to persuade them to open at least on Sunday afternoons. But the Lapps will not be dissuaded from their commitment.

"We feel there is a special blessing when we honor the Lord's day," says Christ. The restaurant should be profitable operating only six days a week because Sunday is the Lord's day. You need church, Sunday school, and time with family."

Dolly takes note of the fact that this policy has been good, not only for their family, but for the families of their unusually long-term employees. Many have been with them for twenty and thirty years. "They don't want us to change," she says with a smile. "We've talked about it with our kids, and they're not going to change it either."

Like the Lapps, David and Barbara Green of Oklahoma City place principle above profit when it comes to honoring God. Hobby Lobby Creative Centers, the Green's enormously successful hobby and craft business, operates 212 retail stores in 23 states, with sales approaching $1 billion annually. The firm employs approximately 10,000 people in six related companies. While Hobby Lobby competes successfully in virtually every area of business, it has one notable exception. Its large and attractive stores are often the only ones in malls across the country to be closed on Sundays.

"We come from the standpoint that we just think its better for families," the 57-year-old entrepreneur said in an interview with northern Illinois' *Daily Herald* newspaper. "We're here to honor God, not dollars." When Mr. Green makes such a statement, he means it. The Green's accountants estimate that acting on their convictions may cost the company upwards of $100 million dollars a year in lost sales. Yet, the company has enjoyed steady growth since its inception in 1970. "It just proves that when you honor God, He gives you blessings," Mr. Green told the *Daily Herald*.

The Lapps and the Greens have a thing or two to tell Bill Gates. They've discovered a secret to far more than business success. They've learned the eternal principle of the Sabbath rest.

A TIMELESS PRINCIPLE

Chances are that you've seen some of those funny, old, moving pictures about early attempts at manned flight. You know the ones I'm talking about. The scratched, black and white, jumpy images of mustached gentlemen in their Victorian suits flapping wing-like contraptions, peddling belt-driven propellers, and bouncing around ridiculously in useless gyrocopters. Occasionally you'll catch them on a television documentary about manned flight, but more often you'll find them as background material for a humorous advertisement. They are amusing now, but they weren't back then. They were dead serious. In fact, many people actually lost their lives in the search for the secret to flight.

The reason these early aviation pioneers look so silly to us today is that they didn't understand the fundamental principle of flight. Today we understand that their flapping, running, and jumping was useless, but they didn't know it then. In hindsight, the joke is on them! It wouldn't be until the Wright Brothers learned how to apply Bernoulli's principle of pressure differentials using a curved wing edge that take-offs stopped appearing as a clown act and the course of human history was changed. Before this amazing discovery, those erstwhile aviators could never have succeeded because they weren't dealing with reality. They had a faulty theoretical model, so they could never get their contraptions to work.

I use this analogy to make this Fourth Commandment point: Discovering the meaning of the seventh-day rule is a lot like the Wright Brothers' breakthrough. It is all about the way we are made, the way the universe in which we live is constructed, and how we as God's creation are to function in it. As Orville and Wilbur found out, in order to function successfully, we must understand certain principles and know how to apply them.

WHAT IS THE SABBATH?

The Western custom of beginning the work week with Monday makes it necessary to remind ourselves that Sunday is not the last day, but rather the first day of the calendar week. However, the biblical Sabbath occurs on Saturday. The Sabbath should not be confused with the Christian practice of worshipping on "The Lord's Day," which is the first day of the week, also the day of the Resurrection of Christ.

The seventh day of the week is Saturday and is called the "Sabbath" in the Fourth Commandment. The reason for this is because "Sabbath" is derived from the Hebrew word *sha'baht* meaning "to cease, desist, or rest." It was on this seventh day, the Bible tells us, that God rested. (See Genesis 1-3, especially 2:2-3.) He did so not because He was physically tired, but because the creation was complete. There was nothing more to add and no need to improve it. God was well pleased with the final product and ceased His activity.

This seventh-day rest became an important symbol, both to the ancient people of Israel as well as believers today, because it speaks of spiritual rest. The Sabbath recalls the fact that it was God, not man, who created and therefore sustains the world. That's a huge burden off our shoulders! While secular humanists, New Age devotees, and other utopians believe they are responsible to build a perfect world, the Word of God clearly indicates that we are to simply do what we are instructed by the Creator and He will do the "world building."

We are talking about the difference between owning your own company and being an employee of someone else's business. In the first instance, if you are the owner, you can never simply lock the door and walk away at night. You carry the burden of the company with you 24 hours a day, 7 days a week, all year round. The employee, on the other hand, only follows orders and does the work they are told to do by their superiors. They are responsible for their particular job, but not the overall success of the company. This is the way it is in God's economy. I am responsible to obey His rules and serve Him in the particular duties assigned to me in a way that glorifies God and pleases Him. He is responsible for the rest. After all, having designed the world, He knows best how to run it!

This also has implications for the way in which we "work out our salvation." (See Philippians 2:12.) Many people believe that we must strive to be holy in order to please God. While the Bible makes it clear that we are to shun sin and pursue holiness (see 2 Corinthians 7:1; Titus 2:12), the apostle Paul told the Philippian Christians, "It is God who works in you both to will and to do for His good pleasure" (Philippians 2:13). This means that we cannot achieve a sinless state in and of ourselves. We must trust Jesus Christ who "appeared once and for all at the end of the ages to do away with sin by the sacrifice of himself" (Hebrews 9:26 NIV).

Notwithstanding these facts, the Sabbath day retains a unique place in the many object lessons of Scripture. It is a grand mnemonic device, a physical reality that reminds us of important truths. When you read the account of creation in the book of Genesis, you will note that each of the six days in creation marches on as if in a parade toward the last day, the Sabbath. This was the crowning day of that first week, and it ends with a divine pronouncement making it holy or consecrated. (See Genesis 2:3; Exodus 20:8,11.) The Hebrew word that is used for both is *Kahw-dawsh*. It literally means "to be clean."

In the dusty, dirty ancient world, it generally took extraordinary measures to keep something clean. The implication here is that the Sabbath is extraordinarily important and deserves special treatment. To accentuate this fact, during Bible times a violation of the Sabbath brought with it the most severe of punishments. The Law of Moses states:

> **You shall keep the Sabbath, therefore, for it is holy to you. Everyone who profanes it shall surely be put to death; for whoever does any work on it, that person shall be cut off from among his people.**
>
> EXODUS 31:14

The rabbis, who recorded the oral tradition of Judaism, considered the Sabbath as the very soul of creation. They believed that the seventh day anchored the earth, and that before the appearance of the seventh day, creation was shaky and unstable. Today, many Orthodox Jews assert that the Sabbath gives permanence to an otherwise temporary world.[2] In their minds, insulting the Sabbath causes great injury to everyone and everything.

Christians also believe the Sabbath to be vitally important. The New Testament broadens the definition of the Sabbath, however, from one particular day of the week to any day dedicated to spiritual, emotional, and physical refreshment:

> **One man considers one day more sacred than another; another man considers every day alike. Each one should be fully convinced in his own mind.**
>
> **He who regards one day as special, does so to the Lord.**
>
> ROMANS 14:5-6 NIV

Some Christian theologians argue that the "sign" of the Sabbath (as a mark of the covenant between God and humankind; see Exodus 31:13) has been replaced by the sign of the cup Jesus offered at His last Passover meal with His disciples. (See Matthew 26:27-29.) The cup symbolized the New Covenant. Regardless of how you interpret these verses, it doesn't change the principles associated with Sabbath rest. Whether a sign or merely a vestige of that sign, we may still learn from the important place the Sabbath holds in God's ongoing relationship with His creation.

IMPORTANCE OF THE SABBATH

The Catholic Catechism instructs the faithful that "the Sabbath is for the Lord, holy and set apart for the praise of God, His work of creation, and His saving actions on behalf of Israel."[3] Martin Luther linked respect for the Sabbath to holding God's Word as sacred because it speaks to a day of corporate worship and learning about spiritual things.[4] John Calvin, the Dutch Reformer, referred to the "singular honor" that the Sabbath holds among all the precepts of God's Law.[5] And John Wesley, founder of Methodism, said in reference to the Ten Commandments, "Every part of the law must remain in force upon all mankind, and in all ages."[6] D. L. Moody, the American revivalist of a century ago, concurred with Wesley, writing, "The Sabbath was binding in Eden and has been in force ever since."[7]

The Sabbath is important because it teaches about the nature of God and the nature of human beings. Its regular appearance every week forces us to continually face questions about the origin of things, the meaning of life, and our place in the world. For those who want to brush these matters away, it just doesn't work. As long as the sun rises in the morning and sets at night, we're going to have to deal with the great questions of life. When watching the beauty of a crimson sunset, we are provoked to ask, "Who made all of this?" *There's got to be something more out there!* is the feeling one gets when gazing up into a spray of stars across a desert sky.

The observance of a weekly Sabbath forces us to think about how small and fragile we really are in comparison to the universe in which we live. In the New Testament, St. Paul warns that we should not think of ourselves more highly than we ought to think. (See Romans 12:3.) It's easy to get a big head, especially when we think we're the be-all and end-all of our existence. Think again! We're all smaller than the tiniest microscopic organisms when compared to the innumerable galaxies.

Considering all of this, it seems only reasonable that we should devote one day out of our week to think about and address these things. Of course, neither Judaism nor Christianity limits spiritual exercise to just one day. Cultivating a relationship with God necessitates much more than a weekly check-in. God calls His people His bride (see Isaiah 49:18), and it is ridiculous to think of trying to build a strong marriage by visiting one day a week! Every day has spiritual duties attached to it, including prayer and Bible reading, not to mention daily obedience to the Commandments. Still, a common day for believers to join together in worship, study, and service to God and their fellow man is irreplaceable.

Something special happens both to individuals and to a group when people of like minds and hearts gather together. All you have to do is observe a large religious gathering to see evidence of this. A stadium full of thousands of participants praying, singing, and worshipping together generates a level of faith that one person alone cannot possess. The same is true for a small chapel with only a dozen assembled. The fire of faith is fanned when believers come together.

Many references in the Old and New Testaments refer to the congregation of God's people:

> I will declare your name to my brothers; in the congregation I will praise you.
>
> PSALM 22:22 NIV

> Let us not give up meeting together, as some are in the habit of doing, but let us encourage one another.
>
> HEBREWS 10:25 NIV

A STAGING GROUND FOR SERVING

It is the day of worship that is the center of activity for all faith traditions. It is this nucleus of community life that generates highly effective ministry. The worship meeting, whether it takes place in a church building, rented hall, or private living room, is where new believers are born. In the gathering of saints, wherever it takes place, new members are received, congregates are instructed, resources are marshaled, and gifts and skills are dispatched to meet human needs. It is here that the Lord is present in a unique way,

> **For where two or three are gathered together in My name, I am there in the midst of them.**

MATTHEW 18:20

Personal spirituality and growth are not the only benefits of regularly gathering together, however. A greater amount of service to others can be accomplished by a group. This is especially true of charitable acts. The more people there are in the assembly, the more resources there will be to care for the needy and the poor. This is a particularly important aspect of Sabbath responsibility.

> **Six days do your work, but on the seventh day do not work, so that your ox and your donkey may rest and the slave born in your household, and the alien as well, may be refreshed.**

EXODUS 23:12 NIV

Jews have historically practiced extraordinary hospitality at Sabbath meals, inviting the poor and the lonely to join them at the table. Christian tradition has also emphasized the Sabbath Day of worship as a time to visit the sick and the elderly, in keeping with the Church's biblical and historical mandate to minister to the needy. Hospitals, orphanages, schools, and substance abuse programs all have religious beginnings that stem from this Judeo-Christian ethic. Today, religiously observant conservatives are the most generous subgroup within the population as a whole.[8] And this spirit of generosity is best promoted when the body of Christ comes together.

> **For this is what a pure and undefiled service in the eyes of God the Father consists in: that a man should take care of orphans and widows in their distress.**

JAMES 1:27 GNC

I will always remember the day when I was serving as an associate pastor to a large congregation in New York City and a letter arrived from Ed Koch, who was the mayor at that time. In his inimitable and colorful style, the mayor rebuked the clergy of New York for not taking care of the homeless. He said they were not his problem, but the problem of the city's churches and synagogues, quoting the Old Testament prophet Isaiah,

> **Is not this the fast that I have chosen? to loose the bands of wickedness, to undo the heavy burdens, and to let the oppressed go free, and that ye break every yoke?**
>
> **Is it not to deal thy bread to the hungry, and that thou bring the poor that are cast out to thy house?**
>
> ISAIAH 58:6-7 KJV

The mayor went on to offer city money to any congregation that would open its facilities to house indigents for which the city did not have space. Our church already had such a program, but several others did take him up on the challenge.

I bring this situation up to remind us that it is the Sabbath-minded, God-directed church that will seek out God's will as a matter of worship. The more seriously we take the day of worship, and the more that we participate with others in it, the sooner we will begin to resolve the vexing problems of poverty, homelessness, broken families, the abandonment of children, and the elderly in our society.

Mayor Koch was right. These urgent human needs are not primarily the business of government. In fact, government does a pretty poor job of caring for people in distress, especially the poor. One study found that less than 35 cents of every welfare dollar makes its way directly to those in need.[9] This waste of resources is compounded by a depersonalized and disinterested system that deals with nameless, faceless masses instead of individuals and families.

Private, faith-based outreach programs run by churches and other religious institutions spend far less than what government programs do, while achieving far greater success. For instance, the national average spending for government-subsidized homeless shelters is $22 per person per day. In contrast, Catholic Sister Connie Driscoll operates the St. Martin de Porres House of Hope in Chicago at an average cost of $6.73 per person per day. And her success rate in helping the homeless achieve independence and permanent housing is an astounding 94 percent![10]

These programs can do what no government agency can hope to achieve. They are generally staffed by highly motivated, even passionate volunteers and are established in either no-cost or extremely low-cost facilities. They also enjoy the potent assistance of three incomparable resources that government has foolishly shunned: prayer, conversion, and spiritual motivation—all of which are celebrated Sabbath activities.

THE SABBATH IS FOR FAMILY

Adults are not the only ones whose lives change by setting aside a day to worship and reflect. The most powerful governors of human behavior are internal, not external, and these internal controls are most effectively impressed on young people at home, by both word and example. The home, even more than the Sunday school, is the place for spiritual and moral instruction to take place. (See Deuteronomy 6.)

Next in importance to our relationship with God is our relationship with our family. When families can get together, the effects can be good. Families are strengthened by a renewed commitment to Sabbath observance. Saturdays and Sundays, at least for now, still offer the best time for family members to be together.

We have a rule in the Schenck house that Sunday is for two things: worship and family. We find that with all the demands that compete for our time and attention, we must have a disciplined time on the weekly calendar to be together as a family, or it just won't happen. For a family, separation on the weekend should be the exception, not the rule.

This premium on family time is not optional. The American family is in deep crisis. Depending on how you read the statistics, anywhere from 10 percent to nearly half of marriages currently end in divorce. This is wreaking havoc on children. We'll explore this more fully when we look at the Seventh Commandment, but suffice it to say here that the break up of a family exposes children to a host of life-long problems they would not face otherwise.

> The evidence is now overwhelming that the collapse of marriage is creating a whole generation of children less happy, less physically and mentally healthy, less equipped to deal with life or to produce at work, and more dangerous to themselves and others.[11]

Divorce is only the beginning of the problem. More and more young women and men are producing children for which they are not properly prepared. Teen pregnancy and the demise of the family in the urban centers of America have thrown unprecedented numbers of children into the courts and into the guardianship of the state. According to the Kids Campaign run by the Benton Foundation, the number of children in foster care has increased 65 percent during the last ten years, and each year 25,000 of these kids "graduate" foster care at age eighteen with no permanent families!

Families don't have to dissolve and cause this kind of negative impact on children. Half of American fathers say they don't spend enough time with their children.[12] In fact, the average parent spends only 17 hours a week with their children, leaving them to be brought up by day care centers, government institutions, or, worse yet, television producers. According to an article in *The Dayton Daily News*, March 3, 1995, half of our children watch more than two hours of television a day, but three-fourths of them say that if they could choose between spending time with their families and watching television, they would choose family time.

The American Public Welfare Association reports that substitute care for children is growing 33 percent faster than the U.S. child population in general! The fallout of this kind of neglect is well documented. Increased drug and alcohol abuse, crime, promiscuous sexual behavior, depression, and suicide among young people are directly correlated to the condition of their families. The condition of their families, in turn, is affected by their worship habits.[13] So the activists can beat their chests and wave their signs as much as they want, but the fact is, a nonreligious family life increases the risk that a child is going to have serious problems.

A Sabbath day for worship, service, and family is almost a sure protection against many problems and a boon for society. Churchgoers are more likely to be married, less likely to be divorced or single, and more likely to manifest high levels of satisfaction in their home lives.[14] Regular religious practice contributes substantially to the formation of strong moral convictions and sound judgment. Most significantly, regular involvement in spiritual activities such as worship, Bible study, and prayer meetings nearly inoculates adults and children against a host of personal and social problems that threaten them and the communities in which they live.[15] The facts are clear: The family who prays together, *indeed*, stays together.

PREVENTATIVE MEDICINE

There remains one more benefit to "Remembering the Sabbath Day," and it has to do with our health. As I have already mentioned, we have certain limitations that make us dependent on one another and, most importantly, on God. The Sabbath reminds us regularly that this is true. How? By cultivating within us what I call an "attitude of gratitude," which relieves the work-day pressure of feeling that everything rests on our shoulders.

Once we understand our place in the scheme of things, we realize that it is a position of both strength and weakness. As the crown of God's creation, we enjoy extraordinary capabilities and prerogatives. Yet, to counterbalance those strengths, we also have plenty of limitations. Human beings can do truly amazing things, but we can't do everything. This realization has important ramifications in many areas. Learning to depend on God strengthens our spiritual well-being, reduces stress and anxiety, helps us to cope with crises, and contributes to overall good mental health.

Dr. Kenneth Ferraro, associate professor of sociology at Purdue University, published a study in 1993 demonstrating that the best means for attaining mental and physical fitness may be a robust spiritual life. Religious practice is not a cure-all for every disease or physical anomaly, but Dr. Ferraro did find that people who worship regularly and participate in religious activities get sick less often than those who don't attend church. An earlier Johns Hopkins University research study concluded that regular church attendance significantly reduced incidents of cardiovascular diseases, the leading killer of older Americans.[16] These positive health effects were said to extend to a variety of illnesses, including colitis and different types of cancers, and even contributed to increasing life span in general.

Healthy people contribute to a healthy society. In fact, comprehensive studies on the social effects of religion have shown that 81 percent of regular church worshipers have proven to be a positive benefit for society. Only 4 percent showed negative effects.[17] Therefore, behavior contrary to the Ten Commandments has proven to be extremely costly.

Health insurance premiums have skyrocketed to pay for the bitter fruits of sin, including teen pregnancies, abortions, drug abuse/

alcoholism rehabilitation, and the spread of sexually transmitted diseases, especially AIDS. Taxes in some places have been pushed up to unbearable levels due to increases in prison populations, the construction of new prison facilities, police recruitment, training, and equipment. And billions of dollars disappear without any apparent benefit because so much time is wasted in public schools due to the lack of discipline in the classroom and the fear of violence on the part of both teachers and students. These social pathologies could be virtually wiped out and the money wasted on them put to better use if we would simply embrace the principles behind the Fourth Commandment: "Remember the Sabbath day, to keep it holy."

There is simply no substitute for an internal governor of human behavior. The surest cure for the dangerous and problematic behaviors now rampant in our country is an internal respect for God and His law. America's second president, John Adams, said, "We have no government armed with power capable of contending with human passions unbridled by morality and religion."[18] By reminding us of our highest obligations, the Sabbath points us individually and collectively toward overall healthier lifestyles that contribute to our national good. Spiritually, mentally, and physically healthy individuals mean healthy families. Healthy families mean healthy communities. And healthy communities mean a healthy nation.

Just ask Christ and Dolly Lapp. They'll tell you. They live happy and successful lives by Jesus words:

The Sabbath was made for man, and not man for the Sabbath.

MARK 2:27

THE HONOR FACTOR

CHAPTER FIVE

Joe Bowles is a large man with a pumpkin-shaped face and a heart as big as his massive hands. We are driving around Columbus, Ohio, in his four-wheel drive Chevy Blazer, and he is telling me his story. I am here on a speaking engagement at a large church. Joe, a corporate executive, has been assigned as my host. This is one of the great joys of my life, meeting new people and hearing their stories. I collect other people's life stories like some people collect stamps. It's as much a hobby for me as it is a continuing education in the ministry. The "stuff" of ministry is the "stuff" of people's lives, so I sit and I listen.

Tonight, I am hearing an amazing account of a son's love for his aging parents. Had it been a made-for-TV movie, it would be the sort of tale that you might dismiss as unbelievably sentimental. But this is not TV. This is real life.

The Bowles family are hardworking people. Joe and his five brothers and sisters spent most of their childhood years in breezy farmhouses. He can remember winters in which the snow would blow up from between the floor boards in the kitchen. No one complained. In the

Bowles' home complaining was reserved for much worse than a little snow in the kitchen.

Joe describes his father, Robert, as having been a strong, heavy man with dark red hair. "Dad was not at all religious," he says in his soft-spoken manner, with only a hint of a farm-boy accent. "But he cared deeply for his family and he would do anything to provide for us children. Sometimes he held down as many as three jobs at once."

The Blazer turns a corner and so does the conversation. "But Dad could get really angry." Joe notes with a wince. "He could at times be explosive. He and I got into a fistfight when I was 16. I knocked him down to the ground. We didn't talk much after that."

Phyllis Bowles is locked in Joe's memory as an angel. These were the early 1950s, when Pentecostal Christian women like Joe's mother wore their hair as long as nature would allow it and tied it up on their heads in a bun. He smiles as he reminisces about her simple, handmade dresses and her love for singing hymns and playing the piano.

"There were always other kids at our house," Joe recalls wistfully. "Mom never seemed to mind. At mealtime she would just cook a little extra. Dad was like that too. He had a dump truck and tools and everybody would come over to borrow them. My parents were always giving."

After Joe's dad became ill with heart disease and diabetes and could no longer work, Joe remembered the vow he had made when he was twelve years old. He would take care of his parents just the way they took care of him and the other kids.

One night, while trying to sort out his parents' long neglected financial records, Joe discovered that his father was deeply in debt. To avoid embarrassing them, he offered to buy out his father's considerable collection of woodworking tools for an amount equal to their outstanding obligations. His father, Robert, accepted in a businesslike manner. Then they shook hands and Joe paid the bills, but the tools remained in his parents' shed.

Next, Joe arranged a family conference call during which the brothers and sisters settled on a plan. Suzie, being closest geographically, would check in with her folks on weekdays. Joe and his wife, Judy, who is a nurse, would travel the two hours from their home on weekends to monitor Robert's medications and sugar levels. The other four kids, who were living too far away to assist in practical ways, agreed to pitch in funds to hire additional help for after hours.

"Dad and I made peace before he died," Joe announces crisply as we roll to stop at a red light. "I made sure of that." It has started raining, and I think I see a tear in Joe's eye. He turns on the windshield wipers and strokes his cheek with a finger.

Another resolution that guided the decisions made by the Bowles children was a determination to keep their parents out of nursing home care as long as they possibly could. When Phyllis exhibited symptoms of Alzhiemer's disease the same year that her husband passed away, it made this resolution more difficult to keep. Still, each child was determined to stick to it. Joe and Suzy developed a rotating schedule of care for their mom. All but those who lived too far away took part. They would drive in, fly in, and sometimes even temporarily move in, to be sure that she had all the help she needed. Joe and Suzy searched out the leading authorities on the treatment of Alzhiemer's, spending hundreds of hours and thousands of dollars.

When remaining in the house that she loved became a danger to Phyllis, Joe's younger brother, David, offered to take her into his North Carolina home. The family and her doctors agreed that this would be best. David and his wife then renovated a spare bedroom, designing it to look as much as possible like the bedroom that Robert and Phyllis occupied together for so many decades. When David claimed his mother's belongings, he was careful to take note where

WORD
FIVE

"HONOR YOUR FATHER AND
YOUR MOTHER, THAT YOUR
DAYS MAY BE LONG UPON THE
LAND WHICH THE LORD YOUR
GOD IS GIVING YOU."

EXODUS 20:12

each photo, momento, and other items were placed, replicating the setup exactly in her new room.

Joe's story comes to a close with Mrs. Bowles taking her first ever plunge into a hot tub at David's house. As we pull up to the front door of my hotel and unload my luggage, I feel a debt of gratitude to Joe and his family. Suddenly my love for my wife, children, and for my own parents has deepened. I only hope that I can be as faithful to them as the Bowles have been to one another.

◢

The tender and devoted care that Joe Bowles and his brothers and sisters showed their aging parents is the epitome of the practical side to the Fifth Commandment. Their actions exemplify the high calling of this moral edict. But it would be a mistake to see this commandment as simply a charge to properly treat our loved ones. As noble as it is in itself, our behavior towards those closest to us must spring from a larger passion, a greater ethic, a more comprehensive principle.

"Honor your father and your mother" takes us to the second table of the Decalogue. Now we will look at the "horizontal" commandments—our duties and obligations to our fellow human beings. Jesus summarized this second table with a directive from the Old Testament book of Leviticus, "Love your neighbor as yourself" (Leviticus 19:18). (See also Matthew 22:39; Mark 12:31.) The Hebrew word used here for neighbor, ray-ah, can be interpreted to mean anyone living in very close proximity to us, especially blood kin.

While mother and father are the focal points of this commandment, they also represent the larger family. As we will see more fully in the Seventh Commandment, the family is the basic unit from which communities grow. The nuclear family surrounded by the extended family becomes the clan or the tribe. These were the foundation stones to nations. You can't have countries without neighbors, and you can't have neighbors without first having families.

It has always struck me how the command to honor God heads the top of the first table in the traditional placement of the Commandments, and the command to honor parents heads the top of the second table. Together, they give us our top two priorities in life: God above all else, then family. Everything else comes after these two.

In God's economy, the family plays an enormously important and incomparable role. The family is to offer unconditional love, protection, and lifelong companionship to its members. It is to be the first church, the first school, the first hospital, and the first government.

The family is where children learn to appreciate the different roles people play in life and the distinctions that exist between male and female, young and old. It is in the family that children also learn how to resolve conflicts, how to communicate their ideas and their feelings, how to enjoy life, and how to endure pain. The confines of family life provide the safest parameters in which to discover acceptable and unacceptable behavior. In short, the home is the principal place for spiritual, emotional, and moral training.

Of course, not every family will accomplish all of these things. Some will utterly fail at them. But the principle remains true, and we must aspire to it. We must honor our mothers and fathers, even those who fall severely short of God's intention. In doing so, we affirm the indispensable place that the family occupies in human development. Even when the family is broken, important lessons about life continue to be taught and learned. Families are not perfect, just as nothing in life is perfect. We live in a fallen world, so we live in fallen families. But even fallen families are made up of individuals who are valuable in the eyes of God and are therefore to be shown honor.

WHO ARE OUR PARENTS?

Before we discuss exactly how to honor our parents, we need to more completely identify just who we are talking about. For some, Mom and Dad are the two people to whom we were born and who raised us. For others, it can be confusing. Are adopted children obligated to honor their birth parents in the same way they honor those who raised them? What about dysfunctional, negligent, or abusive parents? What if we don't even know our parents or have long been estranged from them?

These are all very real questions, especially today when so many children are raised outside of a two-parent, opposite sex, marriage-bound model. Divorce, single parenting, and a growing number of so-called LGBT (Lesbian Gay Bisexual Transgendered) families have redefined who parents are and how we are to relate to them. Still, it is possible for all of us to honor our parents, no matter what their condition, behavior, or our relationship to them. It won't mean the same thing in each case, but where there is God's will, there is always a way to obey it.

As I see it, parents can be defined as three kinds of people. There are 1) biological parents, 2) legal parents, and 3) nurturing parents. In most cases, the parents to whom we relate are all three. This is the ideal. However, you may have adoptive parents who nurtured you and biological parents whom you may not know anything about. If one of your parents remarried after a death or a divorce, you have a stepparent. If you were raised by some other relative or adult, you have both biological and surrogate parents. Sometimes a court or other legal agency will appoint a legal guardian for a child. But *mother* and *father* are verbs as much as nouns. So while this person may have parental authority in the eyes of the law, that status does not always equate to an emotional or spiritual bond with the one who is in their charge.

Clifton Taulbert, a successful entrepreneur and active churchman from Tulsa, Oklahoma, tells a beautiful story of being brought up by his maternal great-grandfather, whom he called Poppa, and others in his extended family in his book, *Once Upon a Time When We Were Colored*. Clifton's happiness as a child and his later success as a Christian man, husband, father, layman, and businessman illustrates how even unusual family configurations can substitute effectively for the conventional mother-father-child structure.

"Poppa and I were very close," Mr. Taulbert writes.

> I had been born in his house, as were my mother and her mother before her. My mother was unmarried when I came into this world, and when she later married, it was felt that I would be better off living with Poppa and his wife, Ma Pearl. Even though I was not raised by my mother, she lived within walking distance of Poppa's house. I spent a great deal of time with her as well as with my other aunts and uncles, enjoying the benefits of an extended family. By the time I was five, Ma Pearl had become too sick to take care of me and I went to live with my great-aunt, Ma Ponk. I built my world around Poppa and he protected me from the harsher realities of our complex social environment.[1]

The reader of Cliff Taulbert's story sees how the character instilled in Mr. Taulbert's "multiple" upbringing saw him through some challenging times and eventually provided him with the fortitude necessary to achieve success. His family experience and his subsequent exploits demonstrate that God can and will bless different family structures. The biblical ideal is the mother-father-child unit, but it is becoming increasingly less common in our American culture. While I will later make an argument as to how we can and must return to the ideal, we must also deal with present realities. The important elements in determining just how this commandment relates to your situation is to look at the roles played by those in various parental positions in our lives.

Parents are found among those who nurtured and equipped us for life. They shouldn't be too difficult to identify. Your "mother" and or "father" took care of you, saw to your most important needs, imparted their wisdom to you, and launched you into adulthood. Most often these will be your birth parents, but whoever he, she, or they may be, the ones who prepared you for life deserve your honor first. Beyond them are those who contributed to your other needs. Perhaps you have a biological parent who contributed to your expenses, whether for clothing, education, or some other material requirement. This person or these persons are next in line for receiving honor, but it needs to be proportional. In other words, the greater the input into your life, the greater debt of gratitude owed to them. Though expressed differently in each case, it is important that those who played parental roles in your life receive some form of appropriate affirmation from you.

How Do We Honor Parents?

What does it mean to honor our parents according to the fourth of God's Ten Commandments? To answer this, once again we have help from the original Hebrew word used here. Honor is translated from *kah-vode*, which literally means "to be heavy" or "to add weight." In ancient times, something that was heavy was thought to have greater value. Precious stones and metals were appraised mostly by their weights. Even people were sometimes judged according to how heavy they were. In the Bible, parents are given great *weight*.

Parents are the beginning of every family and therefore embody the family as no other two persons can. Every family begins with two parents. Even Adam and Eve were formed by the hands of the one who said of Himself, "I am a Father to Israel" (Jeremiah 31:9) and "As a mother comforts her child, so will I comfort you" (Isaiah 66:13 NIV). God himself was their parent.

Our Lord Jesus, who was conceived of a virgin mother, referred to God as His Father, but He also had an earthly father in Mary's husband, Joseph. Every human being has at least a biological mother and a biological father. Therefore, in honoring the family, we must begin with its progenitors.

The ancient Jewish rabbis teach that parents are to be honored because they are partners with God. They cooperate with God by having children. God is the author of life, but parents are the medium through which He chooses to bring new life into the world. Parents don't always do a good job of being God's partner. My wife and I have certainly made our mistakes. We are human beings and are therefore frail. In fact, too many parents are more than frail. They can be destructive, inflicting injury on their children. Nevertheless, parents remain in their stations as a representation of divinity, even if in greatly diminished form. They may bungle everything after conception or birth, but they are still worthy of honor as the earthly source of our lives.

At least in a physical sense, there are no two human beings more intimately connected to us than our natural, biological parents. Like it or not, we are inextricably tied to them. We are literally made of and from them. We are "bone of their bone and flesh of their flesh." (See Genesis 2:23.) Even after separation from our parents in adulthood and through marriage, we continue to carry in our bodies and minds our parents' genetic code, along with many of their emotional and personality traits.

I realize that this doesn't make it any easier for a child (grown or not) whose parents abused or abandoned them to understand or obey this commandment. But, it is possible to honor unworthy parents, not only because God commands it, but for our own well-being.

BEARING THE GOOD WITH THE BAD

Sue H. deliberately summons pleasant memories of her father when asked about him. She will recount with endearment how she visited with him in the serenity of the orchid house that he kept on the back of their property in Miami, Florida. Recalling the deep purples and brilliant yellows of the flowers that oddly share memory space with the odor of the fish emulsion used to feed the plants, she can still hear the soft crush of the building's pine bark covered floor under her feet.

The orchid house seemed the only place where Dad welcomed Sue's presence. Her images of him at other times and in other places are accompanied by sadness, fear, and mystery. It wasn't until Sue was 25, seven years after her father's death, that she learned he had made his living as a bookie, profiting from illegal wagers. Perhaps this was why he was so invisible to her when he was outside of the orchid house.

For most of her childhood, Sue's dad and mom ignored her and her two older brothers. By the early evenings, their parents were in alcoholic stupors. There was never any talk of homework, let alone help with it. It seemed that only the occasional outburst of anger broke the painful silence, and Sue's brothers received most of the negative attention that ensued.

The vacuum left by this absence of a mother and father's presence led Sue into an insatiable quest for love and attention in her teenage years. Drugs, alcohol, and promiscuous sex took their toll. Never having found the peace that she so desperately craved, Sue finally gave in to despair. As a young adult, she spent many days sobbing uncontrollably. She was suicidal. Then she met Rob, who would one day become her husband. Rob introduced her to his Episcopal priest, who explained to Sue that the only person who could help her was Jesus Christ. As a result, Sue was born again. As she grew in her faith, her life changed radically for the better.

Many years later, during a women's retreat for her parish church, Sue shared the memories of her past. Her listeners learned of a father's comforting pleasure at his daughter's meager catch on a fishing expedition, and the rare interest with which he cleaned each of her tiny sunfish. The fun of cooking and eating the fish together was also described with great delight. What Sue's listeners didn't hear, however, is how rare this moment was in her life.

When Sue speaks of her mother today, she talks of her mom's sense of humor, her entertaining Texas drawl, and her amazing talent in the kitchen and as a hostess. She even credits her mother as being the model and resource for the skills that eventually launched her into a successful career in restaurant management.

In Sue's public conversation about her parents, there is no criticism, bitterness, or resentment, nor is there any talk of abandonment or blame. Sue is not in denial about these painful realities, but she has made a conscious decision to honor her parents' memory by recalling the good times, as few as they may have been, and telling others about them. This has brought peace into Sue's heart.

Not every situation lends itself to the resolution that Sue discovered. If you were completely separated or alienated from your natural parents, you need not pretend that they are more than they were to you. If you do not know who they are, you can simply thank God for who you are and for the fact that you had parents who gave you life. If you do know them, and they have had no active role in your upbringing, then you might send them a note on your own birthday saying, "It's my birthday, and I wanted to thank you for helping me get here!" Of course, there can be legal and other dangers involved with some estranged family members, so be sure to get professional and pastoral counseling before making such a contact. On the whole, though, a kind and winsome word can heal many family wounds.

If your biological parents played a minimal role in your upbringing, a simple thank you for the things they bought you or the education they provided you with may be all that is required. As I noted before, you don't have to treat someone as more than they really are to you, but you should acknowledge them for what they have done on your behalf, if for nothing else than the fact that they were there for your conception!

Those parents who were involved in your life, caring for you, disciplining and training you, loving and respecting you, are deserving of the most complete honor. To return to our word study, "honor" in the Bible means to give weight. This is the first clue as to how to honor those parents most worthy of it. To give them weight means that they factor heavily in your priorities. To put it simply, they matter to you. In terms of time, energy, effort, attention, and even expenditures of money, your nurturing parents are on the top of the list. Jesus' precept applies here, "To whom much is given, from him much will be required" (Luke 12:48). If you are given much by God, then you are to give much back. The same with parents. If your parents gave you much, then they most certainly deserve much in return.

For those who have parents appointed by the courts or other legal guardians, and this is the extent of your relationship to them, your obligation is simply to obey them until you reach the age of legal emancipation. (See Colossians 3:20.) Once this is achieved, you should certainly thank them for having assumed that important responsibility, but you needn't feel obligated to do more. Of course, we should follow the leading of the Holy Spirit in every case. Should He prompt you to do more, to show extraordinary kindness beyond what these individuals are entitled to, by all means be obedient! But don't suffer with a guilt complex if you haven't done more than is required of you.

AMERICA AND HER PARENTS

There was a time in America when parents were accorded an unparalleled place in American culture. They were revered by their descendants and highly esteemed in their communities. Children were taught to heed their parents, and those who didn't experienced some pain. There was zero tolerance for disrespect to your elders or back talk of any kind. Grandma and Grandpa sat in a position of honor at the family table. They could be found at the center of those elongated family photos, like an emperor and empress, surrounded by generations of family members. When grandparents became too frail to care for themselves, there was no question about whether their adult children would take them in. The only legitimate concern was whose house was the largest. Grandchildren, watching their moms and dads honor their parents, in turn learned how to do the same, preserving the indispensable institution of the family for the next generation.

The founders of our nation understood the importance of this principle and how critical it was to building an enduring American civilization. They were informed in their ethical and philosophical convictions by biblical moral instruction. John Quincy Adams, sixth president of the United States, expressed the attitude of his generation in a letter to his son:

> The law given from Sinai was a civil and municipal as well
> as a moral and religious code; it contained many statutes . . .
> of universal application—laws essential to the existence of
> men in society.[2]

This Law of Sinai, the Ten Commandments, was just the precursor to many more guidelines on morality. There are hundreds of passages in the Bible that deal with families and family life. Birth, death, marriage, relationships with relatives, and even sexual relations are major themes throughout Scripture. And, in addition to the Fifth Commandment itself, there are other explicit admonitions regarding respect for parents:

Every one of you shall revere his mother and his father.

LEVITICUS 19:3

My son, keep your father's command, and do not forsake the law of your mother.

PROVERBS 6:20

Children, obey your parents in the Lord, for this is right.

EPHESIANS 6:1

These are what guided public policy on the family in our nation for nearly two-hundred years. But then came the radical sixties, when the value of parents and grandparents took a nosedive. The "old man" and "old lady" were suddenly seen as irrelevant, bothersome, and an imposition.

Now, thirty years later, in some ways those rebellious attitudes have been institutionalized and mainstreamed. A recent front cover article in the trendy teen magazine for girls, *Sassy*, teased readers with this lead, "Do you really hate your parents? Like, who doesn't? How to deal with your detestables."[3] And nowhere is this disregard for parents more pronounced than in the growing contempt for the elderly. Another article, originally published in *The Wall Street Journal* and reprinted in the *Cortlandt Forum* medical journal, asked about the cost of caring for a 90-year-old patient suffering from multiple health problems. The piece was entitled, "Was it worth it?"[4]

THE NEW DISPOSABLE PARENT

One evening in April of 1996, the Howard family of Neosha, Missouri, gathered together for an unusual activity. They could have fired up a backyard barbecue, played a game of Monopoly, or just sat around the kitchen table gabbing about neighbors and relatives as so many midwestern American families do. Instead, the Howards mixed up a concoction of orange juice, alcohol, and sleeping medications. They then administered the toxic brew to 76-year old Velma Howard, who was suffering from amyotropic lateral sclerosis, commonly called Lou Gehrig's disease.

While her husband and children looked on, Mrs. Howard fell into unconsciousness, a plastic bag was placed over her head and tied at the neck. At the time that charges were filed against the woman's husband and son, it was not known whether the poison or the lack of oxygen had killed her. But before the two men came to trial, federal judges in California and New York struck down state laws against assisting a suicide and prosecutors dropped the charges. As of the writing of this book, those charges have not been reinstated, even though a subsequent U.S. Supreme Court ruling found no right to suicide in the Constitution.

Mrs. Howard's murder-suicide was not an isolated incident. No one knows precisely how many older Americans commit suicide with the help of family, friends, or physicians, but the sense is that the number is growing exponentially. Incidents of so-called euthanasia, in which doctors or others act to terminate a life without the participation of the victim, also seem to be increasing. A study published in the *New England Journal of Medicine* showed that as much as 54 percent of physicians in Washington State, where this issue has been vigorously debated, approve of legalizing the killing of patients.[5]

In a lawsuit entitled *Compassion in Dying* v. *State of Washington*, the Ninth U.S. Circuit Court of Appeals struck down laws against suicide for the terminally ill in Washington State. That decision was later overturned by the U.S. Supreme Court, but in doing so, the higher court carefully left a door open to reconsider the matter and perhaps legalize suicide in the future. The most disturbing element of the Ninth Circuit Court's decision came in what Judge Stephen Reinhardt wrote for the majority about reasons for the terminally ill to end their lives:

> We also realize that terminally ill patients may well feel
> pressured to hasten their deaths . . . out of concern for the
> economic welfare of their loved ones. Faced with the
> prospect of astronomical medical bills, terminally ill patients
> might decide it is better for them to die before their health
> care expenses consume the life savings they planned to leave
> for their families . . . we are reluctant to say that . . . it is
> improper for competent, terminally ill adults to take
> economic welfare of their families . . . into consideration.[6]

Compare this easy solution to the demands placed on us by the
suffering of our loved ones with the selfless and tireless devotion of
the Bowles' children. Their sacrifice is viewed more and more as
backward, as if no self-respecting babyboomer would allow
themselves to be sucked into such an obligation. The sixties "me"
generation has come home to roost. Parents are there to provide for
me when I am unable to do so for myself. Once I'm on my own, so
are they!

The fruit of this war on parents can now be seen in its deadly effect
on children. The astronomical jump in teen suicides is just one
factor. Teen television shows, films, music, and art also bear witness
to this terrible decline. As disillusionment and alienation grow
among America's youth, families move farther apart. Children are
home less, move far away in adulthood, nursing homes have taken
the place of in-law apartments, and families no longer gather for the
death watch. A telephone call from a dispassionate hospital
employee has replaced the last words of a dying mother.

In contrast, the Fifth Commandment elevates parents to a place of
supreme value in our eyes and moves us to treat them with the
utmost care and respect. The importance of the parent-child
relationship and this commandment in the eyes of God can be seen
vividly in the Old Testament book of Exodus. The impudent child
who would raise his hand against his mother or father was considered

to be such a serious threat to ancient Israel's social order, the child was to be executed. (See Exodus 21:15-17.)

In the Church, when our natural families fail us, God has provided a substitute family in the body of Christ. The apostle Paul captures the dynamic of the church family for a young pastor, Timothy, when he writes:

> **Do not rebuke an older man, but exhort him as a father, younger men as brothers,**
>
> **older women as mothers, younger women as sisters.**
>
> 1 TIMOTHY 5:1-2

This is what Jesus promised to those alienated from their family members by their devotion to Him,

> **"[N]o one who has left home or brothers or sisters or mother or father or children or fields for me and the gospel**
>
> **will fail to receive a hundred times as much in this present age."**
>
> MARK 10:29-30 NIV

This "hundredfold family" is composed of our brothers and sisters in Christ and our elders in the faith.

ALBERTO

Alberto was twelve years old when he was abandoned by his family in one of Mexico City's huge inhabited garbage dumps. I met him while supervising a medical team that was part of Operation Serve, a Christian humanitarian relief organization that I founded in the early 1980's. When the boy strayed into missionary doctor John Seaman's makeshift clinic, an assistant noticed that he couldn't breathe properly. After examining Alberto's nasal passages, the doctor carved out a small pile of solidified glue that was commonly inhaled as a cheap intoxicant by kids like Alberto. As the blockage was removed, Alberto's eyes brightened with appreciative relief.

The last time I saw Alberto was toward the end of the same day. He wandered into the clinic, and one of our team members walked him over to get a bath and new clothes. Operation Serve ministered to thousands of children like Alberto and, to be frank, I forgot about the incident. Then, eight years later I received a surprising note from a student at the Polytechnic Institute in Mexico City.

"Dear Brother Roberto," he wrote.

> Do you remember me? I was living like an animal in the garbage dumps when your people found me. You helped me a lot. I met Jesus and the church adopted me. They put me in Christian school and I graduated with special honors. Today, I am studying computer science in college. I am getting perfect grades! I want to thank you for helping me to find a loving family of so many brothers and sisters. I want to serve the Lord when I am out of school. God bless you! Alberto.

God gave Alberto a new family in place of the one that had not wanted him.

WHY HONOR PARENTS?

In light of Alberto's experience, we might wonder why he would ever show his parents any kind of respect. Their abandonment of him to a place as frightening and as dangerous as a garbage dump would seem to disqualify them forever from receiving such honor. But Sue H.'s experience illustrates how we can find a way to treat our parents in a manner that follows the spirit of this commandment, whether or not they are worthy of it. This enables the wounded child to attribute value to a parent whom they might otherwise despise. It also affords them the opportunity to extend mercy to that erring parent. This very act makes the child a better person. Showing mercy benefits the one giving it most of all. In His Sermon on the Mount, Jesus said there is a special reward for those who act with this sort of kindness,

Blessed are the merciful, for they shall obtain mercy.

MATTHEW 5:7

There is an even larger reason that this is important. The treatment of parents by their children, and by extension the attitude of society toward the family, is of utmost importance. In many ways it sets the pattern for the rest of human culture. We might say that as it goes with parents, so it goes with all authority. The implications of this are self-evident.

The Catechism of the Catholic Church says much about this commandment and its reach into all areas of our lives:

> [The fifth] commandment is addressed expressly to children in their relationship to their father and mother, because this relationship is most universal. It likewise concerns the ties of kinship between members of the extended family. It requires honor, affection, and gratitude toward elders and ancestors. Finally, it extends to the duties of pupils to teachers, employees to employers, subordinates to leaders, citizens to their country, and to those who administer and govern it.[7]

This understanding of the critical place that the treatment of parents occupies in all of life pervades Christian history. It held a prominent place in Martin Luther's table of duties.[8] John Calvin declared children, "unworthy of the light in paying no deference to those to whom they are indebted for beholding it."[9]

If for no other reason, we should honor our parents because God commands it. However, when God commands something, He does so for good reason, and there is most certainly good reason to honor our parents. I've already mentioned that, at the very least, they gave us life. What they did after that may be questionable, but the reason we exist is because two people participated in bringing us into existence, and one of them bore quite a bit of pain and inconvenience and in some cases took consider-able risk in that process. This is reason enough to be grateful.

Nothing comes cheaply, least of all life. Your life unquestionably cost someone—namely your mother—and one would hope that your father invested something as well. If in any way he was negligent in doing so, you still carry something from him in your genetic code. The reason you have the faculties and traits you have is because your parents endowed you with them. You carry something from them and have hopefully made good with it. Your parents gave something to you that you can use for the raw material of your life. This is reason enough to thank and honor them.

GUARDIANS OF CIVILIZATION

There are, however, many more reasons than these to honor our parents. Parents pre-figure God in our lives. Parents are to nurture, protect, instruct, guide, and correct their children. The duty of parents is to prepare their children for life so they can succeed and find happiness. Parents are also to be the guardians of civilization. They teach and enforce acceptable standards of behavior so that others in the human community can live without threat.

Not all parents are faithful to these responsibilities, and some who try fail in their attempts to carry them out. However, their very existence as parents remind us that their earthly duties, whether or not they fulfill them, are merely shadows of God's benevolence towards us. He is our ultimate father and mother:

> **Though my father and mother forsake me, the Lord will receive me.**
>
> PSALM 27:10 NIV

Parents are also the repositories of wisdom. Wisdom has been defined as the accumulation and practical application of knowledge. This is enormously important for individual lives, the life of a whole people, and for cultures and civilizations. There are literally thousands of years of experience deposited into your parents. This too is reason to "give them weight."

The oft quoted adage, "Those who forget the past are doomed to repeat it," is one of the main reasons for our problems today. Human beings experience no new moral dilemmas. They may come cloaked in newer technology or terminology, but they're the same old problems. For example, the current debate over physician-assisted suicide is centuries old. The Greeks debated this before the time of Socrates. In fact, some of the court briefs and judicial rulings in assisted-suicide cases draw on references going back over three thousand years!

Those who have gone before us possess the knowledge of what worked and didn't work in addressing these situations and much more. If they didn't live through something themselves, they may have gleaned something from someone else's experience, or they were entrusted with knowledge from their parents' or great grand-parents' experiences. This makes the parent a wealth of information, information that we cannot, and often should not, learn firsthand.

The 1960's set American culture far back because a whole generation seemed to dismiss the wisdom of their predecessors with a wave of the hand. The result was catastrophic. Parents in the 1950's knew that premarital sex would bring pain and suffering because those who went before them discovered this to be true. Syphilis was a killer centuries before AIDS. Illegitimate children suffered long before the appearance of the modern urban ghetto. Marital infidelity, multiple partners, and easy divorce all caused great pain long before the *Jerry Springer Show* made them popular pastimes. And homosexuality brought about physical and psychological injury, illness, and death millennia before the Stonewall riots gave birth to the gay rights movement.

By dismissing the knowledge, experience, and instruction of our elders, we place ourselves at a serious disadvantage in approaching the great challenges of life. We'll find that we must learn all these sometimes painful lessons over and over again, wasting precious time and resources. On the contrary, should we build upon their foundation, we will deal with whatever comes our way in a quicker, more effective and successful way. We owe it to our children, grandchildren, and all who follow to receive as much wisdom as we can from our predecessors. All of us will be happier and better for it.

The Only Reason

This bears repeating: The best reason for honoring parents is because God commands us to do it. In the end we need go no further than this: God commands us to treat our parents with respect and deference. He instructs us to give them great value and to treat them accordingly. This commandment is so important that St. Paul notes in the New Testament that it is the first commandment with a promise,

> **Children, obey your parents in the Lord, for this is right.**
>
> **"Honor your father and mother," which is the first commandment with promise:**
>
> **"That it may be well with you and you may live long on the earth."**
>
> EPHESIANS 6:1-3

The success of the Israelites as a nation was linked inseparably to their treatment of their forebears. The Bowles of Columbus, Ohio, knew something that the Howards of Neosha, Iowa, did not. It is the law of reciprocity. In His Sermon on the Mount, Jesus said,

> **Just as you want men to do to you, you also do to them likewise.**
>
> LUKE 6:31

The way we treat our parents, family, and neighbors is the way we will be treated. The children and grandchildren who learned how their ailing grandmother Howard was put to death will have that powerful image imbedded in their minds for the time when their own parents, siblings, or children experience similar suffering.

Here's to the Bowles! They give us the right model for how to treat those who go before us. Here's to the mothers and fathers and grandparents and great grandparents who make investments of love and care in generations to come.

Listen to your father who begot you, and do not despise your mother when she is old.

PROVERBS 23:22

AMERICA'S
HEART DISEASE

CHAPTER SIX

"**M**s. Stevens, your mother is gravely ill. Her condition will require surgery and a long period of convalescence." The young doctor is speaking in a near whisper, so Laura leans in close until he can feel her breath on his face. Realizing this, he repeats himself slightly louder and she backs away.

"As you were told by our options counselor, because of your mother's age and status, she qualifies as a C-11 patient." He maintains the higher volume, but touches her elbow momentarily, indicating that they should move further away from the door to the "Que Room"— short for Qualification Examination Room—where Laura's mom lays resting on a metal table.

"I can't remember what C-11 is," Laura announces, nervously shaking her head while she demands the information with her eyes. He is sure that she must remember the conversation of only a few moments ago, but is annoyed by the fact that he is unable to tell whether her feigned ignorance is because she is angered or saddened by the news. These are always awkward experiences for him, and he wishes that the "options counselors" would do a better job of closing the decision process before he has to get involved.

"C-11 is a fifteen-year, end-of-life classification." He modulates in and out of his gravelly whisper again. "That means that neither your private insurer, nor Medisure (the new government health care subsidy program) will pay for treatment. The bill could exceed $250,000. Now maybe you're people of means, but I'm sure you have better ways to spend your money. You may want to consider obitiatry. We can schedule a procedure for as early as Tuesday morning."

"Obitiatry?" Laura stumbles over the word. "You have to remind me what that is." She vaguely remembers that the hospital admissions clerk used the same term, but her mind wasn't on the conversation that day.

"Obitiatry is termination under a physician's direction," he answers matter-of-factly.

Laura bites down on the thumbnail she's been playing with for the last several minutes. Her eyes drop to the floor as she assimilates what the doctor has just said. "No," she says determinedly.

The young doctor is surprised. Ms. Stevens appears well-educated. He doesn't expect such an irrational response. Even wealthy people who can afford this kind of care rarely spend it on their aging parents anymore. He lifts his brow and takes a deep breath, preparing for a more persuasive presentation, but Laura preempts it.

"No . . . No. I have to talk to the family about this." Laura turns to leave without waiting for the doctor's acknowledgment and without seeking anyone's permission. Neither does she ask about her mother's immediate disposition. She simply hurries down the corridor, the echoing clickety-clack of her high heels slowly fading in volume. She disappears around the corner as the elevator bell sounds. Back in the room, the doctor orders patient 5706-C11 to a bed on the holding floor.

Two days later, on Tuesday morning, a BMW station wagon turns the corner onto Front Street and quickly wheels up to a nondescript door at Gaylord Hospital. A male attendant in blue hospital scrubs and a female security guard emerge from behind a simple aluminum-framed door with darkly tinted glass. They hurry Ms. Stevens inside, looking nervously around as the three disappear behind the door.

Once inside, the attendant leads the way down a long corridor that ends at a sliding door with an intercom speaker mounted nearby. The attendant presses a button on the speaker box and mutters something unintelligible. The door opens and Ms. Stevens is whisked into a cold, sparsely furnished viewing room, about the width of a double-wide closet. A one-way mirrored window allows her to see into another room where her mother now lays peacefully on a pneumatically controlled bed. A single shaft underneath slowly elevates her to near chest level. An IV is attached to her right arm.

A hospital chaplain dressed in a black blouse and banded white collar now appears. On her left shoulder, she is wearing a small, circular gold pin depicting an inverted triangle. The pin symbolizes the unity of all religions, sexual equality, and gender equality—three pillars of the hospital's chaplaincy program.

"Well, are you ready Ms. Stevens? Did you do those meditation exercises?" The chaplain asks. Her voice is pleasant, but distant.

"Yeah, I guess so. When do you start this?" Laura replies as she places her purse on the only table in the room and then picks it up nervously.

"They'll start momentarily," the chaplain says without looking Laura in the eye. "May I read you a line from a poem?" Without waiting for Laura's answer, the chaplain opens a small leather-bound book with a gold-colored ribbon marking a particular page. "This life we have is but a ship for navigating the universal sea. When morning comes we will disembark and walk the peaceful shores."

"Thank you," Laura says, so quietly that she is barely audible. "Can we start this now?"

The chaplain raises her finger to someone beyond the glass whom Laura cannot see.

"In just a moment she'll be feeling much better, and this time she won't have to worry about any pain coming back. You've made a very courageous decision, and it really is the best for everybody. You know that, right?"

Laura doesn't answer. She simply stares through the darkened glass and cries silently.

◢

This fictionalized story of Ms. Stevens and her mother is not far from reality. What many American citizens do not realize is that another country has run the full gamut when it comes to euthanasia. Euthanasia has been practiced in Holland for the past 20 years. Here is what those 20 years have produced:

> The Van der Maas Survey is the official study of euthanasia commissioned by the Dutch government. . . . More requests for euthanasia came from families than from patients themselves; furthermore, families, doctors, and nurses were involved in pressuring patients to accept euthanasia by a feeling that the patient's situation was "hopeless."[1]

According to this survey, patients rarely have the choice to die; instead they are told they must die or are simply killed through the consent of their doctors and families. In 1990 there were 13,506 cases of euthanasia by omission [omitting food or treatment] in Holland, but "8,750 (65%) were killed without patient consent. Also in 1990

WORD
SIX

"YOU SHALL NOT MURDER."

EXODUS 20:13

there were 11,800 cases of active euthanasia. We know that 5,941 individuals out of 11,800 were killed without patient consent."[2]

In December of 1998 the *British Medical Journal* reported on a Dutch palliative care doctor (a doctor who specializes in patient pain management) who explained to the House of Lords in Great Britain that "in 1995, there were 900 cases of non-voluntary [*sic*] euthanasia reported. As many as 25 percent of those patients were killed without requesting death, even though they were fully or partly competent."[3] In these cases, death by choice has been replaced by an atrocity most reporters avoid calling murder, but the human soul refuses to lie to itself:

> Almost 80 percent of Dutch general practitioners have now had "experience with" euthanasia. Many physicians refuse, on ethical grounds and religious grounds, to kill their patients; those who do kill "often report nightmares afterwards."[4]

The aftereffects of assisted suicide and nonvoluntary euthanasia haven't been studied as yet, but this report suggests that many families and physicians are experiencing guilt and spiritual crisis as a result.

DOCTOR DEATH MAKES A HOUSE CALL

America is also beginning to entertain legalizing assisted suicide. As I write this, Dr. Jack Kevorkian, who coined the term *obitiatry*, has littered the state of Michigan with his victims' cadavers. Kevorkian is the former pathologist turned "Doctor of Death" who has become a Robin Hood of sorts among those who appreciate his work. He brazenly committed murder after murder with his deadly gas machines and lethal injections to "assist" his "clients" in killing themselves. Dr. Death left so many bodies in motel rooms that the motel association complained during his reign about the cost of cleaning up after his visits.

During a luncheon in Washington, D.C., sponsored by the American Center for Law and Justice, I sat with Richard Thompson, the first prosecutor to take on Kevorkian. He told our table about the evidence he had amassed against the doctor and his cohorts, including proof that Kevorkian had killed at least one victim without her permission. Thompson never got to try Kevorkian because he lost his next election largely due to Kevorkian's ghoulish popularity.

The twisted doctor finally went too far by allowing one of his assisted deaths to be filmed and aired on national television. He was indicted by a Michigan court and eventually convicted of second degree murder. He was sentenced to 10-25 years in prison. Without a renewal in our current American psyche, however, Kevorkian could go down as the first "martyr" pioneer of euthanasia legalization. An ABC poll conducted in March 1999 showed that 55 percent of Americans believed that the jury should not have convicted him.[5] Should American culture progress more toward the purely utilitarian view of life Kevorkian and his accomplices have broken ground to popularize, there will be whole industries of death that will prey on the lonely and the depressed.

If you think this claim is outlandish, take yourself back to the medical practices of the mid 1950s. Who could have imagined then that within twenty years a crime as serious as *abortacide*, the term once used for the intentional abortion of a pre-born infant, would lead the list of health care services in most yellow pages? At that time abortionists and their ilk were hunted down, prosecuted, and jailed. When caught, they lost their medical licenses, if they had them at all, and were cast out to the margins of society.

Today, abortionists are touted by the media as heroes. Dr. George Tiller of Wichita, Kansas, famous for the crematorium that he maintains to dispose of his routinely aborted full-term babies, has been honored as a special guest of President Clinton at the White House.[6] A few administrations earlier, Tiller would have been prosecuted and jailed.

The Bible places the highest value on human life and requires that we protect, promote, and preserve it. But the fact of the matter is, as a society we have lost respect for the incomparable value of human life. God doesn't allow us to take innocent life under any circumstances. Deciding whether a person lives or dies is simply not within our human purview. Therefore, God's Sixth Commandment, "You shall not murder," indicts those such as Kevorkian who take the matter into their own hands.

WHAT IS KILLING?

The taking of human life, no matter what the circumstances, is always cast in the negative in Holy Scripture. It is understood that the intentional premature death of a person is the consequence of something gone awry, something evil, something inauspicious. Whether sanctioned or unsanctioned, the killing of human beings is always regrettable. Yet, not all killing is morally wrong. War, capital punishment, and killing in defense of life are allowed for and given guidance in the Bible. But they are never celebrated.

The common translation of the Sixth Commandment, "Thou shalt not kill," is often misunderstood. In Hebrew this brief sentence reads, *Lo t'ratzach*. *Lo* is the Hebrew word for no. This other word, *ratzach*, appears 49 times in the Old Testament.[7] Although it is used to denote a variety of situations in which killing may take place, its essential meaning is the taking of an innocent human life. However, it doesn't refer simply to an innocent life; it is more accurate to say a *judicially* innocent life. This is an important distinction because the prohibition extends to the protection of not only those who are actually innocent of a capital crime, but also to those who have not been proven guilty of one. In other words, it goes directly to the biblical principle that the accused is innocent until proven guilty, a concept that our nation adopted in the Constitution.

This prohibition against taking innocent life is itself a very pro-life statement. It indicates emphatically that we should respect and treasure all human life, avoiding anything that contributes to the loss of innocent life, whether that loss is caused intentionally or accidentally. The Bible is extremely clear about this. In Numbers 35:16-18, 21, and 30, the point is made that a person who kills with premeditation, as opposed to one who kills accidentally or without hatred in their heart toward the victim, is to be put to death. Similarly, Numbers 35:31 refers to the use of the death penalty in the case of someone who has intentionally committed *ratzach,* but the term *ratzach* is not used for the death penalty in this instance, though it is in the preceding instances.

Hebrew has a variety of words for killing in general and other specific circumstances, but they do not appear in the Sixth Commandment. The context and limited use of *ratzach* specifically instructs us to avoid taking human life under any circumstances, but recognizes that there may be some situations (war, the execution of violent criminals, self-defense, etc.) when it is regrettably necessary. It is our obligation, however, to work to make these necessities as rare as humanly possible.

The Sixth Commandment has nothing to say about killing in other instances. For example, it says nothing about capital punishment. *Ratzach* is used on only two occasions to describe the execution of a convicted criminal, but in each case the context of the language gives clear moral justification for the act. Neither does this commandment address killing in self-defense, in the defense of another, the killing of soldiers during time of war, the slaughter of animals, or hunting. What is prohibited here is murder, the willful taking of an innocent human life.

THE SANCTITY OF ALL HUMAN LIFE

The essence of this prohibition not to kill is the protection of the individual right to life. Every human being, regardless of their age, sex, ethnicity, or condition of dependency has the inherent right to live. It is not something which we struggle to achieve. The Founders recognized this supreme human right and enshrined it in the Declaration of Independence: "We are endowed by our Creator with certain inalienable rights, among them the right to life."

An endowment is a gift. A gift is something freely given. It is not based on any prerequisite criteria, merit, qualification, or capacity to reciprocate. Such is the gift of life. Only God gives life; therefore, only God can say when it is to be taken away. Every person receives this gift by simple virtue of their humanity. And because our humanity itself is something outside our control, no one can decide when or what makes someone a human person.

This was the great error of slavery. The United States Supreme Court dared to interlope in the sacred arena of human personhood in the 1857 case of Dred Scott, declaring that a slave was not a legal person. Though later nullified by an act of Congress, the Dred Scott case set up a precedent for government decrees of human personhood, portending great danger for anyone out of favor with the judicial elite. Apparently not learning its lesson from the Scott case, the U.S. Supreme Court once again took away the personhood of an entire class of Americans in 1973.

Jane Roe v. *Henry Wade*, was a case involving an anonymous pregnant woman whose lawyers took on the district attorney of Dallas County, Texas. The losers in the *Roe* case were the pre-born, their mothers, and every American citizen. It was in 1969 that Norma McCorvey, poor, pregnant, and unmarried, fell into the hands of two young and ambitious lawyers. They wanted a volunteer to challenge a Texas law against abortion with a view toward striking down similar laws in all 50 states. Uneducated, unskilled, drug addicted, and alcoholic, Norma was gullible and compliant. She delighted in the attention.

But the activists who championed her cause in public privately reviled her as an embarrassment to their movement.

On January 22, 1973, Norma was granted her right to abort by a 7-2 majority of the justices, long after she had given birth to a baby girl and had surrendered her for adoption. But millions of other babies would die in *Roe's* aftermath. Well aware of the pro-choice movement's love-hate relationship with her, and tortured in her own conscience as a result of her decision, Norma spent the next 22 years in deep depression. Then, as I wrote in Chapter II, she received Jesus Christ as her Lord and Savior and began to be restored. Today, she works to undo the atrocity that was committed in her name through her full-time ministry, *Roe No More.*

THE FIRST HUMAN RIGHT

The *Roe* decision bore an eerie similarity to the *Dred Scott* decision involving slavery. In *Dred Scott*, the Court pronounced that slaves were human, but not persons; *Roe* pronounced that pre-borns are human, but not persons. *Dred Scott* said that "Negroes" only became legal persons after they were set free, and that before then they had no legal rights; *Roe* said that a baby only becomes a legal person after being born, and that before then the baby has no legal rights. *Dred Scott* also declared that a slaveholder had the right to choose what to do with his own property; *Roe* also declared that a woman has the right to choose what to do with her own body—including the killing of a fetus gestating in her womb. The arguments are identical. If you simply substitute different names, dates, and places into the slavery debate, you come out with the debate over abortion. Denying personhood to human beings was wrong in 1857, and it is wrong now.

The Bible, like the Declaration of Independence and the Constitution it informs, makes it clear that you cannot have your right to life taken away, neither can you voluntarily give it up.

"Inalienable" means it can't be alienated from you in any way, neither by your own will nor the will of someone else. In other words, a human being has nothing to say about the giving and taking of life. This is solely God's territory. And God has made provision for the ending of human life. The Bible allows for both the execution of criminals and self-defense.[8] But neither of these can be construed as human license to willfully take innocent human life or to circumvent proper judicial process by engaging in vigilantism.

A VERY SCARY GUY

The Bible prescribes a course of action in bringing perpetrators to justice. This includes credible charges, witnesses, evidence, and an objective review before judgment. In our system we duly deputize, train, and monitor law enforcement personnel to protect the citizenry and apprehend criminals. We maintain courts where charges are formally lodged, investigated, prosecuted, and defended. This is our criminal justice system. It is not a perfect system, but after traveling to more than 35 nations, I can say that, on the whole, I have confidence in our court system.

When someone takes it upon themselves to enforce the law and punish the guilty, particularly by death, they take on an enormous responsibility. This is why the Bible does not condone singular acts of retribution. I may know that someone is guilty of capital murder, but I can't possibly know all the circumstances surrounding that person's guilt. Neither can I divorce myself from my own passions. This is why the Scripture is explicit,

> **No one is to be put to death on the testimony of only one witness.**

NUMBERS 35:30 NIV

Shortly after I arrived in Washington, D.C., a reporter from a major magazine interviewed me for a story about my new ministry assignment on Capitol Hill. When she was through with her writing, she sent out a photographer to take a few pictures of me with my family. "Ya' know, you're a pretty scary guy, Reverend," the photographer said as he moved around, squatting and focusing.

I was puzzled by his perception of me. I didn't know how anyone could be afraid of me. My 5' 11" build is average, and I am hardly muscular. As a kid I was always teased for my scrawny arms and skinny legs. I was never an athlete, preferring the school library to the gym, and I can remember only twice being in a fight. Both times I lost miserably. Consequently, I have tried to be a peacemaker rather than a combatant. So the photographer's comment was a little perplexing. "Why would you say that?" I asked.

"We'll, you're the kind of guy that would pick up a gun and shoot an abortion doctor," he deadpanned.

Wrong again. I've fired a gun only three times in my life, and I can remember each instance. Once when I was twelve, I killed a small bird on an amateur hunting expedition. It proved so traumatic, I never wanted to use a firearm again. I did, but only on a hated old Datsun sedan that I had junked on a friend's farm. He offered me a .22 caliber rifle to put the car out of its misery and I gladly fired away. The final time was when a police officer with whom I was visiting wanted me to feel what it is like to shoot a .38 pistol. I obliged, but was not impressed with the experience. Firearms make me nervous, so I leave those duties to others.

On the day abortionist David Gunn was killed by a deranged Michael Griffin in Pensacola, Florida, I quickly responded by organizing a press conference, denouncing the violent act, and calling for anyone entertaining similar sins to repent and seek pastoral counseling. My clear and unequivocal statements were broadcast nationwide that night as part of the lead into CNN's popular show, *Crossfire*. Obviously, this photographer had not seen the broadcast.

I asked him, "You know about the Ten Commandments, don't you?"

"Yes," he answered matter-of-factly. "What does that have to do with anything?"

"Well, I wondered if you felt obligated to obey them."

He looked at me as if I were crazy. "No." He answered. "That code was for an ancient culture. We can make our own moral judgments and decide for ourselves what is right and wrong. Those are personal things. They shouldn't be decided on the dictates of some ancient philosophy."

"Then you aren't beholden to a moral code?" I asked, shaking my head incredulously.

He shrugged his shoulders, as if to ask, "What's the big deal?"

"For example," I continued, while ironically changing my posture and position to comply with his directives, "you wouldn't be obligated to the Seventh Commandment banning adultery?"

"No," he said dismissively. "People define the parameters of their own relationships. Some people have more open relationships than others. They aren't so insecure that they're possessive of another person."

"Would that describe the kind of relationships that you have?"

I knew I was stepping over a line by asking such a direct question, but he brought it up.

"I guess so," he answered nonchalantly as he dug into his canvas bag.

"Well," I observed, "if you're not obligated to the commandment against adultery, then you're not obligated to any of the Commandments."

"I guess that's right," he said, fidgeting with his camera.

"Well, I *am* bound to obey the moral law," I continued. "No matter what I think of an abortionist's guilt, I cannot take justice into my own hands. You, on the other hand, seem to be bound only by the law of the land. If the inconvenience of being prosecuted and punished were lifted, who knows what you would do to people you don't like . . . people like me."

He paused to look up at me.

"You know," I said, "you're a pretty scary guy!"

LIFE IS SACRED

The moral law of God transcends all other laws, and this law is abundantly clear. Once again, it explicitly proscribes the willful taking of *judicially innocent* human life. What does it mean to be *judicially innocent?* It means that no charges, evidence, or witnesses have been presented which show that this person has committed an offense. Most people believe the principle that someone is innocent until proven guilty originated with the Founders of our nation, but this isn't true. The Bible called for convincing evidence and objective witnesses against an accused person thousands of years before the Founders ever thought of it. (See Deuteronomy 19:15.) This process is indispensable, and it is the best protection against an irreparable mistake.

The focus of the Sixth Commandment, then, has to do with the protection and sanctity of all human life at every stage of development, from conception until natural death. It declares that no judicially innocent human being is ever subject to the will of another when it comes to the right of that person to exist. Abortion, euthanasia, suicide, and all acts of deliberate and unwarranted homicide are violations of this commandment because they involve the devaluation of another human being.

Robbers shoot their victims because the concealment of their crimes or the ability to take what they want is deemed more valuable than their victims' existence.

Suicidal paraplegics judge the value of their lives by their utility.

Judges allow comatose patients to be starved and thirsted to death because their care is too burdensome for their family.

Little babies are deliberately breach-birthed and pierced in the base of the skull with a suction nozzle because they are feared to have a congenital defect that will leave them imperfect.

These terminations of human life are justified by a self-centered culture that doesn't want to be bothered by the demands of caring for one another. The most insulting bumper sticker I've ever seen is the one that reads, "Every child a wanted child." This slogan, put out by pro-abortion groups, suggests that unwanted people shouldn't be allowed to be born.

Whenever I pass a car with that obnoxious slogan splashed on it, I think of a foster child, bounced around from institution to institution, looking out over the dashboard of some social worker's car, only to read that she shouldn't have been born in the first place. Wanted by others or not, happily conceived or not, every person has inherent worth and is entitled to the same dignity and status as other persons!

The Dump

During my first ministry visit to Mexico, I was taken to the large inhabited garbage dump outside Mexico City where I met Alberto, whom I mentioned previously. Thousands of tiny children are virtually enslaved in the waste processing business in this burgeoning mega city. They live literally in, on, and off piles of putrefaction. Like pack animals they sort and haul bundles of paper, metal, and glass to

Judge Roy Moore, who battles the ACLU over his display of the Ten Commandments in his Alabama courtroom, addresses the media at a Ten Commandments Ceremony on the lawn of the U.S. Capitol.

ROB SCHENCK INTRODUCES HEIDI JOHNSON, A SURVIVOR OF THE COLUMBINE HIGH SCHOOL SHOOTING, AT A TEN COMMANDMENTS YOUTH RALLY ON CAPITOL HILL.

SEVERAL HUNDRED CHRISTIAN YOUNG PEOPLE AND THEIR YOUTH PASTORS ATTEND A SPECIAL TEN COMMANDMENTS DAY RALLY IN THE HISTORIC U.S. SENATE CAUCUS ROOM ON CAPITOL HILL.

CATHOLIC DEACON KEITH
FOURNIER LEADS IN PRAYER
AT A TEN COMMANDMENTS
LEADERSHIP DINNER ON
CAPITOL HILL.
AMBASSADOR ALAN KEYES,
STANDING TO THE RIGHT OF
DEACON FOURNIER, LATER
ADDRESSED THE GROUP.

ROB SCHENCK ASKS REV. BILL MURRAY, SON OF THE ATHEIST MADALYN MURRAY O'HARE, TO GIVE THE CLOSING PRAYER AT A CAPITOL HILL NEWS CONFERENCE.

THE FORMER "JANE ROE" OF THE INFAMOUS ROE V. WADE SUPREME COURT DECISION WAS BAPTIZED IN AUGUST 1995. SHE MADE ONE OF HER FIRST PUBLIC APPEARANCES AS A CHRISTIAN AT OUR NATIONAL MEMORIAL FOR THE PRE-BORN AT GEORGETOWN UNIVERSITY IN WASHINGTON.

ROB SCHENCK AND A
DELEGATION OF CHRISTIAN
LEADERS PRESENT THE TEN
COMMANDMENTS TO THE
"AMERICAN MOSES,"
CHARLTON HESTON, FAMOUS
FOR HIS ROLE IN THE CLASSIC
FILM, THE TEN
COMMANDMENTS.

PRESENTING THE TEN COMMANDMENTS OUTSIDE THE WHITE HOUSE AFTER THEY WERE REJECTED BY PRESIDENT CLINTON. FOLLOWING THIS NEWS CONFERENCE, THE ADMINISTRATION "RECONSIDERED" AND INSTRUCTED US TO "DROP THEM OFF AT THE MAIL ROOM" ACROSS THE STREET.

"DROPPING OFF" THE TEN COMMANDMENTS AT THE WHITE HOUSE MAIL ROOM. THE CLERK'S HANDS TREMBLED AS HE HANDLED THE STONE TABLETS!

House of Representatives
Majority Leader Richard
Armey receives a set of
the Ten Commandments
for display in the U.S.
Capitol. Moments later
a gunman opened fire
downstairs, killing two
police officers. Rob and
his ministry team were
instantly conscripted by
Capitol security agents
to counsel witnesses to
the tragedy.

CONGRESSMAN ROBERT
ADERHOLT OF ALABAMA
ADDRESSES A NEWS
CONFERENCE AFTER PASSAGE
OF THE TEN
COMMANDMENTS DEFENSE
ACT, WHICH ALLOWS STATES
TO DISPLAY GOD'S WORD IN
PUBLIC BUILDINGS.

SENATOR RICHARD SHELBY
OF ALABAMA SPEAKS IN
SUPPORT OF THE TEN
COMMANDMENTS AT A
CAPITOL NEWS CONFERENCE.

ROB WELCOMES SENATOR JIM
INHOFE OF OKLAHOMA WHO
CHALLENGED AN AUDIENCE
OF PASTORS AND POLITICAL
LEADERS TO "LISTEN FOR THE
VOICE OF GOD" AND "GET ON
THEIR FACES AND PRAY."

RETIRED NEW YORK STATE
SUPREME COURT JUSTICE
WILLIAM OSTROWSKI
ADDRESSES A GATHERING OF
CHRISTIAN LEADERS NEAR
THE WHITE HOUSE.

ROB SCHENCK, "IN
UNIFORM," PRESENTS THE
TEN COMMANDMENTS TO
LEADING DEMOCRATIC
SENATOR JOSEPH LIEBERMAN
(D- CT) AND THEN VICE-
PRESIDENTIAL CANDIDATE
AND REPUBLICAN ACTIVIST
JACK KEMP.

CONGRESSMAN TODD
TIAHRT OF KANSAS RECEIVES
THE TEN COMMANDMENTS IN
HIS CAPITOL HILL OFFICE.
RECIPIENTS AGREE TO DISPLAY
THE COMMANDMENTS IN
THEIR PUBLIC OFFICES. MORE
THAN 200 COPIES OF THE
COMMANDMENTS ARE NOW
DISPLAYED ON CAPITOL HILL.

LAUGHING WITH RABBI
YECHIEL ECKSTIEN OF THE
CENTER FOR JEWISH AND
CHRISTIAN VALUES. WITH
US IS MICHAEL JONES,
EDITOR OF *CULTURE WARS*
MAGAZINE, FOR WHICH
I SERVE AS A CONSULTANT.

A HISTORIC GATHERING OF
CHRISTIAN LEADERS
ASSEMBLED IN THE U.S.
SENATE RUSSELL BUILDING
TO PRAY FOR THE NATION.

THE HONORABLE ROY S.
MOORE, THE "TEN
COMMANDMENTS JUDGE"
FROM ALABAMA, AND HIS
FAMILY RELAX WITH THE
SCHENCKS AND THEIR
FAMILIES AND MINISTRY
TEAM MEMBERS.

trucks for recycling. As I walked through this Dantean scene, with fires burning and noxious smoke billowing into the sky, I spotted a little boy with a blistered face and torn clothing sitting forlornly on an overturned trash barrel.

We had brought doctors, dentists, and childcare workers with us that day to offer what assistance we could, while telling these children of God's love for them. As I drew close to this boy, I crouched down and extended my hand, using my limited Spanish to introduce myself and to tell him that God loved him.

"God doesn't love me," he shot back bitterly. "You see that sick dog over there? He is worth more than I am." I assured him that wasn't the case, but it was going to take some real persuasion. The world around him seemed to be shouting, "You should never have been born!"

Whether in a garbage dump in Mexico, a ghetto in Calcutta, a tenement in East Los Angeles, or still in the womb, every human being possesses the supreme dignity of God-given human person-hood, no matter what ethnicity, ability, or disability they may have. Nothing can diminish this state, and every effort must be taken to preserve it.

PROMOTING LIFE

It is important to point out that the Sixth Commandment is much more than simply a prohibition against heinous crimes. While it clearly prohibits abortion (the willful termination of life in the womb), suicide (self murder), euthanasia (physician induced death), infanticide (the starvation, dehydration, strangulation, or other killing of infants), and all acts of malicious homicide (murder), it is also a positive directive. It mandates us to pursue those things that preserve and enhance life.

Choose life, so that you and your children may live.

DEUTERONOMY 30:19 NIV

Choosing life involves more than merely rejecting death. It calls on us to promote those things that contribute to the well-being of all persons. It means fostering life. The Westminster Confession of Faith, first published in 1646, has been called the greatest of all Protestant creeds. It states that the duties required in the Sixth Commandment are:

> All careful studies, and lawful endeavors, to preserve the life of ourselves and others by resisting all thoughts and purposes, subduing all passions, and avoiding all occasions, temptations, and practices, which tend to the unjust taking away of the life of any; by just defense thereof against violence, patient bearing of the hand of God, quietness of mind, cheerfulness of spirit; a sober use of meat, drink, physick [medicine], sleep, labour, and recreations; by charitable thoughts, love, compassion, meekness, gentleness, kindness; peaceable, mild and courteous speeches and behavior; forbearance, readiness to be reconciled, patient bearing and forgiving of injuries; comfort and succouring the distressed, and protecting and defending the innocent.

In short, what the Westminster divines recommended was a positive, well-balanced life and temperament. To these learned theologians, the life ethic is simple: Concentrate on spiritual, psychological, and physical health. Don't do things to excess. Keep all things in moderation. In every case give attention to what helps people to go on living happy and wholesome lives.

There is one aspect to promoting life that can easily be lost in this list: *how we treat others*. To value life means to value people. When we treat others wrongly, we devalue the meaning and dignity of their lives. Jesus warned,

> You have heard that it was said to those of old, "You shall not murder, and whoever murders will be in danger of the judgment."
>
> But I say to you that whoever is angry with his brother without a cause shall be in danger of the judgment.
>
> MATTHEW 5:21-22

The apostle John was vivid about what Jesus meant:

> Whoever hates his brother is a murderer, and you know that no murderer has eternal life abiding in him.
>
> 1 JOHN 3:15

Advancing the cause of life means being at peace with our family, neighbors, and friends. Grudges, resentment, prejudice, racism, bitterness, and hatred work against the ethic of life and in the end hurt all parties involved in the conflict.

Another aspect to promoting life is also quite obvious: the love and care of children. Children exemplify life in a way nothing else can. My twin brother, Paul, and his wife, Becky, have seven children. Twins Miriam and Marta, who are the second youngest, are filled with an incredible amount of energy. When they play with each other there is so much activity between them that it appears they are multiplying in front of your eyes! Paul and Becky often joke that the girls' cells are still dividing and that they're likely to turn out as quadruplets! Paul is a brilliant minister and a pro-life apologist of international renown. Still, he will tell you that nothing is more important than the priceless investment he and Becky make in the love and nurture of their children.

It grieves my brother and so many others that during the last several decades there has been a growing anti-child sentiment in America. Despite a lack of evidence, groups promoting zero population growth, birth control, and abortion have scared people into thinking that there will soon be too many mouths too feed and too little space to house the world's masses.⁹ (I always wonder why it is that these traveling troubadours of trouble always seem to have enough to get by themselves, but when it comes to the "threatening" generation behind them, there won't be enough food or space to contain them!)

This anti-family philosophy is especially pronounced in Washington, D.C., where powerful government forces and organizations exert pressure and influence on politicians hungry for their endorsements and contributions. The heady culture of our nation's elitists also has an affinity for the psuedo-science and class contempt shown by the so-called population control experts.

As my wife, Cheryl, and I drove our kids around Capitol Hill those first days of organizing a new congregation for my denomination, we were perplexed by the absence of children in the playgrounds and parks. Capitol Hill is actually a residential area with quite a few homes, and the weather is mild, making almost any day a play day. But we hardly ever saw any kids outside. One day, I asked a longtime resident of the area about it. "Oh what, raise kids here?" he said, surprised that I would even ask. "First of all, this is one of the murder capitals of the world. You don't want kids here. Second, most of the couples up here are professionals. They're not married. They don't have any intention of getting married, and they don't want the responsibility of kids. If they do get pregnant, they get abortions. And the rest are gay."

How sad, I thought. Here we were in the shadow of the Capitol dome, mere blocks from the Supreme Court and a few short miles from the White House. The noticeable lack of children among the dwellings of those who made the Capitol tick loomed as a prophetic symptom of America's heart disease!

Love of children is a godly virtue that stems back to the first order given by God to humankind: "Be fruitful and increase in number" (Genesis 1:28 NIV). As a people, it is not only our duty and obligation to procreate, it is also our joy. From conception to birth, through all the stages of childhood, rearing children is one of the greatest joys human beings can experience. With a daughter and son in college, I'm having a ball. Not that it's been easy. I assure you, it hasn't. But I wouldn't trade anything for it. Even for those who have not been given the gift of children, the pleasure of investing in a young person through your friendship, concern, or guidance is unparalleled. Love of children is love of life!

Fostering life also means enjoying life. The very word "life" in Hebrew, *chai,* is multidimensional. *Chai* means breath, well-being, health, strength, vitality, spirit, and prosperity. The New Testament Greek equivalent, *zoe,* has been defined as "life intensive." Jesus said, "I have come that they may have life, and that they may have it more abundantly" (John 10:10). Whoever said that life for the believer has to be a burden? I enjoy life, and I really enjoy people who enjoy life. What could make life more enjoyable than to know the Lord of life?

So many people spend their days in an anxious pursuit of the meaning to life. For those who know God, this is a settled matter. There is no time to waste on asking the same redundant questions over and over again. Knowing God's will and understanding His expectations free us from the fear of the unknown. Relationships mean more; jobs, tasks, and responsibilities have purpose to them; and we find ourselves driven by a much grander mission than just getting through a day or collecting a paycheck.

Lovers of God are lovers of the life He has given to us. Before God ever gave humankind a no, He gave us a big YES! Let me remind you of that. Remember, God's original edict was to eat: "Of every tree of the garden you may freely eat" (Genesis 2:16). So we can rejoice in the fact that God's creation is for our enjoyment! Friends, family, food, strength, imagination, and humor come with all of the pathos, tears, and pain. This is the stuff that makes us so much more than plant or plankton.

LIFE FOR ALL

Finally, yes, we should do those things that enhance life for ourselves, but more importantly, the life of God is all about enhancing the life of others. Selfless service to others is the way to a happiness and fulfillment that is otherwise impossible to know. The New Testament speaks directly to this aspect of the spiritual life:

> **Let each of you look out not only for his own interests, but also for the interests of others.**
>
> **Let this mind be in you which was also in Christ Jesus,**
>
> **who, being in the form of God, did not consider it robbery to be equal with God,**
>
> **but made Himself of no reputation, taking the form of a bondservant, and coming in the likeness of men.**
>
> **And being found in appearance as a man, He humbled Himself and became obedient to the point of death, even the death of the cross.**
>
> PHILIPPIANS 2:4-8

A new international survey by Independent Sector, which monitors giving, finds that 56 percent of adults serve as volunteers. The number of those volunteering—youths as well as elders—comes to 109 million. Independent Sector found that 90 percent of Americans volunteer when asked and 81 percent give money when asked.[10] These are impressive numbers. It says a lot about the generosity of Americans. It also says a great deal about the spiritual, emotional, and social well-being of these people. Volunteers consistently show higher levels of happiness and motivation than those who don't volunteer. They also have more vibrant social lives.

The most common excuse for not volunteering is lack of time, but let's put this in perspective: If Jesus, through whom the very universe was made (see John 1:3), had time to dirty Himself with the needs of humanity, who are we to say that we are busier than He? Ministry, from the Latin word *ministratum,* means service. Ministry to others is a mark of spiritual maturity. In fact, it is the very thing that we are called to do as Christians.

And He Himself (Jesus) **gave some to be apostles, some prophets, some evangelists, and some pastors and teachers,**

for the equipping of the saints for the work of ministry, for the edifying of the body of Christ.

EPHESIANS 4:11-12

Service goes together with spiritual maturity, so you simply can't get away from it. And it is spiritual service, whether to the needs of body or soul, that improves the lives of others. It is not enough to be philosophically pro-life. We must marry our convictions to practical, hands-on work. This is what my good friend Richard Exley calls "blue collar Christianity." In his book of the same title, he writes:

In our house, Christianity wasn't a moral code, church membership, or a way of behaving in public. It was a lifestyle—love with its sleeves rolled up! If there was a job to do we did it. If there was a need we did our best to meet it. Pleasing God and serving others was our highest goal.[11]

Whether you serve at the community soup kitchen, crisis pregnancy center, nursing home, hospice, elder-care center, or in your local church nursery, you contribute to the celebration and strengthening of God's gift of life. And life is something we simply can't take for granted. It is wonderful and powerful, but it is also very fragile. This is why it is precious. It must be respected by all, including those in the health care professions, in government, and in the courts. It must be guarded, taught, and promoted by those who understand and treasure it. Most importantly, its disposition must be left in the hands of the One who authored it.

L'chaim! To life!

> **The Spirit of God has made me, and the breath of the Almighty gives me life.**
>
> JOB 33:4

WHEN THE VOW
BREAKS . . .

CHAPTER SEVEN

It was August 17, 1998, and it was arguably the worst day in President Bill Clinton's life. He was sitting before a closed circuit video camera in the White House Map Room giving testimony before the grand jury investigating allegations that he had lied under oath about a sexual affair with a young intern. His face was sullen, his voice at times strained. Beads of sweat hung above his brow. The normally composed and extraordinarily gifted communicator was obviously nervous and uncomfortable. The sight of a United States president in such a compromising situation made it a miserable day for all Americans. How had it come to this?

President Clinton had been riding high in the second year of his second term. His job approval ratings had never been better. The economy was good. America was at peace with the world. Gas prices were low. People were generally happy. After considerable dissension over his provocative policies surrounding gays in the military and socialized medicine, Clinton was now steering a somewhat moderate course. It seemed that the tumultuous days of his controversial presidency were over.

Whitewater, an investigation into shady land deals that he and his wife, Hillary Rodham Clinton, had engaged in while he was governor of Arkansas, was running out of steam. Some thought him to be the most conservative Democrat in 30 years, and politicians in both parties seemed to be learning to live with him. Then catastrophe struck.

Linda Tripp, a forty-two-year-old career civil servant, was reported in the newspapers to have given a tape to Kenneth Starr. Starr had been the special prosecutor in both the Whitewater matter and a second investigation surrounding a sexual harassment suit filed against the President by Paula Jones, a one-time Arkansas state employee. The now infamous recording contained conversations between Tripp and a former White House intern named Monica Lewinsky.

Lewinsky claimed to have had an 18-month Oval Office affair with the President, and that he had subtly encouraged her to be evasive about it if she was ever subpoenaed to testify in the Paula Jones case. Tripp reported the information to Starr's office, and Starr subsequently obtained court approval to wire Tripp so she could officially record future conversations with Lewinsky. The resulting allegations were despicable and humiliating to the President and to Miss Lewinsky. In the end, not only would the President have to explain the lewd and immoral relationship, but his other actions, if true, left him vulnerable to prosecution and impeachment.

The political damage control was bedazzling. Mr. Clinton's defenders fanned out across the country and over the airwaves to nullify the accusations and quell the rumors. The First Lady took to national television to blame a "vast right-wing conspiracy." Mrs. Clinton made appearances on morning talk shows, explaining that she and her husband understood each other, suggesting that they had been through this before and had worked out an arrangement despite his infidelities.

The President denied the allegations, choosing his words carefully and saying that he had "no improper relationship" with Miss Lewinsky. In an infamous finger-wagging news conference, Mr. Clinton stated emphatically that he had "no sexual relationship with that woman, Miss Lewinsky." Anonymous sources were quoted in the media, explaining that Mr. Clinton didn't consider the kind of sexual acts that he was being accused of as constituting adultery or a "sexual relationship." Reports out of the grand jury investigating the allegations added that Mr. Clinton and Miss Lewinsky's behavior involved "incomplete sexual acts."

In the end, Mr. Clinton would be impeached by the House of Representatives and acquitted in a Senate trial. The judge in the Paula Jones case would later find him guilty of civil contempt for willfully obstructing justice by repeatedly making false statements under oath in her court. More accusations by various women would follow, including one of a hotel room rape. Yet, no one really appeared to care. In many ways America seemed a nation incapable of shame. In fact, Mr. Clinton's affair and the ensuing response of the American people serve as a social commentary on our disregard for the Seventh Commandment.

There are many voices in secular American culture who would today dismiss sexual fidelity within marriage as outmoded and narrow-minded. They believe that keeping to one man or one woman is prudish and unrealistic in a sexually sophisticated world. Prime-time television shows depict extramarital sexual relationships by a margin of eight to one.[1] Films seem to do so even more frequently. So many public personalities have been exposed for their infidelities, the newspaper reports about them are buried on pages with grocery coupons, if they make it as a story at all. A new science called "socio-biology" propounds that all males are polygamous by nature, especially the most powerful or "alpha" males like President Clinton. But experience bears out that adultery constitutes a real moral crime and places innocent people in emotional and even physical jeopardy.

WORD
SEVEN

"YOU SHALL NOT

COMMIT ADULTERY."

◣

EXODUS 20:14

WHAT IS ADULTERY?

Was Mr. Clinton right? Does adultery mean only one thing? The Bible's answer is an emphatic NO. Adultery covers much more than a completed act of sexual intercourse by a married person with someone other than their spouse. It is a violation of trust in the deepest sense.

As we saw in our study on the Fifth Commandment concerning parents, we have no closer neighbors than our own family. In the case of marriage, there is no person closer than one's spouse. All this is to say that to the ancient Israelites, God came first; spouse and family were a close second. The Seventh Commandment reads in Hebrew, *Lo Na-aaf*, literally, "no apostatizing." To apostatize means to abandon one's principles or promises. This is a clear reference not only to the pledge of fidelity between a husband and wife, but to the underlying principles that give rise to such pledges. Once a promise is spoken, there is a moral obligation to walk responsibly and emphatically keep it.

In biblical times, marriage was a long process, involving many stages. The road to marriage during that period began in early childhood, as parents carefully trained their children to assume their eventual roles as husbands, wives, and parents to their own children. In the Hebrew world, life revolved around two things: God and family. One's attachment to both began as early as birth.

The whole of Jewish religious instruction, based on the first five books of the Old Testament, known as the *Torah*, bears out the supremacy of God and His will in the individual's life. The corner-stone of the Jewish law is found in Deuteronomy 6:4-5,

> **Hear, O Israel: The Lord our God, the Lord is one.**
> **You shall love the Lord your God with all your heart, and with all your soul, and with all your strength.**

This took in the totality of one's life, emotions, intellect, and physical behavior. Jesus later identified this as the "first and great commandment" (Matthew 22:38). The second, He said, was like it, "Love your neighbor as yourself" (Matthew 22:39), a direct reference to Leviticus 19:18.

The ancient Jewish wedding ceremony beautifully illustrates this conviction. It consisted of four principle elements: The betrothal, ring, *ketubah* or marriage contract, and cohabitation. The elaborate marriage ritual began after a bride and groom were pledged to each other, sometimes at the arrangement of parents and at other times by their own choosing, but always with parental blessing. This often occurred when the couple was very young, and so the boy and girl were set aside for one another. Dating was unheard of, and the only real romance, as we think of it, surrounded the preparation of oneself for a successful marriage.

In their early teenage years, the boy and girl entered the period of betrothal, a sort of engagement time during which they were to practice strict celibacy. In fact, only virgins were eligible for marriage. The consequences of losing one's virginity were severe, and elaborate schemes were sometimes cooked up by parents of a girl who had lost her virginity so that it could not be detected before or after the marriage act.

The wedding itself began with the bride waiting at her father's house, surrounded by friends. The bridegroom and his attendants would come by night to escort her through the main streets of the village in a torchlight procession to the home of her future in-laws. She was considered the queen of her wedding day. Bearing a crown and wearing a showy dress, she was often carried aloft on a litter, a sort of sofa-bed mounted on two poles borne on the shoulders of the attendants.

When they reached their destination, the bride became the center of a grand celebration that included the music of exotic instruments.

Women sang of the bride's beauty. Men chanted of the groom's bravery and strength. The fragrance of wine, perfume, and roasted nuts filled the house. The parents pronounced blessings over their children and the feasting lasted for a week.

At the height of the festivities, the bride and groom would stand before their witnesses and read from the *ketubah*, a legally binding document that set forth the terms of the marriage, including the promise of the nuptials to be faithful to one another. They would then set their seals to the contract in hot wax and enter the *cheder*, or bridal chamber, to physically consummate the marriage.

This spectacular ceremony survives today in part in the Orthodox Jewish culture and in some Arab and Bedouin traditions. I once happened on such a ceremony while traveling in the Middle East. From a desert roadside, I could see a large Bedouin tent that was rippling from the festive music and merriment inside. The people were arrayed in brightly colored outfits and dancing joyously inside and outside the tent. A marriage contract hung prominently on a nearby tent pole. My hosts told me that the party would continue for several days. As I gazed into the centuries-old scene, it gave me an appreciation for the significant place marriage occupied in the biblical period.

Of the three great life events in Scripture—birth, marriage, and death—marriage is regarded as the most important.[2] This sets the stage for understanding marriage as the normal state of life and the basic unit of society.

Marital love involves a deep exchange of spirituality, emotions, personalities, desires, goals, dreams, and all those other things that make up personhood. Scripture defines marriage as a literal blending of two lives into one:

> **For this reason a man shall leave his father and mother and be united to his wife, and they will become one flesh.**
>
> GENESIS 2:24 NIV

The protection of this union and its most vital component, sexual fidelity, is at the heart of the Seventh Commandment. Violations include any sexual behavior outside the marriage covenant, including intercourse, fornication, and, because marriage is restricted to one man and one woman, homosexual sodomy. (See Leviticus 18:20; Romans 1:26-27; 1 Corinthians 6:9; 1 Timothy 1:10; Jude 7.) The New Testament Greek word *porneuo*, and its Old Testament Hebrew equivalent, *tznah*, used in these passages, denote every form of sexual activity between persons for the purpose of arrousal and gratification. Perversions are also covered under these terms, including bestiality (sex with animals), sex between blood kin, and between relatives by marriage (incest), prostitution, and rape.[3]

◪

Pam is trembling so badly she can barely stand. Still, she speaks confidently and authoritatively. "Is my husband here?"

The woman at the apartment door has a surprised smirk on her face. Pam's husband, Ted, sheepishly looks around the doorframe. He pats the woman on the arm and prepares to step out into the hall, but something snaps inside Pam. "You may as well just kiss the *****!" she yells, turning on her heels and bolting down the stairs. As she runs out the door to the parking lot, she can hear the echoing laughter of the woman's voice.

After eighteen months of what she describes as "hell on earth," Pam has had enough. "How could it have ever come to this?" she constantly asked herself. It wasn't supposed to be this way. Pam had grown up in a Christian family. She was active in the church youth group and played in the church orchestra. She was a good student and achieved excellent grades.

At sixteen, Pam began to date. She believed strongly that premarital sex was wrong and always told the boys who wanted it, "No, not until marriage." But when her sister introduced her to Ted, her feelings for him became so intense that she crossed over the line. After each episode of sexual intimacy, she resolved that she wouldn't do it again. She asked God for forgiveness, but could never accept it. Then, at seventeen, Pam was pregnant.

The couple was married in Pam's home church in Bremerton, Washington. Though the relationship was off to a difficult start, the young newlywed had high expectations. She truly loved Ted, and she believed him when he said he would love only her. After all, neither had ever been intimate with anyone else, and Ted had had a sudden conversion to Christianity.

The day of their wedding Ted talked about his spiritual life with Pam's pastor. He told the minister that he had not been raised to be religious, but that he now wanted to become a Christian. So, only moments before they exchanged vows, Ted pledged his life to Jesus Christ.

The couple left the brief service with new hope in their hearts. Then, after a quick two-day honeymoon in an inexpensive hotel, Ted flew off to attend Air Force Tech School at Chanute Air Force Base in Rantoul, Illinois. After graduation, Ted was assigned to Mountain Home, Idaho, where their son, Ted Jr., was born, and later a daughter named Ashley.

The next few years were full of fun, love, and adventure. Pam and Ted built new friendships and enjoyed an active social life. As time passed, though, parties began replacing church activities and the couple drifted away from their spiritual commitments.

When Ted received orders to go back to Chanute Air Base, he and Pam returned to church life. They loved the little congregation they found there, and had built a family-like relationship with the pastor and his wife. Pam and Ted were active in nearly all of the church's ministries. Ted was even elected to the board of deacons.

Then Ted was transferred to San Antonio, where he was placed on a special inspection team. He was away continuously, and even when he was home he suddenly seemed distant and uncommunicative. He withdrew emotionally and physically from Pam, often staying up until the early morning hours to avoid sleeping with her.

When orders came for him to take special training at an Air Force base in Colorado, Pam remained behind in Texas until the children were out of school. In the meantime, Ted received word that he would be going to Hill Air Force Base in Layton, Utah. By now, Pam realized there was something terribly wrong in their marriage. What she didn't know was that Ted had met a young clerk at the air base in Colorado with whom he was now having an affair. Eventually the girl told Ted that he was too old for her. After it was over, Ted confessed to Pam. He explained it as an "affair of the heart," and insisted that they had not had sexual intercourse.

Pam was deeply hurt, but wanted to forgive and forget. She told Ted that once school was out, she wanted to travel with the children to a reunion at their beloved church in Rantoul, Illinois. Ted agreed to meet them there and to drive the family to Utah following the reunion.

At the reunion Pam saw her close friend, Nicole, who had recently visited with Ted while on a business trip. In a cathartic moment, Ted had told Nicole that he was having another affair and planned to ask Pam for a divorce. Nicole felt she had to do something with this information, so she shared it with her pastor. They decided to tell Pam together.

Before Ted arrived, the pastor and his wife asked Pam to come with them to a private room. Waiting in the room was Nicole, who immediately told Pam everything. Pam was devastated. She literally reeled, as if struck with a heavy object, zigzagging around the room and bumping into walls and furniture. She felt like a caged animal with no route of escape.

When Ted arrived, he was confronted by Pam and the pastor. Ted admitted to the second affair and told them that he didn't want to be married anymore. He then left before the reunion began. Pam walked through the next few weeks in an emotional fog. She found an apartment and was able to furnish it with the generous help of the church.

After awhile, Ted called. Pam feared he had been drinking. He was in deep distress and despondently confessed that his affairs had been the worst decisions of his life. He said he had "learned his lesson" and that he now needed Pam and the children more than ever. After what she had been through, Pam told him she needed some time to think about it. She eventually decided to go back to him, but not until he promised to return to church, seek counseling, and submit to an AIDS test. He agreed to all three.

Once in Utah, Pam wanted assurance that his illicit relationship with the other woman was over. To test his sincerity, she asked Ted to show her where the woman lived. Ted pointed out an apartment complex adjacent to the base, but would not be more specific. So Pam continued to worry.

It wasn't long before a series of strange phone calls confirmed to Pam that the relationship had not ended. One evening, Ted told her that he had to go back to his office on the base. Suspicious, she followed a little later in her car. She did not see his motorcycle in its normal parking space at the office, so she drove to the apartment complex where the woman was said to live. There was his motorcycle, parked behind a van.

A neighbor helped Pam find the woman's apartment. That's when she confronted both of them at the door. Most of the incident is a blur, but she remembers being more angry and hurt than she had ever been in her life. Her whole world was shattered. It was as if the floor had collapsed underneath her. She was absolutely devastated. She felt alone, angry, and insecure.

Shortly thereafter, Pam and Ted were divorced. The next few years proved to be extremely painful and difficult for Pam and her children. Money was tight and caused her constant anxiety. She eventually remarried and presently enjoys a stable Christian marriage, but the unfortunate emotional scarring remains. She still can't speak of the traumatic experience without a quiver in her voice. Her son is now married and she sometimes fears for the future of his family because, "history repeats itself."[4]

WHAT'S WRONG WITH ADULTERY?

Everything is wrong with adultery!

Any act that tears at the physical oneness of marriage and comes between husband and wife to separate them crushes the confidence and trust of the violated mate, as we have just heard from Pam's story, and violates the sacred fidelity established by God in marriage.

For Pam and Ted, the undoing of their relationship began before they were even married. Their infidelity to the principles of Scripture (see Ephesians 5:3; Colossians 3:3,5; Hebrews 12:16) in committing premarital sex was indicative of Ted's future infidelities. But the abundance of real-life stories of so many like Pam and Ted in American society today could be compiled into a voluminous encyclopedia. Adultery destroys. In the book of Leviticus, the language regarding the offense is specifically physical:

> **Do not have sexual relations with your neighbor's wife and defile yourself with her.**
>
> LEVITICUS 18:20 NIV

The rabbis took this literal admonition even further than Leviticus 18:20. They taught that by logical extension, any relationship, real or imagined, which distances one spouse from the other pollutes or adulterates the holy union between husband and wife. This is why Jesus said that adultery can be in the mind:

Whoever looks at a woman to lust for her has already committed adultery with her in his heart.

MATTHEW 5:28

Adultery violently rips at the fabric of marriage by rupturing the vows that hold the family together. Political activist David Horowitz tells the story of his conversion from Marxism to Reagan Conservatism in his fascinating autobiography, *Radical Son*. In it, Horowitz relates the horrific misery and pain that he inflicted on his wife and children, not to mention his own life, through his adulterous behavior. He confesses all this irrespective of any religious convictions about adultery, which he says he does not possess. Here is how he describes the agony in the aftermath of his affair:

> I still wanted to be the good husband and father, though I was neither. I couldn't let go of my past that was dead, but I couldn't breathe life into it, either. I wanted to split myself in two, letting one half continue with the old life, and sending the other on to see if it could make a new one. But the more I struggled with these dilemmas, the tighter the knots became. I had created my own prison, and it had no exit.[5]

The universality of suffering caused by adultery is itself evidence that it is not an invention of prudish religious believers. In fact, it runs contrary to human nature and the desire God has placed in us for undivided love, security, and spiritual oneness for ourselves and for our families. Furthermore, there is an interesting link between the Sixth and Seventh Commandments. The Sixth protects the sanctity of life itself, while the Seventh protects the steward and guardian of life, which is the family. The sequence of these commandments suggests to us that the home, founded upon marriage, is the most sacred earthly thing next to life itself.

It can be argued that marriage is based on natural law because its rule of conduct is inherent in human nature. This explains why it exists in virtually every society regardless of religious belief. But the biblical concept of marriage, as we have seen, is much more than this. Marriage in the Bible has, at its core, a spiritual or theological meaning:

Neither is man independent of woman, nor woman independent of man, in the Lord.

For as woman came from man, even so man also comes through woman; but all things are from God.

1 CORINTHIANS 11:11-12

The apostle Paul compared marriage to the very union of Christ with His Church:

For this reason a man shall leave his father and mother and be joined to his wife, and the two shall become one flesh.

This is a great mystery, but I speak concerning Christ and the church.

EPHESIANS 5:31-32

This spirituality of the marital union is the reason adultery is treated so severely in the Bible. The late and venerable Oxford don and Cambridge professor, C. S. Lewis, alluded to this special dimension in his classic book, *Mere Christianity:*

The Christian idea of marriage is based on Christ's words that a man and wife are to be regarded as a single organism. . . . The male and female were to be combined . . . not simply on a sexual level, but totally combined. The monstrosity of sexual intercourse outside marriage is that those who indulge in it are trying to isolate one kind of union from all other kinds of union . . . [Y]ou must not isolate that (sexual) pleasure and try to get it by itself, any more than you ought to try to get the pleasures of taste without swallowing and digesting, by chewing things and spitting them out again.[6]

The husband-wife union, which in time normally leads to the mother-father-child matrix, is like a cell from which all other social systems develop. If there is something wrong with this building block, the flaw will be repeated and amplified throughout the social system. The further it extends, the bigger the problem gets, until it threatens to dismantle the entire social order.

THE SACREDNESS OF MARRIAGE

Marriage in general has existed since the very beginning of human civilization, and virtually every culture and society practices it in some form. It is a universal institution whereby men and women are intimately joined together in a special kind of dependence for, among other things, the establishment and maintenance of a family. It also provides a framework for the expression of powerful sexual drives, for the care of children and relatives, for regulating lines of descent, and for the governing of inheritance. It clarifies roles and responsibilities between sex and age and satisfies the personal needs of affection, status, and companionship.

The *Book of Common Prayer* refers to marriage as "instituted of God" and a "holy estate." The *Catholic Catechism* states unequivocally that "God himself is the author of marriage."[7] And the *Westminster Confession* adjures that it is the "duty of Christians to marry only in the Lord."[8] Jesus affirmed the permanency of marriage with few exceptions when He said,

> **They are no longer two but one flesh. Therefore what God has joined together, let not man separate.**
>
> MATTHEW 19:6

The Seventh Commandment is not to be taken lightly. Until recently, adultery was universally considered an extremely serious crime. For centuries perpetrators were punished by fines, imprisonment, and, in Bible times, death. Why? Not because it pleased the killjoys, but because adultery is an affront to God. The betrayal involved in this particular sin produces an extremely serious breach of trust that is devastating to its victims, particularly to women and children.

THE DEVASTATION OF ADULTERY

As a minister, I have prepared many couples for marriage. Part of that process is asking each person to share with me and one another their highest expectations for their marital relationship. Without exception, mutual fidelity, honesty, and genuine love for each other are on the top of their lists. It is these top-of-the-list ideals that adultery obliterates.

Adultery violates the most fundamental element of human relationship: trust. With only bizarre exceptions, the offending party acts without the consent or knowledge of the spouse who is violated. This means lying and deception are necessary in order to carry it out. In fact, adultery usually requires an elaborate web of lies and often forces the violator to become a veritable actor to keep the dirty secret from coming out.

When two people give themselves to one another spiritually, emotionally, and physically, it makes them vulnerable in a way nothing else does. Therefore, the injury that is sustained when that vulnerability is exploited is almost always fatal to the marriage because marriage is, in large part, defined by the protection of that vulnerability. When this most basic pledge is broken by a husband, wife, or both, it deals an extremely serious, if not irreparable, blow to their bond.

Suspicion, doubt, and lowered self-esteem often spell the end of the marriage relationship. And just because someone may have gotten away with adultery or survived it as a married couple doesn't mean that they survived the trauma intact. The scars of this sin change the equation between a husband and wife. While God can and does miraculously preserve marriages through the generous forgiveness of one or both partners, the burden of working through this pain is something no couple should have to endure.

When a marriage does fail because of adultery, the resulting divorce hurts everyone involved. In her book, *The Abolition of Marriage*, Maggie Gallagher refers to the aftermath of divorce as "downward mobility." She points to research indicating that "post-marital culture is associated with persistent decline" for both men and women. Areas affected by this downward decline include health, finances, physical safety, psychological security, education, and job employment status. For women who do not remarry and who also have children, the results are particularly negative. According to Mrs. Gallagher, these single mothers are nine times more likely to experience "deep poverty."[9]

In case some may think that living together before marriage or after divorce is a solution to this problem, look again. Cohabitation as a trial run does more to threaten the marriage. Couples who live together before they marry are 33 percent more likely to divorce than couples who don't. Contrary to popular myth, virgin brides are less likely to divorce than women who lost their virginity prior to marriage.[10]

The best reason for women to avoid shacking up, though, may be physical safety. Live-in boyfriends are far more likely to beat their partners than are spouses. They are also more likely to use drugs.[11] And in what may be the most damning revelation about men who will not marry their partners, the Heritage Foundation found that a child who lives in a home with her mother and her mother's boyfriend is 73 times more likely to suffer fatal abuse than a child living with her married biological parents![12]

Children affected by divorce are generally more susceptible to life-controlling problems such as drug and alcohol abuse, early sexual experiences, depression, and even suicide.[13]

IT'S TIME TO FACE THE TRUTH

Adultery is dangerous to everyone involved. AIDS and other sexually transmitted diseases permanently debilitate and even kill unsuspecting sexual partners. I'll never forget looking into the face of one young bride whose husband had infected her with AIDS. She died a terrible death while still madly in love with him. Crimes of passion also follow marital betrayal, so jaded lovers can be even more deadly than a lethal virus.

I've often wondered how an adulterous affair could be so attractive as to exact such a steep price from its participants and inflict such cruelty on its victims. The only answer I can come up with is that adultery is a supreme act of selfishness. It says, "This is for *me*. No one can understand why, but *I* need this."

The Bible tells us that the secret to truly happy and healthy human relationships is looking "not only to your own interests, but also to the interests of others" (Philippians 2:4 NIV). It's about considering others better than yourselves. (See Philippians 2:3.) Marriage is about giving; adultery is about taking.

In contrast to the self-serving sexual hedonism which was born in the selfish 1960s, marital fidelity and the sexual purity that precedes it says, "Look, you can trust me. What I say is what I mean when I say I will be faithful. What I share with you spiritually, emotionally, and physically is just for you. Furthermore, I pledge to be there to help you. You can trust me in the little things, and you can trust me in the big things. Even when I may not feel like it, I am willing to be held to account for my obligations to you and to our children. I pledge myself to your safety and welfare before witnesses so that I may be held to the words of my mouth." This is the essence of the marriage contract.

The words of the traditional wedding ceremony are barely appreciated today, but they capture in poetic verse the highest and happiest of all human relationships. In the old Anglican prayer book, bride and groom announce their pledge to one another, ". . . to have and to hold, from this day forward, for better for worse, for richer for poorer, in sickness and in health, to love and to cherish, till death do us part, according to God's holy ordinance."

STRONG MARRIAGES MEAN A STRONG NATION

If America wishes to survive, we must champion and strengthen marriage. We must demand of the arts and entertainment industries that they portray marriage positively, and we must reward them with our praise and patronage when they do. We must work to elect school boards who understand how important it is for children to be told that chastity until marriage and fidelity once married are the surest ways to happy and successful lives and families. And we must urge our elected and appointed government officials to model healthy marriages, enact legislation that supports lifelong marriage, and formulate tax regulations that are marriage friendly. We need to be generous to nonprofit organizations that bolster the family and encourage our churches to reach out with effective ministries to married couples.

The tragedy of Pam's experience, which I shared in this chapter, is played out with alarming regularity in our country. Too many marriages in the United States end in divorce, and many of those divorces are caused by infidelity. The subsequent emotional fallout is often devastating. So let there be no mistaking the fact that adultery is a deadly wound that few marriages can survive.

Today we are witnessing the destructive effects of adultery and subsequent divorce in the psychological suffering of children and the breakdown of family structures, which ultimately can turn classrooms into war zones and erode the order in America's schools. We see the exasperation and exhaustion of single parents, mostly mothers, who must cope with excruciating demands without relief to recover their spiritual, emotional, and physical strength. And we have seen the demoralization of men and women as a result of easy, no-fault divorce laws, which undermine the social stability necessary to a successful future. When either spouse can simply end the marriage without justification or challenge, the marriage and the family that go with it become as disposable as a paper cup.

The Founders understood that marriage forms the moral and social superstructure of a safe and prosperous human community. In a famous quote, Elias Boudinot, President of the Continental Congress in 1783, said,

> Good government generally begins in the family, and if the moral character of a people once degenerates, their political character must soon follow.

THEREFORE, strong nations require strong families, and strong families require the Seventh Commandment!

Marriage is honorable among all, and the bed undefiled; but fornicators and adulterers God will judge.

HEBREWS 13:4

COLLARED CRIMINALS AND TRUSTY THIEVES

CHAPTER EIGHT

Jack removes the envelope from the small pile of mail and draws in a deep breath. It is from his former employer. He has lost sleep waiting for it. What he is about to read could lead to his exoneration or to imprisonment. He had written to this man two weeks ago, confessing that he had stolen money from the cash deposits he drove to the bank each day as part of his job. After he received Jesus Christ and entered seminary, he felt that confession with an offer of restitution was the only responsible thing to do.

This letter to Jack's employer wasn't his only attempt to right the wrongs of his past. Jack had been a heroin addict and had committed many crimes to feed his habit. After a dramatic Christian conversion he made the rounds, confessing to police officials and offering to repay his victims. So far, none of them wished to prosecute, and this letter was his final act of contrition.

His school advisors warned him that, being a married student, he was taking a huge risk. Should the company decide to prosecute, it could have grave consequences for his family. As a full-time student with a part-time job and a family to care for, there was no way he could afford an attorney if legal action ensued. If they were to sue him for the entire amount, that would put his family out of house and home. He proceeded to send the letter anyway.

Now Jack calls to his wife, Pat, and asks her to come into the kitchen. When she sees the envelope, she nervously goes to the sink and begins washing dishes. It is her way to work off the tension they are both feeling. *Could Jack really go off to jail?* she wonders.

Slipping his thumb under the flap, Jack slowly tears the envelope open, nearly ripping its contents. He pulls out a single sheet of paper, pausing for only a second as he considers the possible outcomes of his well-intentioned *mea culpa*. As he slowly separates the top gummed portion of the envelope to remove its unnerving contents, he can't help wondering if it was foolish of him to have started something that he might not be able to finish. Hands trembling, he unfolds the letter and clears his throat. He begins reading aloud to Pam. "Dear Jack . . . Thank you for your letter indicating your actions while in our employ. The figures from the deposits were adjusted by our accounting department," Jack looks over at Pam, then finishes reading, ". . . and there is no need to address this matter further."

"Is that it?" Pat asks in a surprised and delighted tone, pausing from her frenetic washing to move over and look at the letter herself. Jack turns the envelope upside down and shakes it, thinking perhaps he missed a second page. Nothing else is there. Two sentences; that's it. Jack and Pam hug one another. Their ordeal is over.

Despite his relief, Jack can't help but wonder how the company can afford to write off this kind of internal theft. After all, as he told Pat before he wrote his confessional letter, "I couldn't have been the only one who stole money from the company."

◢

WORD
EIGHT

"YOU SHALL NOT STEAL."

◢

EXODUS 20:15

Jack is right. Roughly one-third of employees in the United States admit to having stolen from their companies. Two-thirds say they benefit by abusing sick leave or falsifying time cards.[1] Future prospects are no better. According to a *U.S. News and World Report* survey, 34 percent of college-age students say they will steal from an employer if given the opportunity.[2]

Every year in America, some $15 billion worth of property is stolen in connection with reported crimes.[3] That's more than the total gross domestic product for the nations of Kenya, Luxembourg, and Uruguay combined![4] And this figure doesn't include crimes that go unreported or remain undetected. White collar crime, like Jack's, is particularly difficult to quantify since such a broad range of crimes come under this general classification.

WHAT IS STEALING?

Everybody knows what stealing is, you may be tempted to think. But this isn't necessarily so. In a day when words are redefined to serve the politically correct culture, and when relativistic concepts of right and wrong prevail in most educational institutions, stealing isn't so easy to define for many Americans.

The Eighth Commandment reads in Hebrew, *Lo t'gahnaf.* The Hebrew word for steal, *gahnaf*, means to take by stealth or to carry away secretly. In other words, it refers to any transaction that must be kept hidden from the owner of whatever is being taken. The implication here is that the "taker" does not have permission or legitimate right to do the taking. When someone takes something that doesn't belong to them, it must be done without the other party being warned or prepared for it. This is the point of the prohibition.

I'm not talking about personal business that must on occasion be kept private or commercial activities that must remain confidential. These, like many government transactions, are often kept secret to protect the parties involved, to preserve a competitive edge, or to ensure safety and security. What I am talking about are actions that cannot be announced beforehand because to do so would surely cause the targeted party to assume a protective response. Generally speaking, if a confidential or classified business transaction is legitimate, there is always some sort of record kept, and the reciprocal party is at least partly informed. If you have to keep your activities secret even from those directly involved, you are probably breaking the spirit, if not the letter, of this injunction.

What exactly, then, is covered under the prohibition against stealing? Let's begin with the obvious. *Ganaf*—stealing—covers all conventional types of theft: burglary (breaking into a home or building to commit theft); robbery (taking property directly from another using violence or intimidation); larceny (taking something without permission and not returning it); hijacking (using force to take goods in transit or seizing control of a bus, truck, plane, etc.); shoplifting (taking items from a store during business hours without paying for them); and pickpocketing and purse-snatching.

The term *ganaf* also covers a wide range of exotic and complex thefts. Jack's pilfering of deposits is a form of embezzlement (the fraudulent taking of money or other goods entrusted to one's care). There is extortion (getting money from someone by means of threats or misuse of authority), and racketeering (obtaining money by any illegal means). In his book, *Trusted Criminals*, Professor of Sociology and Criminal Justice David Friedrichs of the University of Scranton, enumerates several broad categories of crimes that are in one way or another related to white collar stealing: Corporate Crime, Occupational Crime, Governmental Crime, State and Corporate Finance Crime. These include Technocrime, Enterprise, Contrepreneurial Crime, and Avocational Crime. Each of these has numerous subsets. They are too nuanced to define in detail here, but this partial listing gives you a sense for the breadth of this sin.

There are, in fact, an infinite number of ways to steal, and they don't end in taking property or money *per se*. For example, we hear talk of stealing *intellectual* property. That is ideas, creative material like music or song lyrics, artistic concepts, movie plots, etc. The protection of these nontangibles is the basis for trademark and copyright laws. If I come up with an idea for a television show, that idea belongs to me. If someone takes and uses that idea for gain without my permission, it is stealing.

These are only the more obvious aspects to the prohibition of stealing. There is a more subtle dimension as well. *Ganaf* also encompasses deception and exploitation. This includes what we know as swindling, cheating, price-gouging, and defrauding. Here's how it applies. If I intentionally exploit someone's ignorance, using it to my advantage, I rob them of the benefit of being reasonably informed. For example, let's say I sell a particular product. As an experienced salesperson, I learn to size up potential customers. Should I determine that my potential buyer doesn't know much about my product, and I use that deficiency to extract from that person more money than I normally would from another better informed customer, I am probably breaking this rule.

A more blatant example is when a supplier, manufacturer, or retailer out-and-out lies about a product or service, making false claims as to its quality, benefits, effectiveness, and usefulness. In this case, the promoter of the product or service withholds the truth from the prospective buyer, essentially stealing from them the capacity to make an accurate decision in an environment of reality.

Too often, government officials perpetrate this kind of deception and exploitation. Politicians who make promises during their campaigns, only to intentionally break them after they are elected, are stealing the confidence and hope of their constituents. The same is true when it comes to manipulating budget numbers and double-talking about cutting one tax while raising another. Both forms of behavior are condemned by the Seventh Commandment.

This stealing of the truth is perhaps the most alarming development in our post-Christian culture. Too many politicians, news commentators, social activists, advertisers, educators, lawyers, and even religious leaders routinely use dishonesty, sophistry (the tricky use of language to make something sound true that is really false), and hyperbole (deliberate exaggeration) to play their victims as fools. The object of this form of ideological theft is to get constituent "customers" to part with their beliefs, values, convictions, and common sense.

This sort of stealing of the truth is especially prevalent in sexual politics, where heterosexual misbehavior such as adultery is excused as no more than a *sociobiological* trait that is an "inherent flaw" in the species.[5] Homosexuality is similarly excused as a predisposition that one is born with and can do nothing about. Even pedophilia (sex imposed on a child by an adult) is being incrementally justified as an irrepressible drive connected with virility.[6]

The so-called world population crisis, which has been debunked by numerous scientific studies,[7] nonetheless continues to frighten grammar school children who are warned by their teachers of future global catastrophes. Even organizations as sophisticated as the United Nations are taken in by the alarming and unsupported projections of private groups whose motives for making predictions of population disasters are suspect. For example, "You have wealthy white men spending hundreds of millions of dollars to contraceptualize, sterilize, and abort poor brown, yellow, and black women in developing worlds. That's scary!"[8] says Steven Mosher, president of the Population Research Institute in Falls Church, Virginia, a nonpartisan think tank dedicated to objectively presenting the truth about population-related issues.

Revisionist history (the rewriting of the history-maker biographies and historical events to conform with the academic revisionist's own ideological bias) is another way in which people, particularly children, are robbed of the truth. During the last two decades school children and college students have been fed a steady diet of anti-American propaganda masquerading as historical analysis. Heroes of the past are fictitiously vilified and their motives are cynically questioned.[9] Add to this the pseudoscience of Darwinian evolutionary theory that has reigned unchallenged in the biology departments of virtually all major universities for the last fifty years[10] and you have several generations of students who have been denied access to objective facts, thereby disconnecting them from reality and brainwashing them into compliance with the mission of social radicals. The results of this assault on the minds of young Americans can be seen in the incapacity of most Americans to reason through a moral crisis and resolve moral questions.

BRINGING IT HOME

Nowhere have more people been defrauded of the truth than in the proliferation of so-called "gaming," or what used to be called legalized gambling. This entire industry is built on lies and deception. Except when they are required to do so by law, gambling businesses never inform prospects of their real chances of winning. When they do, it is in muffled tones and rapid-fire speaking as a trailer to a recorded commercial or in excruciatingly small type in a newspaper or other printed ad. The reason is because they must fool you into believing that you'll be the next winner. The more they can convince you of that fantasy, the greater their revenues. Never mind what the real odds are! Such information may give you reason to think again about wasting your hard-earned money on something with a minuscule chance of return.

But Americans sure enjoy a good wager. We now spend more money on games of chance than we do on food or clothing.[11] There are many forms of gambling, from the relatively harmless amusement of bingo to the dangerous and even deadly world of high stakes gambling. The games may vary in the way they are played, but their common denominator is the effect on their victims: Beguiled by the exhilarating risk, imaginations of instant wealth, and guarantees of success, the vast majority of players are bamboozled out of their money with no return except, perhaps, a cheap thrill. And the consequences can be devastating. Experts say that nearly seven million Americans may be addicted to gambling, which can lead to crime, bankruptcy, divorce, and even suicide.[12]

John Jackson is the dashing, articulate, and much loved assistant pastor at the Come Alive! New Testament Church in Medford, New Jersey. There is nothing about him that would clue you into the nightmare that he once lived which nearly cost him his life. He grew up in a Christian home. His dad was a Baptist minister. And when he went off to Brigantine on New Jersey's Atlantic shore to attend Stockton State College, John's parents felt secure that all would be well for their son.

John's parents didn't know about the recreational habits of Stockton students, however. Dubbed "the other Atlantic City," Brigantine hosted just one source of amusement for bored or stressed-out kids: slot machines. Soon, John was visiting the local casinos with rolls of quarters. At first, he spent $10 to $20 at a sitting, a fair amount for an unemployed college kid, but nothing that he couldn't later recover.

In spite of his best resolutions to the contrary, however, the fever soon got the best of John. Within months he had used up his entire student loan and government grant. The pay-off never came, and he started drinking to anesthetize the pain. Ashamed and afraid, John wandered out into the ocean one night, standing knee-deep in the foaming water, dreaming of swimming off into the horizon and oblivion beyond. Only the grace of God spared him from taking the plunge. Dazed and depressed, he returned to his off-campus apartment to search frantically for the Bible his mom had sent with him when he left for school. Finding it, he read it for hope and comfort. That's when John decided he needed help if he was to ever overcome his gambling and consequent drinking problems. He returned home to recover and rebuild his spiritual life. Later he married and returned to Stockton to finish the education he had abandoned.

John's experience is not unique. A Harvard University study says two million teenagers in America are struggling with gambling addiction, which is twice the rate of adults.[13] Twenty-two percent of pathological gamblers of all ages attempt suicide.[14] Virginia Congressman Frank Wolf's House Commission on Gambling found that for 25 percent of adult abusers, gambling leads to divorce or separation. It has also been found that domestic violence and child abuse skyrocket when gaming tables and slot machines arrive in a community.[15]

STEALING IS STEALING!

There is something obvious here. To steal means to take something from someone else in a way that they would not permit you to do if they were fully informed about it. There is no more protected secret in the gaming industry than the fact that the odds are overwhelmingly against you. But even worse is a reason that doesn't seem to matter anymore: The fact that there must be an enormous number of losers just so there can be one winner. In fact, the more losers there are, the better the "take" for the gambling interest and that one, rare winner.

Gaming, gambling, lotteries, slot machines, and other games of chance are precisely the kind of "slight of hand" banned by the Eighth Commandment. There was no need for God to wait for university studies, congressional commissions, or investigative reporters to tell Him that enriching oneself by fooling people out of their hard-earned money would hurt individuals, families, and communities. The Bible clearly speaks against gambling. The prophet Isaiah thundered against the false gods of good and bad luck when he indicted those who "forsake the Lord, who forget my holy mountain, who set a table for Fortune and fill cups of wine mixed for Destiny" (Isaiah 65:11 RSV). In its *Issues and Answers* paper on gambling, the Southern Baptist Convention says it well:

> While the Bible contains no "thou shalt not" in regard to gambling, it does contain many insights and principles which indicate that gambling is wrong. The Bible emphasizes the sovereignty of God in the direction of human events (see Mathew 10:29-30), gambling looks to chance and good luck. The Bible indicates that man is to work creatively and use his possessions for the good of others (see Ephesians 4:28), gambling fosters a something-for-nothing attitude. The Bible calls for careful stewardship; gambling calls for reckless abandon. The Bible condemns covetousness and materialism (see Matthew 6:24-34), gambling has both at its heart. The moral thrust of the Bible is love for God and neighbor (Matthew 22:37-40), gambling seeks personal gain and pleasure at another person's loss and pain.[16]

WHY STEALING IS WRONG

Most human beings know when they are doing someone "dirty" by taking advantage of them. The New Testament explains this by noting that the requirements of the law are "written on their hearts, their conscience also bearing witness" (Romans 2:15). Unfortunately, the New Testament also warns that repeated violations against our God-given conscience can dull our sensitivity to evil and destructive acts. So let's spell it out.

The common denominator in any type of stealing is this: One party benefits by taking or appropriating to themselves without permission, dishonestly, and in a secret or surreptitious way what belongs to another party. Stealing is a one-way transaction with one of the parties in the dark about it until it is in progress or already done. One person gains; the other loses. In the game of stealing, the score is always 1-0. Yet, not everything in life is fair. So what is it that makes stealing morally wrong?

This may sound like a ludicrous question, but it is being asked, mostly in classrooms across America. In a speech entitled "Are We Living in a Moral Stone Age?" delivered at Michigan's Hillsdale College, Clark University philosophy Professor Christine Hoff Sommers said,

> [T]oday's young people live in a moral fog. Ask one of them if there are such things as "right" and "wrong" and suddenly you are confronted with a confused, tongue-tied, nervous, insecure person.[17]

We're now into a third generation of students steeped in moral relativism—the idea that standards of right and wrong differ according to circumstances and individual preferences. This theory asserts that there are no moral absolutes. Among secularists, materialists, agnostics, atheists, Marxists, and pragmatists, the question must be asked, "What's so wrong with stealing?"

Presumably they would answer, "It breaks down the social order." But would it always? Stealing property may, in fact, be perceived to empower some. During the urban riots of the late 1960s, some voices were suggesting that aggrieved minorities ought to be able to loot stores at will. According to them, this would equalize economic class distinctions and provide reparations for class bias.

The violent stream of the 1960s secular left, groups like the Weathermen Underground and the Black Panther Party, regularly engaged in holdups and bank robberies to fuel their political movements. In their minds, stealing from the few contributed to the greater good of the whole. Vestiges of this thinking remain today, particularly among baby-boomer age faculty on state college and university campuses. In a morally relativistic culture, all prohibitions are up for question.

When it comes to stealing, there are some very good reasons why God forbids it. Rabbi Robert Kahn has written,

> What we possess is in a way a part of ourselves. Steal my clothes and I go naked, rob me of my food, and I go hungry, cheat me out of my house and I go shelterless, burgle my tools and I can no longer work at my trade, abscond with my savings and I lose my security.[18]

I will add one more important loss that results from stealing: trust. The foundation for all of life is trust. As an infant, I learned to trust that my parents, or some other competent caregiver, would feed me when I felt hunger pangs. I came to expect that my diapers would be changed when they became uncomfortable. I was able to go to sleep at night knowing that someone would rock me and protect me. As I grew older, I learned that my father worked so we could have a house which was warm in the winter, and that my mother labored to prepare the food we would eat. When I was older still, I learned that I could count on my parents for encouragement and for important information and advice. As a result of these lessons learned at home, I transferred that confidence to my friends, schools, employers, and yes, even to the government. Our most inner, personal security is tied to our ability to trust the people and things around us.

In short, most of us learn early that there are certain things we can count on. This is one way in which humans are very different from animals. Dogs, for example, are anxiety driven. They repeat the same worries over and over again. We have a small dog at home, and small dogs are the worst when it comes to nervousness. At dinnertime every night, Zachariah will sit staring at the kitchen counter where his food is prepared, obviously distraught that it may never arrive. But it does. Despite his haggard brooding, out comes the same concoction in the same blue bowl at about the same time as the night before. I often look down at him in that neurotic state and say, "You have a problem with trust!" He just wags his tail with delight as he scampers over to the bowl to chow down on his unappetizing gruel. As surely as the next day will come, we will repeat the exercise.

Not all of life is predictable, of course. There are plenty of uncertainties for all of us. Most tragic in all of life's conundrums are the children raised in completely chaotic environments, where crying does not bring a breast or warm bottle and where dirty diapers (if they have diapers at all) only lead to the agony of rashes and infections. These children are victims of a certain kind of theft: the theft of human warmth, security, and provision.

I've worked with such children in Operation Serve, which provides medical care and humanitarian relief to thousands of children who live in the world's massive inhabited garbage dumps. Many of these children are abandoned to the dumps. Others are raped and brutalized by the other inhabitants. All are exploited by those who profit from their cheap labor. In one country in which our teams were working, the children did not have access to drinkable water. So I went to a local official whom I was told could authorize the installation of a clean waterline into that area. When I appealed to him, he lifted up a computer printout and asked if their names were on the tax roles.

"No," I said indignantly. "Of course not. These are children who have no parents. Of course they are not on the tax roles."

"Then they are ghosts to me," he said, going back to his work. "I cannot do anything." When I offered to pay for the line with funds from our organization, he remained intransigent. We eventually found a water truck business that was willing to risk severe penalties by going in unauthorized, but not until we had paid a very sizable *propina* or tip to the boss.

Everything has been stolen from the children of the dumps—their innocence, their self-esteem, their wonder and excitement about life—everything. To them, nothing and no one can be trusted. This is the greatest robbery of all.

My point here is that whenever one party steals from another, trust is undermined and the relationship, or potential relationship, is ruined. In addition to the immediate loss as a result of the theft, the very mind and disposition of the victim is injured. Fear, suspicion, and cynicism replace the positive characteristics of faith, confidence, and optimism. Once again, stealing what a human being needs most to develop into a healthy and whole person is theft of the worst kind.

STEALING FROM AMERICA

There is a lesson here for politicians and all those who form and promote public policy. The wasteful, deceitful, and avaricious practices of government are bringing about a growing discontent among the American people that at times borders on rage. While most American citizens must carefully and punctiliously watch how they spend and manage their money, government budgets are routinely violated in the most flagrant and outrageous ways. Officeholders have too long exempted themselves from laws to which the rest of the citizenry must adhere. When the public demands an accounting, what it gets too often is prevarications. Meanwhile, current taxes increase and new taxes are added to the already heavy burden. More and more Americans are becoming aware that they are not getting anything near a fair return for what they are paying into the public treasury. As the nation's largest nonprofit corporation, the federal government owes taxpayers commensurate benefits, and knowingly failing to do so constitutes stealing.

The negative effects of such pervasive stealing are incalculable. Everyone pays when a crime is committed, not just the immediate victims. A robbery in the elevator of an office building can rob every-one who works there of a sense of personal security. Auto thefts drive up insurance premiums for every policyholder. Shoplifting results in higher prices for all the store's customers, not to mention the intru-sion of surveillance equipment. Extortion and embezzlement bring every employee under a cloud of suspicion. And virtually every U.S. citizen is penalized in the form of higher taxes to cover additional police officers and their upgraded equipment, not to mention heavier case loads in the courts and the construction and maintenance of jails and prisons.

The ancient Jewish rabbis believed that virtually all of the moral law was somehow contained in each of the Ten Commandments. If this one is any example, they were right. Nearly every immoral and crimi-nal act is covered under this commandment because, in the end, the whole community loses something to pay for the misdeeds of a few.

Cursing in the name of God steals His integrity. Worshipping idols robs God of His preeminence in our lives. Failing to take time to worship defrauds the Lord of His throne and denies strength and resources to His Church. Making a false accusation steals a person's reputation. Coveting undermines another person's relationship and property rights. Murder steals loved ones from families. Murder also robs neighborhoods of their innocence and companies of valued employees. It takes friends and companions away and denies the human family the gifts, talents, and contributions of a unique person.

Even acts as seemingly innocent as premarital sex steal something from the perpetrators and the society around them. When sex is played like a sport, it denies the participants the deep pleasure that accompanies knowing the act is reserved only for one's spouse, the one we truly love and devote ourselves to for life. For society, it often means a host of costly problems, from the treatment of sexually transmitted diseases and subsidizing prenatal care to the astronomical costs incurred in the criminal justice system.

In summary, the Eighth Commandment, "You shall not steal," applies very obviously to robbing someone through the act of taking goods from a store without paying for them, breaking into and taking the contents out of someone's house or car, or illicitly obtaining someone's credit cards or bank account numbers. From petty pilferage to grand larceny, it's all outlawed by this commandment. It applies to employees who cheat their employers, deliberately withhold their maximum productivity, and take long lunch breaks that do not directly benefit the company. It covers the unauthorized use of company phone lines, facilities, vehicles, or expense accounts. It also applies to misrepresenting a relationship or position for personal advantage and addresses employers who unduly withhold benefits, promotions, or information to which employees are entitled by mutual agreement.

This principle also works the other way around. I've known of people who make false claims against companies with whom they have done business. While serving as a youth minister with a New York church, I counseled a young man who told me that he had a habit of buying electronic equipment, removing expensive components from inside, then returning them as defective! At the time of our conversation, his scam had been discovered by only one of the hundreds of businesses he had victimized.

A misguided clergyman in the Church of England once caused an uproar in that country when he announced that the commandment against stealing did not apply to taking things from large multinational companies. He claimed they were impersonal and that the poor should be able to steal from them without penalty. The clergyman conveniently left out the many people who invest in these companies who are hurt. Stockholders are real people who must provide for themselves and for others. Many families keep their children's college funds in mutual accounts that are tied to the stock market. Even a modest amount of theft can negatively affect stock values and can therefore injure an unknowing student who is utterly dependent on that money. Workers in these companies are also affected. Theft reduces bottom-line profits, and profitability determines pay scales, which in turn are detrimental to whether or not a job can even remain in place.

COVENANT

We must remember that the backdrop to the moral law is covenant. Covenant implies a reciprocal exchange of action based on the fulfillment of promises: "I will do this when you do that." The normal terms of exchange for goods and services in the Bible are based on either direct labor or, as in our economy, the exchange of currency that represents an individual or group's labor. The agreement is basically that the first party will surrender work or pay money to the second party, and it can work vice versa. Whether one-way or two-way, both parties should benefit from the arrangement. To keep the agreement just and equitable, both parties should know the terms and approve of them before any agreement can be enforced.

God himself works on this basis. Over and over again in the Bible, God is found promising something in return for actions on the part of human beings. One of the most famous of these promises is found in the Old Testament book of Chronicles,

> **If My people who are called by My name will humble themselves, and pray and seek My face, and turn from their wicked ways, then I will hear from heaven, and will forgive their sin and heal their land.**

2 CHRONICLES 7:14

Another promise of benefit was given to Moses' protégé, Joshua, and involves the moral law directly,

> **This Book of the Law shall not depart from your mouth, but you shall mediate in it day and night, that you may observe to do according to all that is written in it. For then you will make your way prosperous, and then you will have good success.**
>
> JOSHUA 1:8

Blessing in exchange for humility and prayer; prosperity in exchange for obedience to the moral law—this was the essence of God's covenant with the nation of Israel. These same terms extend to other nations, as well as our own. If we follow God's rules and respect the ownership rights of others, including each individual's personal right to the truth, we all will enjoy what is rightfully ours. Ignore these rules, and we will rob ourselves and others of God's richest blessings!

> **He who has been stealing must steal no longer, but must work, doing something useful with his own hands, that he may have something to share with those in need.**
>
> EPHESIANS 4:28 NIV

GOSSIP, RUMORS, AND INNUENDOES

CHAPTER NINE

The Reverend Robert "Roby" Roberson, an avuncular man in his late forties, gets out of his car in front of the Pentecostal Church in East Wenatchee, Washington. "Good mornin, Pastor!" shouts one of the small town's many citizens Roberson has blessed as he jogs by. Wenatchee is a tiny town known only to local residents and the ski buffs who seek out the three hundred plus days of sun and unmatched powder at nearby resorts.

It is a busy Tuesday morning in March 1995. Hundreds of people gather at the church to receive free food and household supplies from the community pantry that is a focus of the congregation's outreach to the poor. Pastor Roberson is known as a man who cares deeply for his flock and his neighborhood. Nothing about him suggests anything less than a man of God whose first mission is to serve his Lord and people in need.

As Pastor Roberson enters his office, a police cruiser wheels around a nearby corner, pulling to an abrupt stop in front of the church. Seconds later two more unmarked cars squeal up alongside it. By now several law enforcement officers in uniform and plain clothes are bounding up the stairs to the church's entrance, interrupting the morning's solace with the squeaking of their patent leather shoes and crackling radios. One holds a legal document in his hand while another motions to have yellow police tape draped across a stair railing, sealing off the building.

Moments later, Pastor Roberson is led out in handcuffs. Crime lab technicians carrying plastic bags with gloved hands scurry to a waiting van. Arrested in front of the group assembled at the pantry, Pastor Roberson is charged with child molestation. He and his wife Connie are soon jailed after a hasty hearing and failing to post $2 million bail. Their four-year-old daughter, Rebecca, is taken into state custody and later forced to undergo "memory recovery therapy." They will not see her during their eight-month detention while awaiting trial.

In addition to the Robersons, more than one hundred other adults related to the church will be accused of conducting bizarre and fantastic ritual orgies in the church's fellowship hall and sanctuary, even during worship services. Sixteen of the church's parishioners will be convicted after plea bargaining at the behest of overwhelmed public defenders and overwrought prosecutors. Church members receive sentences that range between 33 and 47 years in prison. One incarcerated couple will send their daughter into hiding rather than subject her to the interrogations of state workers.

In the end, no physical evidence indicates that any of the accused actually committed a crime. Quite the contrary. What evidence that is produced demonstrates the opposite. For example, carpet samples taken from the church where accusers said sexual intercourse blatantly and violently occurred show no signs of bodily fluids. Social workers, police officials, and prosecutors will be roundly criticized for using pressure tactics in exacting sometimes wildly incredible stories out of frightened children. The only injury ever documented is a bruising sustained by the daughter of the principal police investigator, Detective Bob Perez. She is not one of the alleged molestation victims, and she accuses her father of manhandling her because she would not join in with an accusation of her own against the people of the church.

Within a year, the botched and unprofessional investigation begins to unravel. The Robersons are found not guilty by a jury and appeals courts begin overturning previous "convictions." Detective Perez is placed on administrative leave while several civil suits are pending, including one by Pastor Roberson against the police department.

◢

Pastor Roberson's ordeal seems terribly strange and frightening to most of us today, but in Bible times such injustice occurred routinely without means of remedy. In the ancient pagan world, a simple assertion, a whispered rumor, the pointing of a finger, or even the flashing of an "evil eye" was enough to get one accused, convicted, and punished, often severely and irreparably. While such extreme situations as Pastor Roberson's are rare in the United States today, in many underdeveloped and totalitarian countries there is little of what Americans know as justice. But this does not mean that Americans are free of bearing false witness. Gossip, rumor, and innuendo, each of them a form of false witness, plague our modern culture, and they are every bit as dangerous.

Yahweh-God gave the Ninth Commandment to ensure that individuals would be protected against capricious, vindictive, and untruthful attacks against their character, reputation, and lives. While this Ninth Word is often misunderstood to be a prohibition of lying, it is much more complex. It concerns false accusation and its relation to truth, fairness, and justice. It is binding on all aspects of human relationships, including those that involve relatives and friends,

WORD
NINE

"YOU SHALL NOT BEAR

FALSE WITNESS AGAINST

YOUR NEIGHBOR."

◪

EXODUS 20:16

business dealings, legal disputes and criminal charges, and the civic life of our nation as a whole.

ANATOMY OF A FALSE ACCUSATION

False accusations involve knowingly charging a person or a group with something they did not do. Lying is only the most blatant way to make such an accusation. A lie is when a person intentionally deceives, fabricates a false report, tells a half-truth, or deliberately withholds information in order to injure someone's reputation, dignity, relationships, or freedom. But lying is only one of a myriad of ways to make a false accusation. Whenever we assume that a bad report is true without sufficient information, we violate the spirit of the Ninth Commandment by rushing to judgment. Smearing a person's good name by intentionally disclosing harmful information without valid reason is the functional equivalent of a false accusation. Even insincere or excessive compliments offered for an ulterior motive can come under this prohibition. For example, when employees vainly flatter their bosses with the intention of gaining a promotion or a raise, they break this commandment.

The most overlooked breach of this principle is blame-shifting. This occurs when an individual refuses to take personal responsibility for their actions and instead place the burden on others. The result is that someone else ends up answering for the other person's actions or defending themselves for no reason. Blame-shifting is one of the earliest sins recorded in the Bible. After Adam and Eve disobeyed God and ate from the forbidden tree, they tried to shift the blame to one another and even to the serpent. (See Genesis 2:15-17, 3:11-13.) In other words, they were the first to use "the devil made me do it" defense!

Later in this chapter we will examine where and how these different manifestations of false accusations occur. But for now, let's look at their result, which is the scourge of injustice.

THE FALSE ACCUSATION AND INJUSTICE

At the time in which the Ten Commandments were given, the peoples with whom the Israelites had contact didn't work with the same presuppositions that guide most of us in our thinking regarding fairness. This was especially true when it came to being charged with committing a crime. In many parts of the ancient Near East, nothing more than a single unproved accusation was required to convict an individual of even the most serious crimes. The idea that one was innocent until proven guilty was simply nonexistent. The relatively recent practice of due process of law—the right to a fair and impartial hearing, the presentation of evidence, the right to a defense, speedy trial, trial by jury, and so forth—were born of concepts that did not factor into the Eastern pagan mind. The Founders wrote these safeguards into our jurisprudence based largely on English common law which had its inspiration in Holy Scripture and Christian moral tradition.

Because the ancient practice of "one strike and you're out" placed all power in the hands of the accuser and virtually none in the hands of the accused, justice was often unattainable. In addition, tribal chiefs, rulers, monarchs, and heads of clans regularly played favorites, meting out rewards and punishments subjectively and erratically. They favored the people they liked, while treating those they did not like cruelly. This sort of malfeasance survives in countries like Pakistan.

AYUB

Twenty-year-old Ayub Masih lived in the village of Arifwala, 700 kilometers south of the Pakistani capital of Islamabad. His family is part of a tiny Christian minority in this Moslem country. In the spring of 1996, Ayub was accused by a villager of blaspheming the name of the prophet Mohammed during a dispute over a land grant. On this one villager's single testimony, Ayub and his brother, Samsoon, who was later similarly charged, were both arrested under section 295-C of the Pakistani Penal Code, which bans any insult to the name of "the Holy Prophet." The two brothers were then severely beaten and tortured by police while awaiting trial.

Samsoon was eventually released without explanation. One year later, following a mock trial held in his prison cell, Ayub was sentenced to hang to death. No witnesses beyond the accuser came forward, and no additional evidence was presented to the court. This present day example of fickle injustice is in direct contrast to what the Bible teaches about determining guilt and assigning punishment.

The patriarch Abraham was chosen by *Yahweh*-God to be the progenitor of a great and powerful nation that would practice what is "right and just," (See Genesis 18:19.) "Righteousness" and "justice" are dominant themes throughout Scripture. They are, in fact, the cornerstones of Judeo-Christian morality and therefore the bedrock of the Ninth Commandment. (See Psalm 119:172.)

There are seven words in the Bible that we translate right, righteousness, just, and justice: The Hebrew *yashar, mishpaht,* and *tse-deh-kah* or *tse-dehk* are all used in the Old Testament and mean, "to be straight, direct, unadulterated, even-handed, equal." The New Testament Greek words *dikaiosun, dikaios,* and *euthus* mean the same as their Old Testament counterparts, with the added element of custom or conformity to a standard. The implication in all these words is the existence of an objective or procedural norm. In other words, there *is* a right way to do things. To Job and his comforters, Elihu said of God,

He is excellent in power, in judgment and abundant
justice; He does not oppress.

JOB 37:23

God's way is the way of justice.

PRACTICING JUSTICE

The Bible gives us clear guidelines on how justice is to be carried out.
Whether it is in the courtroom, the legislative chamber, the church,
or the home, all rules of conduct must first conform to God's moral
nature. The Old Testament prophet Micah reminds us of God's
moral nature when he writes:

> He has shown you, O man, what is good; and what does
> the Lord require of you but to do justly, to love mercy, and
> to walk humbly with your God?

MICAH 6:8

Secondly, justice must always be predicated on truth. The *Larger
Catechism of the Westminster Divines* points out our obligation to
speak "the truth, and only truth, in matters of judgment and justice."[1]
The very essence of God's character is truth,

> And you shall swear, "The Lord lives," in truth, in
> judgment, and in righteousness.

JEREMIAH 4:2

Thirdly, systems of justice must conform to the model of Jesus, for He
is the very embodiment of truth,

> I am the way, the truth, and the life.

JOHN 14:6

Once a society's ruling entity complies with these guidelines, the
rules of justice must be announced to all who are bound by them.

He made known His ways to Moses, His acts to the children of Israel.

PSALM 103:7

Jesus told Caiaphas the High Priest,

I spoke openly to the world. I always taught in synagogues and in the temple, where the Jews always meet, and in secret I have said nothing.

JOHN 18:20

"Surprise rules" violate the concept of fundamental fairness. In order to be held accountable, I have to know the standard to which I am held. I must also be able to understand the rules and to apply them to my life. God said through Moses,

Hear, O Israel, the statutes and judgments which I speak in your hearing today, that you may learn them and be careful to observe them.

DEUTERONOMY 5:1

Justice demands that more than one witness be presented against the accused.

One witness is not enough to convict a man accused of any crime or offense.

DEUTERONOMY 19:15 NIV

If it is one person's word against the other, only the strongest will prevail. This is neither right nor fair. Justice means that every party has equal weight in a dispute.

Differing weights and differing measures—the Lord detests them both.

PROVERBS 20:10 NIV

Witnesses must also have firsthand knowledge of what they are testifying about. Rumors, innuendoes, unsubstantiated assertions of facts, hearsay, exaggerations, and so forth disqualify a witness because they aren't based on absolute truth. As a story is passed along, the story-tellers will either wittingly or unwittingly attach their own spin to it. This colors and corrupts the truth, often obscuring it completely.

To achieve justice, rules or laws must be applied at all times, evenhandedly and without prejudice. (See Leviticus 19:15.) Laws targeting one group as opposed to another are generally not "straight" or "direct," as our word study indicated they must be. Instead, they zigzag through personal preferences and favoritism. These laws protect or satisfy one class of people at the expense of another.

INJUSTICE IN THE MARKETPLACE

My twin brother, Paul, and I fought a seven-year battle in the federal courts over this very issue. We had been conducting street evangelism in front of abortion clinics in our home city of Buffalo, New York, passing out Christian literature and Bibles to women and men coming and going from several abortion businesses. In response, a group of abortion clinic owners banded together to find a federal judge willing to sign an order to stop our outreach. They found their man in Judge Richard Arcarra, who had questionable ties to the abortion industry.

Judge Arcarra signed into law an order drafted by pro-abortion activists from the extremely liberal University of Buffalo School of Law. The order banned pro-lifers from offering literature, Bibles, or prayer to anyone claiming to be coming from or going into an abortion clinic at any time and in any place. My brother and I knew that this was a blatant violation of the First Amendment guarantee of free speech, so we continued evangelizing. We were eventually summoned to court. Not knowing how to find a constitutional lawyer, nor being able to afford one, we simply represented ourselves. It proved to be a costly mistake. Judge Arcarra did not accept any of our arguments.

Reading about our plight in the newspaper, retired New York State Supreme Court justice William Ostrowski came to our rescue. He took up our defense free of charge, and the case eventually wound its way up to the U.S. Supreme Court. Nationally known constitutional expert Jay Sekulow, a champion of religious liberty, argued our petition before the justices.

In March of 1997, I sat in the front row of the United States Supreme Court as the Chief Justice announced our winning 8-1 decision. Their finding was based almost precisely on the arguments that my brother and I had presented to Judge Arcarra seven years earlier! Christians were once again free to proclaim the good news of the Gospel on public sidewalks, even if they happened to be in front of an abortion clinic.

The collaborative Judge Arcarra had placed cruel restrictions on pro-life advocates while allowing pro-abortion advocates to do whatever they pleased. He based his unconstitutional ban on the content of the speech in question, thus sanctioning a certain set of ideas and opinions. Had we handed out pro-choice literature instead of Bibles, we would have been free to do so. This is fundamentally unjust and constituted an act of oppression.

This is why justice requires an independent and objective trier of fact. Whether an individual or a group, the deciding party must be disinterested in the matter at hand. This does not equate to being unprincipled. Quite the contrary, strong principles are necessary to avoid becoming biased. But it is impossible for a judge, jury, or any other arbiter to get a truly accurate picture if any of them is unable to see the argument on both sides. When emotions, opinions, or personal preferences get in the way, an unbiased outcome is virtually impossible. Our justice system depends on obedience to the Ninth Commandment in order to function justly.

RUMORMONGERING

The rule against false accusations isn't limited to the courtroom or to the criminal justice system. Each time an individual passes along a rumor, makes a derogatory remark, or engages in stereotyping, the end result is the same as if they pointed an accuser's finger.

"Rumors" are unconfirmed stories or reports that enter general circulation and often take on a life of their own. They are generally scandalous and perversely entertaining, but they are rarely accurate. The source of a rumor often becomes vague or altogether unknown as word passes from one individual or group to another. In fact, a good way to determine if something is a rumor is to ask the person reporting it, "May I quote you on this?" The answer to such a question is universally an unequivocal, NO, because no one wants to take responsibility for a rumor! This is what makes them so harmful.

The person or persons who start rumors won't be held accountable for them, so they don't have to defend themselves or their allegations. They throw their bombs into the public square and run the other way, ducking from accountability. So, like death-dealing terrorists, rumormongers are not only harmful and unjust, they are cowardly. Their weapons of destruction are convoluted truths, elongated myths, and innuendoes.

"Innuendo" comes from the Latin meaning "to nod." It refers to an indirect gesture or reference, usually implying something derogatory about someone. Like rumors, the use of innuendo insulates the originator from accountability. The Bible uses strong language to denounce those who engage in this sort of behavior. The writer of Proverbs calls them,

> **A worthless person, a wicked man,**
> **Walks with a perverse mouth;**
> **He winks with his eyes,**

He shuffles his feet,
He points his fingers;
Perversity is in his heart
He devises evil continually,
He sows discord.

PROVERBS 6:12-14

"Gossip" is idle talk about the private affairs of others. It comes from a Middle English word *godsyp*, which means "Godparent." Back in olden times, Godparents were stereotyped as chattering old people who talked too much. This is a good picture of a gossip. To put it bluntly, a gossip doesn't know when to shut up. To talk about someone's private business in the hearing of others denies that person the ability to defend or justify their actions, explain circumstances, or correct inaccuracies. Gossiping hurts people and compromises the high standard of truth that must be the foundation for any civilized culture. It is damaging to the one who spreads it as well as to its victim, and it is against God's Law.

These expressions of untruths do not just affect families, neighborhoods, schools, and communities, which they most certainly do. They also affect the largest spheres of American life. And those wreaking the greatest amount of havoc in this nation's corrupted public arena through the broadcasting and printing of such fallacious misrepresentations have been the news media.

MEET THE REALLY BAD PRESS

The downward spiral in journalistic standards over the last twenty years has been nothing short of breathtaking. Major network television, news agencies, the largest print news organizations, and the arts and entertainment industry have overwhelmed the American psyche with "inventive reality." Facts aren't checked, sources go unnamed, corrections needn't be published, and opinions masquerade as news in stories which are written before reporters are even dispatched to cover them.

I'll never forget when a reporter from a major national magazine interviewed me during a pro-life demonstration. He told me he wanted my comment about the women who seek abortions, but before I could even complete a sentence he said, "Thank you, that's all I need." I explained that I hadn't finished, but he turned away saying, "Reverend, the story's already written. I've got what I need." This man wasn't seeking reportable facts, he was looking for filler to help him make a point he had already developed. When my partial quote appeared in print, I was horrified to find he had set it in a context that made it sound as if I were saying the exact opposite of what I had meant. When I called him to register my complaint, he said, "Reverend, we have our editorial policies. Sorry."

This kind of reckless disregard for the truth is damaging the very cultural fabric of America. When the newspapers, radio, and television news agencies deliberately distort reality, it becomes impossible for the average person to render a proper and informed judgment. They say the first casualty of war is always the truth, and it certainly applies to the culture war.

To be sure, some of this deliberate distortion is motivated by social, political, and even moral (or I should say immoral) agendas. But for the most part it has to do with ratings, readership, and revenue. The greater the controversy, the better the audience. Playing to this prurient curiosity led to one of the worst media abuses of all time.

Richard Jewell had never been arrested or indicted for any crime. He had never been tried in a court of law. Yet for some 88 days he was front-page news and was virtually convicted of detonating a crude pipe bomb in Olympic Park during the 1996 Summer Olympic Games in Atlanta, Georgia.

Immediately after the bomb went off, Jewell appeared on television explaining how he had found a suspicious knapsack and had led people away from it, saving more lives. He was initially dubbed a hero. Then a call was made to FBI officials by a former employer who alleged that Jewell had behaved overzealously as a security guard. An investigation was initiated, and leaks from the FBI soon began to appear in newspapers. The widely-read *Atlanta Journal-Constitution* broke the story that Jewell was a prime suspect with a blazing headline reading, "Guard Denies Role in Blast: Man Called Hero After Bombing Under Srutiny." Information for the story came from "anonymous sources."[2]

The Jewell story was an intriguing one. It had all the components of a fallen hero tale. To augment the scenario, the media portrayed him as an odd, reclusive, paramilitary type who still lived with his mother as a grown man. And there was the clamoring by the public for a solution to the crime. People were nervous. A TWA 747 had recently blown up inexplicably while airborne off the coast of Long Island, and people wanted answers. Jewell provided the FBI with a badly needed suspect and the news media with a much wanted ratings boost.

The media continued to repeat allegations, leaks, and unconfirmed rumors about Jewell, rapidly building a case against him. They camped outside the modest apartment complex where he lived with his mother, setting up banks of cameras, microphones, and broadcast transmission equipment. As far as most of the public was concerned, the only thing left was Jewell's sentencing.

When the FBI announced that Jewell was no longer a suspect, his reputation was already ruined, his life was in shambles, and his aged mother was a nervous wreck. He eventually sued the FBI, ABC News, and the *Atlanta Journal-Constitution*. He settled with each for undisclosed figures, but in the minds of many he will always remain guilty as falsely charged.

ALL POLITICIANS DON'T LIE

The joke goes, "How do you know when a politician is lying? His lips are moving!"

If there is one thing that nearly all Americans have shed during the last 25 years, it is their naiveté about politics and politicians. The optimistic way of looking at this is that fewer people will be vulnerable to being bamboozled by fast talking candidates, career politicians, and bureaucrats. The more gloomy view is that Americans have fast become cynical and resigned about the low moral character of those in public office.

The truth is that not all politicians lie. From my vantage point, working on Pennsylvania Avenue and having visited with and developed personal relationships with many, I can say that the majority of those who serve in government are honest and sincere. This does not equate to being morally upright. There is a difference between an honest and a dishonest sinner. Honest sinners admit to their sin! And there are plenty in public office who do. Dishonest sinners are the ones who won't admit who they really are or the truth of their hidden agenda.

While most politicians are honest and sincere about themselves, this doesn't make political institutions virtuous. There is a serious degrading of ethical standards in our political culture, and we are beginning to pay a high price for it. Second only to the media, politicians routinely engage in false accusations. Making a false accusation is almost fashionable in political campaigning, and I'm not just talking about mudslinging.

"Slander" (making a false statement in the hearing of others that is damaging to another person's reputation); "libel" (writing or publishing such a statement); and "defamation" (making an unwarranted attack on a person's character) are false accusations generally punishable by law. However, these sleazy tactics are used liberally in political conflicts and go unpunished because the courts have largely ruled that public personalities are fair game in rhetorical battles.

There is a much larger way, however, in which false accusations are employed by politicians and other social and political leaders. I call it the art of vilification. This is when political opponents are demonized rather than debated. It is the same as breaking the *ad hominem* rule. Instead of dealing with the merits of an argument, the one who brings the argument is personally attacked in order to gain an unfair advantage or to weaken the effect of their criticisms. In this case, the violation of the Ninth Commandment comes in the deception that is involved. Like blame-shifting, vilifying an opponent is done for an ulterior motive, one that can't be disclosed to the public. The attack is made for a reason other than the one that is cited.

It is important to point out here that there are times when it is appropriate to bring an individual's private sin into public view. John the Baptist was beheaded after he openly rebuked Herod the Tetrarch for taking his brother's wife in violation of the Levitical law. (See Mark 6:17-28.) When the private sin of a public figure affects either directly or indirectly those whom they serve, it is often necessary to bring those sins to light. Exposing their sins publicly not only holds them accountable in the realm where their behavior and principles have the most serious and farthest reaching ramifications, but doing so also becomes instructive to others. This is especially true for those public figures who claim to be Christian. (See 1 Timothy 5:20.)

George Stephanapolous, the one-time senior presidential advisor, tells how President Bill Clinton justified his lifting the ban on homosexuals in the military by telling Senator Robert Byrd, "When the Lord delivered the Ten Commandments, Senator Byrd, He did not include a prohibition on homosexuality."[3] Clinton had already made numerous public statements explaining that his liberal abortion policies were based on his understanding that the soul does not enter a child until the first breath is taken.

President Clinton's flawed interpretations of Holy Scripture resulted in the single most immoral administration in American history. His use of the force of federal government policy and considerable federal funds to relentlessly promote homosexuality as a legitimate sexual practice will have long-lasting effects. And, in spite of his campaign promise to make abortion "safe, legal, and rare," President Clinton went on to unleash a furious push for wider access to abortion in the United States and throughout the world.

This was fresh in my mind when I was invited to attend the Christmas Eve service at the Washington National Cathedral in 1996. I had just sat through several weeks of hearings and votes on a bill to ban partial-birth abortion, a particularly gruesome late-term procedure in which the pre-born child is partially extracted from the mother's womb to have their brain vacuumed out. I had listened to one abortion provider brag on his skill in being able to "find an ankle, a wrist, or a shoulder," to pull the baby into a breach position in order to gain access to the rear of the skull. After a robust number of debates, I watched as both the House and the Senate voted to ban the barbaric practice, only to see it made legal again with a stroke of Bill Clinton's veto pen.

Called the People's Church, the Washington National Cathedral sits majestically atop Cathedral Hill overlooking virtually all of the nation's capital. Each year it draws millions of visitors and dignitaries from around the world to many of its events and services. This is why my wife and I didn't find it strange that there were several levels of security when we arrived. Passing through a metal detector and a search of our belongings, we took our seats in the middle of the cavernous sanctuary. Huge marble columns blocked our view of much of the front seating areas, so we couldn't see the special guests seated in the forward section.

When it came time for communion, my family and I took our places in line. As we moved forward, I looked to my left to see the President, the First Lady, and their daughter seated in the front left row. Nothing had been said about their presence. As our line split between two aisles, I realized that in a few moments I would be standing immediately next to the President as we both prepared to receive communion. A verse from the book of Hebrews tumbled through my mind,

> **All things are naked and open to the eyes of Him to whom we must give account.**
>
> HEBREWS 4:13

The President was still seated as I drew up alongside him. With no one between him and me, I leaned over very respectfully and peacefully said to him, "Mr. President, God will hold you to account."

He looked up at me as if to ask with his eyes, *Did you really say that?* Then he blushed, set his face straight ahead, and deliberately ignored me.

I proceeded to the communion rail, partook of communion, then returned to my seat. In the aftermath, I was asked many times to justify what I had done. My response was simple: Bill Clinton has claimed publicly on many occasions that he is a Christian, that he reads his Bible, and that he prays daily. The apostle Paul exhorted the Galatians in his letter,

> **Brethren, if a man is overtaken in any trespass, you who are spiritual restore such a one in a spirit of gentleness.**
>
> GALATIANS 6:1

It is our duty and obligation to rebuke, exhort, and admonish one another, particularly in the household of God. (See 2 Thessalonians 3:14-15; 2 Timothy 4:2; Titus 2:15.) This includes public officials whose sins and sinful ideas poison the culture and society they influence.

> **Woe to those who call evil good, and good evil;**
>
> **Who put darkness for light, and light for darkness;**
>
> **Who put bitter for sweet, and sweet for bitter!**
>
> **Woe to those who are wise in their own eyes,**
>
> **And prudent in their own sight!**
>
> **Woe to men mighty at drinking wine,**
>
> **Woe to men valiant for mixing intoxicating drink,**
>
> **Who justify the wicked for a bribe,**
>
> **And take away justice from the righteous man!**
>
> ISAIAH 5:20-23

By promoting their falsities, these individuals corrupt the ability of a nation to discern right from wrong, leading many into grave moral error.

SUMMARY

False reports and accusations have cost our nation and everyone of us dearly. If there is any lesson from the past that we must learn, it is that we are never immune to repeating our failures. Great empires have fallen, great cultures have collapsed, and great harm has been done when a people abandon the truth for a lie. False accusation in all of its evil forms, from the gossip exchanged between friends over coffee to the distortion of reality by a self-serving media to the deception foisted upon a whole civilization by its highest court to the sophistry of a fast-talking politician—all these are real and present dangers. They have only one antidote, the Truth. Jesus said,

If you abide in My word, you are My disciples indeed.
And you shall know the truth, and the truth shall make
you free.

JOHN 8:31-32

Much of the world lives under the tyranny of the false accusation. As you read this paragraph, a note will be slipped to a secret police agent in Havana, a complaint will be filed with a Communist party chief in Beijing, a shout will be heard outside a hut in Kigali, and a neighbor, a coworker, or a wife will disappear into the night. Unless we are constantly vigilant to remember and practice in our private and public lives the age-old axiom of "innocent until proven guilty," Americans will find themselves in the same shadow of terror.

"You shall make no false accusations," says God to humanity. And if we know what's good for us, we will heed the directive. When Pastor Robby Roberson and his congregation were attacked and nearly destroyed through the lies of a corrupt American law enforcement official in East Wenatchee, Washington, the truth eventually set the record straight, and both he and his congregation judiciously won out. In other societies, there is no place for trial or truth after the accusations are made. So let us ensure in America that the falsely accused will always have their day in court. And let the perpetrators of slander, vilification, and misinformation understand (regardless of their position) that God will irrevocably and eternally hold them to account.

He who speaks truth declares righteousness, but a false witness, deceit.

PROVERBS 12:17

I SPY WITH
MY LITTLE EYE

CHAPTER TEN

Jessica gazes up at the shadows on her bedroom ceiling. She would normally be fast asleep by now, but her mind is racing. Her thoughts collide with one another, sometimes crossing over like phantom images on a page. At moments she has difficulty associating the current thought with the one just passed. Does it belong to this scenario or one she has already dismissed? She looks to the night stand and focuses her eyes on the dim red numbers of her alarm clock. It is 3:30 A.M.

What is she to do? The anxiety is palpable. Auditions are almost here and she is worried about her daughter, Terra. Her girl deserves to have the lead in the school play and she wants it so badly. What's a mother to do? *If only Mindy was out of the way—then Terra would get it hands down. Only Mindy posed any kind of threat.* "What can I do?" Jessica asks herself aloud. Then the thought comes, *I've got to get rid of her!*

Get rid of her? Is she thinking the unthinkable? Is she kidding herself? That would be too obvious. Who else would have a motive? Mindy's a good kid.

She doesn't have an enemy in the world—except for me, Jessica thinks, chuckling sardonically. *Besides, I couldn't kill anyone,* she reasons. *There are people who kill, but I could never do that. And kill a seventeen-year-old? A girl the same age as my own daughter? No, I couldn't do that. It would be better if someone in her family just keeled over and died. That would take her out of running! She could never compete if that happened.*

What would it take to make that happen? Ah, they're probably all healthy. Someone would have to shoot them or something. I wonder if there's people who do that?

As the sun rises, Jessica realizes that she hasn't slept at all. She feels physically ill, but she knows now what must be done. She has no idea how much it will cost, who to see, or where to find such a person, but she's always believed that where there's a will, there's a way. *Once Mindy's brother is dead, the little challenger will be in no shape to give a good audition.*

On September 9, 1996, Wanda Holloway pled no contest to solicitation of capital murder. Like our mother in the fictitious story above, she wanted her teenage daughter to succeed and achieve her dream, in this case in becoming a cheerleader. She paid a hit man to kill Verna Heath, the mother of her daughter's chief rival for the coveted position on the cheerleading squad, using diamond earrings as a down payment. By the time she pled no contest to the crime, Wanda had already spent six years of a fifteen-year sentence in prison. After one of the jurors for the original trial was found to have been on federal probation at the time, Wanda was retried. This time she received a ten-year sentence, nine and a half of which she will spend on probation.

Legally, Wanda Holloway is guilty of solicitation of capital murder. Morally, she is guilty of coveting. Mrs. Holloway determined to get

WORD
TEN

"YOU SHALL NOT COVET YOUR

NEIGHBOR'S HOUSE; YOU

SHALL NOT COVET YOUR

NEIGHBOR'S WIFE, NOR HIS

MALE SERVANT, NOR HIS FEMALE

SERVANT, NOR HIS OX, NOR HIS

DONKEY, NOR ANYTHING THAT

IS YOUR NEIGHBOR'S."

EXODUS 20:17

what she wanted for her daughter even if it meant selling her own soul. Her story illustrates just how serious this last sin is.

The rule against coveting is generally underappreciated. The majority of us do not know what really constitutes coveting. We think of it as wishing for something we can't afford or being discontent with what we have. While there are elements of both within the sin of covetousness, this offense is one of the most complex and grievous of moral violations. The Bible lists it with vile passions, maliciousness, murder, and violence. (See Romans 1:24-32.) Jesus said, "Out of the hearts of men, proceed evil thoughts, adulteries, fornications, murders, thefts, covetousness" (Mark 7:21,22). And according to 1 Corinthians 6:9-10, unrepented covetousness will exclude a person from heaven:

> **Do you not know that the unrighteous will not inherit the kingdom of God? Do not be deceived. Neither fornicators, nor idolaters, nor adulterers, nor homosexuals, nor sodomites, nor thieves, nor covetous, nor drunkards, nor revilers, nor extortioners will inherit the kingdom of God.**

WHAT DOES IT MEAN TO COVET?

While most people have desired something that they couldn't readily obtain, not many have actually coveted. For example, you're driving through a neighborhood of fancy homes only to find yourself fantasizing about owning one. You may even resolve that you *will* own one. *Stop coveting!* scolds your conscience. You shake your head to snap yourself out of your greedy fantasy. Your conscience continues, *You don't need a bigger house. Be content with what you have!*

While desires for more or nicer things may lead to coveting, they fall far short of it. Desiring something in and of itself is not immoral. In fact, God himself has desires, "For I desire mercy and not sacrifice" (Hosea 6:6). A passionate quest for what is good is considered virtuous in Holy Scripture, "The desire of the righteous is only good" (Proverbs 11:23). Consider Solomon, who was rewarded by God because he desired the wisdom of God instead of material wealth or power. (See 2 Chronicles 1:11.) So desire is not sinful, but it can become covetous when the object of our desire belongs to another, and that is what this Tenth Word condemns.

The Hebrew word for covet used in this commandment is *chamad*. It means "to desire with the intent to own something that can never be rightfully yours." This doesn't mean something that you can't afford. You never know what you may or may not be able to afford in the future. Hard work, skillful money management, or a surprise inheritance can change everything about your economic status. Coveting, on the other hand, refers to pursuing what can never, under any legitimate circumstances, be yours because it belongs to someone else. This is why the commandment qualifies its prohibition with *your neighbor's* house, wife, ox, or donkey. In the reiteration of the Tenth Commandment found in Deuteronomy 5:21, the *New International Version* renders this clause, "You shall not set your desire on your neighbor's house." It means what it literally says—*You cannot possess what belongs to another*.

There is nothing wrong with wanting something *exactly like* what your neighbor has, but you can't ever have what belongs to them until they voluntarily give up their right of ownership. And there are many things that can never legitimately be relinquished. For example, one cannot give up their spouse. (See Matthew 19:5-6.) However, there is nothing wrong with driving through a neighborhood of fine homes and dreaming of someday living in a house like one of them. You may even desire a particular house, provided you are willing to pay whatever price the owner would ask for it.

Once, while preaching in New Jersey, I was hosted by a family whose custom-designed home was the subject of a number of magazine photo spreads. Though they had built it for only $45,000 thirty years before, the owners received regular offers of many times that amount which they routinely turned down. One day a woman rang the doorbell and said to my hostess, "Name your price, I want your house." Just to send her away she answered, "How about a million dollars?" The woman said, "Sold." They closed on the property a month later! At no time in this extraordinary transaction was the Tenth Commandment broken. The woman who wanted the house was willing to pay any price for it, and the owner agreed to sell. You could call this unusual business, but it wasn't covetous.

The Bible says you may even set your desire on a particular person to be your wife or your husband. "He who finds a wife finds a good thing, and obtains favor from the Lord" (Proverbs 18:22). You only break this commandment when the object of your desire is pledged or wedded to another. More often than not, adulterous affairs are rooted in covetousness. A person "looks over the fence," so to speak, and sets their desire on their neighbor's wife—or husband. Because marriage is for life, they can never have their neighbor's spouse for themselves. But if they allow the thinking process of covetousness to develop and grow, adultery and even murder could be its ultimate, deadly fruit.

This is the tragic story of King David and Bathsheba. She was the wife of Uriah, a soldier in David's army. While the nation was at war and Uriah was in the field of battle, David spied the beautiful Bathsheba bathing herself on a nearby rooftop. Lust and covetousness inflamed his heart, and in a despicable moral failing he "took her." A child was conceived, and fear for his reputation and throne caused David to cover up the scandal by having Uriah killed. In so doing, he demoralized his chief general, Joab, and set in motion a series of events that would haunt him the rest of his life. (See 2 Samuel 11-12.)

THE CONSEQUENCES OF COVETING

The consequences of covetousness are incalculable. When it involves sexual attraction, they are particularly devastating. Ask King David or President Clinton. Families are torn apart. Hearts are sometimes irreparably wounded. Children are emotionally and often physically abandoned. Reputations are ruined. And in some instances, lives are taken. Though King David repented of his own complicity in murder, he paid a severe price for his error, leaving the legacy of his moral failures as a focal point of his life and bringing the scourge of incestuous rape and murder to his household and God's kingdom at large. (See 2 Samuel 13-14.)

Coveting, however, is not confined to sexual indiscretions. In business and professional environments, competition is often ruthless when clients, accounts, jobs, positions, titles, and benefits are envied. According to the U.S. Department of Labor, homicide is now the second leading cause of death in the workplace. A number of such murders are committed by employees exacting revenge after being passed over for a promotion.[1] On college and university campuses, social or academic status, scholarship moneys, and other scholastic recognition can cause students and even parents to cross the line between aspiration and obsession. In one case, a student at Harvard wanted a particular roommate so badly that when she was rebuffed, she stabbed the young woman 45 times before hanging herself.[2]

While murderous expressions of coveting are rare, I see other extreme forms of it all around me in Washington, D.C. People with high ambition set their sights on positions of prestige or influence, and they will stop at nothing to obtain them. Lying, cheating, conniving, framing, slandering, and libeling are all somehow justified in the pursuit of the prize. There is no better example of this in recent times than the episode early on in President Bill Clinton's first term that has come to be known as "Travelgate."

In May 1993, the White House abruptly fired seven career employees from the Travel Office, accusing them of mishandling funds.
Though a subsequent investigation would exonerate them, the lives
of all seven would be painfully changed forever. It all began when
Harry Thomason, a Clinton associate, allegedly sought the firings
after Travel Office employees rejected his plan to get the White
House's charter business for a company he partly owned. Thomason
and his wife, Linda Bloodworth-Thomason, had been close friends of
the Clintons in Arkansas and later became successful Hollywood
producers. After President Clinton's election, the couple went to the
White House, taking up temporary residence there to help orches-
trate the public image of the new administration. Thomason quickly
raised unsubstantiated allegations that Travel Office employees were
seeking kickbacks. Billy Dale, head of the Travel Office, was charged
with embezzling travel funds, but was acquitted after trial by jury.

In a subsequent House investigation, David Watkins, White House
Chief of Administration, who actually fired the staff, was asked if he
felt pressure from First Lady Hillary Rodham Clinton, who apparently had made remarks about getting rid of the Travel Office staff.
"Did I feel pressure? Yes, I did," he told Congress. Watkins was later
fired for using a government helicopter for a golf outing, which cost
taxpayers $13,000.

The vilification of innocent public servants, their near bankruptcy
because of legal bills, and the total disruption of their lives was fair
game to those who wanted what they couldn't have. In this case the
coveted booty was huge sums of money associated with presidential
travel. This scandalous behavior on the part of White House opera-
tives may have caused Vince Foster, the president's boyhood friend
and deputy legal counsel, to commit suicide. His body was found in
Ft. Marcy Park on the shores of the Potomac River on July 20, 1993.
Several days later, a torn note was discovered in Foster's briefcase
with what appeared to be talking points on how to explain the

Travelgate controversy to the media. It ended with this lamentation, "I was never meant for the spotlight of public life. Here ruining people is considered sport."

THE ROAD TO COVETING

The road to coveting, and it is sometimes a terribly long and winding one, begins with unbridled desire. Like all of our inclinations, desire must be checked by virtue. "Add to your faith virtue, to virtue knowledge, to knowledge self-control" (2 Peter 1:5-6).

Desire involves a complex array of human capacities, including volition (the engagement of the will), affection, and passion. It is a powerful drive that propels us through many necessary stages in our lives. Marriage and family start with desire. Physical, intellectual, and professional achievements begin with desire. Many medical, social, and technological breakthroughs find their impetus in human desire. But inordinate, ungoverned, selfish desire leads to an equal dimension of human destruction. Wars begin with desire:

> **Where do wars and fights come from among you? Do they not come from your desires?**
>
> JAMES 4:1

Both the Old and New Testaments point out that coveting is the root to many forms of sin, including lying (see 2 Kings 5:22-25), theft (see Joshua 7:21), domestic troubles (see Proverbs 15:27), murder (see Ezekiel 22:12), lust (see 1 Timothy 6:9), greed (see Proverbs 1:19), envy (see Titus 3:3), and sinful jealousies (see 1 Corinthians 3:3). These are also manifestations of desire gone awry and run amok.

Jesus listed covetousness with a host of evils that proceed from a corrupt heart. (See Mark 7:21-23.) So it is clear that evil desire begins with the wrong kind of thoughts. James tells us that sin begins with an evil mental inclination:

> But each one is tempted when he is drawn away by his
> own desires and enticed.
>
> Then, when desire has conceived, it gives birth to sin; and
> sin, when it is full-grown, brings forth death.
>
> JAMES 1:14-15

The great Reformationist John Calvin emphasized that coveting is
principally a sin of the mind.[3] Eve's fall into violating God's command
began with a thought, which became an imagination: "The woman
saw that the tree was good for eating and that it was a delight to the
eyes and the tree was desirable to contemplate."[4] No wonder one of
the first Christian disciplines is the renewing of the mind.

> And do not be conformed to this world, but be trans-
> formed by the renewing of your mind, that you may prove
> what is that good and acceptable and perfect will of God.
>
> ROMANS 12:2

> For though we walk in the flesh, we do not war according
> to the flesh.
>
> For the weapons of our warfare are not carnal but mighty
> in God for pulling down strongholds,
>
> casting down arguments and every high thing that exalts
> itself against the knowledge of God, bringing every
> thought into captivity to the obedience of Christ.
>
> 2 CORINTHIANS 10:3-5

Learning to think right and to control desire is the antidote to the
moral poison of covetousness. Whether on a personal level, as with
one's relationships, personal aspirations, and professional goals; or on
a societal level, as with political or cultural objectives, our thinking
must be tempered with biblical moral sensibilities. The end does not
justify the means. Getting something at all costs is a distinctly non-
Christian, unbiblical, and satanic way of thinking. It was the devil
embodied in the serpent who persuaded Eve to disobey God's

command by appealing to what could be hers, "You will be like God" (Genesis 3:5).

I was once told by a journalist that the most important parts of a story are the lead and last paragraphs. The lead draws the reader into the story, but it is the story's last paragraph that the reader will remember. I don't know if that's what every journalist would say, but it rings true to me. Perhaps this is why this sin of covetousness is identified last in the list of commandments—because this last sin just might produce the downward slippery slide that leads to the nine sins listed previously. It seems to me that virtually all sins begin with this one.

Those who disregard God's moral commands commit this luciferic sin of covetousness. One day in heaven, somewhere in eternity past, Lucifer coveted God's position and sought to overthrow Him. He failed then, but now he thinks he can do it through mankind: A judge orders God's Law to come down from a public building. A teacher promotes alternative lifestyles. A screenwriter takes God's name in vain. A company announces staff meetings on Sunday mornings. An aged mother is abandoned by her adult children. A doctor kills an unborn child. An employee takes home a carton of cigarettes without paying. A news commentator blames right-wing religious fanatics for America's problems. An adoring mother hires a hit man so that her daughter can be a cheerleader. They covet something that can never be theirs—the very place of God.

LEARNING TO BE CONTENT

The lesson of the Tenth Commandment may be summed up in the word, "contentment," the secret of which can't be found in asceticism (self-denial) or concupiscence (self-indulgence). Rather, contentment lies somewhere in the balance between the two. On the one hand, we human beings are promised that we will enjoy the good things of God:

They will feast on the abundance of the seas, on the treasures hidden in the sand.

DEUTERONOMY 33:19 NIV

On the other hand, we are reminded that:

He who loves silver will not be satisfied with silver; nor he who loves abundance, with increase.

ECCLESIASTES 5:10

Like a delicate piece of crystal, we may enjoy the good things of God, but we are not to hold them too tightly. Satisfaction comes in sharing the Lord's bounty, and many times His bounty does not consist in material things. This is the testimony of Agnes Bojaxhiu of Albania, who lived one of the most remarkable lives of all time. We know her as Mother Teresa.

When Agnes was born in 1910, Albania was as politically turbulent as it has been in these last years of the twentieth century. Back then, nationalists were struggling for their cultural identity against a brutal Turkish Ottoman regime. Public floggings were used to intimidate recalcitrant rebels. Times were volatile.

Nikolas Bojaxhiu, an imposing man with impish eyes and a handle-bar mustache, was a prosperous entrepreneur in the city of Skopje. He owned a number of properties, had at one time lucratively supplied a leading physician with medicines, and later traded furs, cloth, and leather. His wife, Drana, spent the many days her husband was away on business keeping an upper middle-class household. Upon his return, Drana always greeted Nikolas with a new dress and freshly coifed hair.

When Nikolas died unexpectedly at 45, the family suffered, but was never deprived. Drana found ingenious ways to provide for her children. She also emphasized that it was the intangibles of love, compassion, and devotion to God that were of the greatest value.

Agnes was eighteen when she announced her intention to join a missionary order of sisters. Her older brother, Lazar, a second lieutenant in the army of Albanian King Zog I, questioned her decision. Agnes defiantly responded, "You may think you are important because you are an officer serving a king with two million subjects. But I am serving the King of the whole world!" Drana Bojaxhiu gave her daughter permission to enter the convent only if she promised to live, "Only, all for Jesus." This became one of Mother Teresa's lifelong mottos.[5]

This exuberance about life never left Agnes. Though willingly dispossessed of her worldly goods, she became one of the most famous women in history. Known as the Saint of Calcutta, she was a Nobel laureate and the founder of one of the largest missionary organizations in the world. At her death in 1997, Mother Teresa owned only a few cotton saris, a cloth bag in which to carry them, and a pair of well-worn sandals. Yet, she was given a lavish state funeral and her body was borne atop the same carriage that once carried Ghandi and Nehru. The rich, the famous, and the powerful came from all over the world to pay her homage.

Though she eschewed those things that money can buy, Mother Teresa valued prayer, love, and smiles. In her seventies she wrote:

Life is an opportunity, benefit from it.
Life is beauty, admire it.
Life is bliss, taste it.
Life is a dream, realize it.
Life is a challenge, meet it.
Life is costly, care for it.
Life is wealth, keep it.
Life is love, enjoy it.
Life is a promise, fulfil it.
Life is sorrow, overcome it.

Life is a song, sing it.

Life is a struggle, accept it.

Life is an adventure, dare it.

Life is luck, make it.

Life is too precious, do not destroy it.

Life is life, fight for it![6]

Occasionally, God will call someone to surrender earthly pleasures in an extraordinary way. Still, as He did with Mother Teresa, God returns such sacrifices a hundredfold:

> **So Jesus answered and said, "Assuredly, I say to you, there is no one who has left house or brothers or sisters or father or mother or wife or children or lands, for My sake and the gospel's,**

> **"who shall not receive a hundredfold now in this time— houses and brothers and sisters and mothers and children and lands, with persecutions—and in the age to come, eternal life."**

> MARK 10:29-30

Mother Teresa knew what she wanted: "Only, all for Jesus." She obtained it, not by coveting what was not hers, but by delighting in what was. She gave up everything she had, but in return received more than any of us could imagine. She led a full life and she enjoyed it.

The Tenth Word teaches us that whether we are called to be a Mother Teresa or one of the many wealthy people who supported her work, we are each called to be content with who and what we are and what the Lord has given to us. If God has given us a desire to succeed in business so that we may be a blessing to His work, to our family, and to others, then we must pursue it with passion! If He has given to us a desire to abandon the comforts of America to take His

Gospel to the bleak and difficult places of the world, then we must hurry towards them! If He has given to us a desire to marry and rear godly children who will witness to righteousness in the earth, then we must do so as unto the Lord! What is most important is that we do whatever we do as unto the Lord and be content in Him.

> **Let your conduct be without covetousness; be content with such things as you have.**
>
> HEBREWS 13:5

EPILOGUE

A number of important events have occurred since I completed the first drafts of this book. As most Americans remember all too well, on April 20, 1999, twelve high school students and one beloved teacher were mercilessly gunned down at Columbine High School in Littleton, Colorado. The two student assailants mocked their victims as they died, poked a gun barrel into the head wound of one while calling him by a racial epithet, and demanded that two of the students declare their belief in God before they shot them. To add horror to horror, the gunmen committed suicide after being cornered by police.

Every such tragedy is too much to bear, no matter how many are injured or wounded, but the Columbine shooting arrested the attention of the entire nation. The disturbing details of the killings, the martyrdom of the two Christian students, and the contemporaneous broadcast of images from the scene made us all feel as if we were somehow personally involved. The public demanded to know how such a thing could happen in a nice suburban school, and the blame game began. Blame for the tragedy was spread around among the parents of the shooters, the school officials who apparently allowed cliques to torment outsiders (which, the gunmen said, led them to seek revenge), and finally to conservative politicians and the NRA for facilitating access to guns by minors.

But something else happened in the aftermath of Columbine. Parents, teachers, and students called for a return to God, prayer, and the Ten Commandments in public schools. In fact, since the shooting, the churches in and around Littleton have been packed for

Sunday services. As if to be a terrible reminder of the grave consequences of repudiating God's moral authority, Columbine dramatically pricked the conscience of the community and the nation. The
spontaneous reaction to the slaughter of so many innocent children
brought a wave of intensely spiritual, completely biblical, and boldly
Christian memorial services, which were broadcast on national
television and reported in publications around the world.

Several of the student survivors launched into full-time Christian
ministry, appealing to young people, parents, and elected officials to
return to God in repentance. I had the privilege of hosting one such
survivor, Heidi Johnson, and her father, Barry Johnson, here in
Washington, D.C. They came at my invitation to help present stone
artwork tablets of the Ten Commandments to the Majority Leader of
the United States Senate and the Speaker of the House in two
private U.S. Capitol ceremonies. We, together with a delegation of
hand-picked clergy from around the country, appealed to the two
leaders of Congress to pass the Ten Commandments Defense Act,
which would allow states to display the Ten Commandments in public buildings, including schools.

Miss Johnson survived the shooting only after hiding under a library
desk while her classmates, including her best friend, Rachel Scott,
were systematically murdered around her. After she was discovered
by the shooters, Heidi was told she would be the next to die, but a
police bullet fired through a window distracted the killers and they
turned away at the last minute. She and her father, along with their
pastor, Billy Epperhart, who buried four of the Columbine victims,
pled with lawmakers to allow God's Word back into the classroom.
Heidi delivered a special two-page letter from the mother of Rachel
Scott, one of the girls who was killed for professing her belief in God,
to the Senate Majority Leader containing a similar message. Her
letter is published at the front of this book.

The event at Columbine High School and others like it in Jonesboro, Arkansas; Paducah, Kentucky; and Conyers, Georgia; have not deterred the so-called American Civil Liberties Union (ACLU) and anti-religious groups like them from continuing their war against Jewish-Christian morality. The ACLU has been joined by the American Atheists, Inc., in opposing the Ten Commandments Defense Act. The Clinton-Gore Administration once hosted the American Atheists for executive level meetings in the White House after they protested belief in God as part of the Boy Scout pledge. Ron Barrier, National Spokesman for the American Atheists, called the Ten Commandments bill "illegal, unconstitutional, un-American, and dangerous."[1]

As I write, the ACLU is in several state and federal courts suing for the removal of Ten Commandments displays in various communities. In Ohio, the ACLU is challenging the placement of religious monuments depicting the Ten Commandments outside high schools in Adams County. The constitutional challenge, filed in U.S. District Court in Cincinnati, was brought on behalf of Barry Baker, a school district resident. A total of four monuments were placed in front of four different high schools, all in Adams County. Baker says he finds the presence of the religious monuments on public property offensive to his sensibilities—never mind that such displays might have made Dylan Klebold and Eric Harris, the Columbine gunmen, think twice about killing innocent kids.[2]

In Downey, California, 86-year-old Edward DiLoreto is preparing to file yet another appeal in his bid to display the Ten Commandments on an advertising board posted on the school ball field's fence which he bought to support Downey High's baseball team. The ACLU intimidated the school's officials into taking down all the ball field signs rather than allowing Mr. DiLoreto's to go up. He says that his greatest prayer is that he will live long enough to see the ACLU's victory reversed and the Commandments back up where kids can read and learn from them.[3]

Yet in view of all this and more, I remain optimistic about the quest to see God's Holy Law once again honored in our nation. While many battles have been lost, there have also been a number of important victories. The House of Representatives passed the Ten Commandments Defense Act by a wide margin. Over 200 elected officials in Washington, D.C., now display the Ten Commandments in their public offices. More and more young people and the vast majority of adults support a return to prayer and the Ten Commandments in schools. The Ten Commandments were the subject of a recent *New York Times* bestseller. Citizen movements to display the Ten Commandments in public buildings are popping up everywhere and gaining strength. And most significantly, the House of Representatives fell just short of a needed two-thirds majority vote on a proclamation for a week of national repentance.

As for Judge Roy Moore, whose story in part inspired this book, he continues his brave fight for righteousness while the Ten Commandments remain prominently displayed in his courtroom. The Judge spends countless days speaking to groups across the country. The *Cumberland Law Review* recently published his brilliant treatise presenting the historical and constitutional argument for the government's acknowledgment of God and His moral law. This treatise will be the basis for Judge Moore's hoped for Supreme Court argument. He graciously allowed me to include it for your edification in the Appendix, and I encourage you to read it.

I also invite you to be one of the many courageous Americans who have joined in the mission to return the Ten Commandments to their rightful place in our culture. It may be late in America, but it's not too late!

Let the mission begin . . .

"Teacher, which is the great commandment in the law?"

Jesus said to him, " 'You shall love the Lord your God with all your heart, with all your soul, and with all your mind.'

"This is the first and great commandment.

"And the second is like it: 'You shall love your neighbor as yourself.'

"On these two commandments hang all the Law and the Prophets."

MATTHEW 22:36-40

ENDNOTES

Introduction

1 "Re-creating the Tablets of the Law" by Alan R. Millard, *Bible Review*, February 1994, pp. 49-53.

2 From the Middle English, *Decaloge*, derived from the Latin, *decalogus* and Greek, *dekalogos*, or Ten Words.

3 *Christian Coalition News*, April 21, 1997, "Poll Finds Americans Want More Religion in Public Life; Want Politicians to Address Moral Concerns," report on results of Luntz Research Corporation Poll. Luntz Research Company, Arlington, Virginia, surveyed a nationwide sample of 900 American adults, selected randomly on April 4-5, 1997. Overall margin of error for the survey is 3.3 percent.

4 "Prayer," Journal of the Senate, Number 1–Regular Session, March 4, 1997.

5 *Stone et al. v. Graham, Superintendent of Public Instruction of Kentucky*, United States Supreme Court, Decided November 17, 1980, from record of October term, 1980, p. 42.

Come Up!

1 *The Five Books of Moses, A New Translation with Introductions, Commentary and Notes* by Everett Fox (New York: Schocken Books, Inc., 1995), p. 372.

I The One and Only

1 The same resolution, with even stronger language, would later pass as an amendment to a budget bill in the Senate, forcing a hostile President Clinton, who was embroiled in a sex scandal, to either sign on to it or use his line item veto power.

2 Moses Maimonides (1135-1204), a physician in the court of Sultan Saladin, was the foremost intellectual figure of medieval Judaism. As a device to help pronounce the "unspoken name," he interspersed the vowels for the Hebrew word *Adonai* (Lord) through the name YHWH, producing *Jehovah*.

3 T. Rees, "God," *New International Bible Encyclopedia*, vol. II (Grand Rapids, MI: Wm. B. Eerdmans Publishing Co., 1956, reprinted 1980), p. 1254.

4 Martin Luther, *Martin Luther's Large Catechism*, translation by Rev. Robert E. Smith (St. Louis: Concordia Publishing House, 1921), p. 580.

5 Martin Luther, *Luther's Small Catechism, with Explanation,* (St. Louis: Concordia, 1986), p. 58.

6 Terry Muck, *Alien Gods on American Turf* (Wheaton, IL: Victor Books, 1990), p. 14.

7 George Gallup, *Religion in America* (Princeton, NJ: Princeton Religion Research Center, 1996), p. 4.

8 To explore how to celebrate the Passover, visit your local library or Jewish bookstore. For a Christian perspective, I recommend two books: *Christ in the Passover* by Ceil and Moishe Rosen (Moody Press) and *Celebrate the Feasts* by Martha Zimmerman (Bethany House Publishers).

9 Christine Hoff Sommers, "Teaching the Virtues," *Imprimis*, November 1991 (Hillsdale, MI: Hillsdale College), p. 3.

10 Ibid.

11 *The Writings of George Washington from the Original Manuscript Sources: 1789 to 1799*, ed. John D. Richardson, 11 vols. (Washington, D.C.: United States Government Printing Office, 1936), pp. 15-55.

12 Benjamin Rush, *Essays, Literary, Moral, and Philosophical* (Philadelphia: Printed by Thomas and William Bradford, 1806), pp. 93-94.

13 Jedediah Morse, Election Sermon delivered at Charleston, MA, April 25, 1799.

14 David Barton, *Original Intent* (Aledo, TX: Wallbuilder Press), p. 173.

15 T. Rees, "God," *New International Bible Encyclopedia*, p. 1260.

16 David Barton, op. cit., p. 327.

17 *Roy S. Moore* v. ACLU *of Alabama, et al.*, Brief of Appellant Roy S. Moore, The Supreme Court of Alabama.

18 David Barton, op. cit., p. 329.

II Mortal and *Pecel:* Making Poison Worship

1 These images were of the cherubim, great angelic beings, which were placed on the Ark of the Covenant, the holy box which carried the presence of God in the Old Testament. The Ark rested in the Holy of Holies, first in the Tabernacle and later in the Temple. Images of similar

beings, the seraphim, were woven into the curtains that divided the Holy place from the Holy of Holies in the Tabernacle. (See Exodus 26:31.)

2 The story of Judah Maccabbee and the revolt against Syria is told in the apocryphal book of I Maccabees. The Apocrypha are those books and portions of books which appear in the Latin Vulgate Bible, as part of the Old Testament, but not in the Hebrew scriptures. With the exception of 2 Esdras, these books appear in the Greek version of the Old Testament which is known as the Septuagint, but they are not included in the Hebrew Canon of Holy Scriptures.

3 Human Rights Campaign Press Release, November 8, 1997, "Remarks by the President at Human Rights Campaign Dinner," *C-SPAN.org*, date accessed: 11/9/97, no web address.

4 For biblical counsel on overcoming same-sex desires, see *Coming Out of Homosexuality: New Freedom for Men and Women* by Bob Davies and Lori Rentzel (Intervarsity Press, 1993).

5 *Everson v. Board of Education of Ewing Township*, 330 U.S.1 (1947).

6 See *U.S. Supreme Court Reports*, 35 L. Ed.2d, p. 177.

7 *Compassion in Dying v. Washington*, 79 F. 3d 790 (1996).

8 Ibid.

9 Ibid.

10 For a full treatment of this argument from a minority viewpoint see *America's Real War: An Orthodox Rabbi Insists that Judeo-Christian Values Are Vital for Our Nation's Survival* by Rabbi Daniel Lapin (Multnomah Books, 1999).

III His Name Is Wonderful

1 Partners Task Force for Gay and Lesbian Marriage, Seattle, Washington. www.budybuddy.com/toc.html

2 The more conventional translation of this name is "The Jealous One," but because this word now denotes a negative character trait in modern English, it is more accurate to its ancient meaning to use "Zealous."

3 *The Five Books of Moses, A New Translation with Introductions, Commentary and Notes* by Everett Fox (New York: Schocken Books, Inc., 1995), p. 371.

4 *Sacred Writings*, Vol 1, "Judaism: The Tanakh" (New York: Book of the Month Club, 1992) p. 115.

[5] *Newsbits*, an internet publication of Coral Ridge Ministries, Ft. Lauderdale, FL, October, 1996.

[6] William A. DeGregorio, *Complete Book of U.S. Presidents* (New York: Barricade Books, Inc., 1993), p. 708.

[7] "A Theological and Moral Analysis of the Current Presidential Administration," by the Ad Hoc Commission for the Theological and Moral Study of the Current Administration, Washington, D.C., The National Clergy Council, October, 1996, p. 22.

[8] President William Jefferson Clinton, *State of the Union Address*, January 24, 1995, public transcript, Office of the Press Secretary, The White House.

IV Holy R & R!

[1] "In Search of the Real Bill Gates" by Walter Isaacson, *Time*, January 13, 1997, p. 7.

[2] Rabbi Chaim Richman, *The Restoration*, July 30, 1995.

[3] *Catechism of the Catholic Church*, Article 3, paragraph 2171 (New Hope, KY: Orbi et Orbi Communications, 1994), p. 523.

[4] *Luther's Small Catechism* (St. Louis: Concordia Publishing House, 1986), pp. 66-67.

[5] John Calvin, *Institutes of the Christian Religion*, translated by Henry Beverage (Grand Rapids, MI: Wm. B. Eerdmans Publishing Company, 1989, 1993).

[6] *The Works of John Wesley*, A.M., John Emory, ed. (New York: Eaton & Mains), p. 221.

[7] D. L. Moody, *Weighed and Wanting* (New York: Fleming H. Revell & Co.), pp. 47-48.

[8] Jennifer E. Marshall, "The Greatest of These Is Love: Faith-Based Alternatives to the Welfare State," *Family Policy Newsletter*, 3-35-96 (Washington, D.C.: Family Research Council), p. 2.

[9] Ibid., p. 3.

[10] Acton Institute for the Study of Religion and Liberty, 161 Ottawa NW, Suite 301, Grand Rapids, MI 49503.

[11] Maggie Gallagher, *The Abolition of Marriage* (Washington, D.C.: Regnery Publishing, Inc., 1996), p. 34.

[12] "The American Family Time Satisfaction Study," Massachusetts Mutual Life Insurance Company and *Family Fun*, November 1993, pg. 5.

[13] Patrick F. Fagan, "Why Religion Matters: The Impact of Religious Practice on Social Stability," Heritage Foundation *Backgrounder* No. 1064, January 25, 1996.

[14] Ibid., p. 1.

[15] Ibid., p. 2.

[16] George W. Comstock and Kay B. Partridge, "Church Attendance and Health," *Journal of Chronic Disease*, Vol. 25 (1972), pp. 665-672.

[17] Ibid.

[18] *The Works of John Adams*, Vol. VI, Charles Francis Adams, ed. (Boston: Charles C. Little and James Brown, 1851), p. 9.

V The Honor Factor

[1] *Once Upon A Time When We Were Colored*, © 1989 by Clifton L. Talubert. Published by Council Oaks Books. Used with permission.

[2] John Quincy Adams, *Letters of John Quincy Adams, to His Son, on the Bible and Its Teachings* (Auburn: James M. Alden, 1850), pp. 22-23.

[3] We contacted *Sassy* to cite the article, and they no longer publish the magazine, nor have they archived back issues.

[4] "Was It Worth It?" from *The Wall Street Journal*.

[5] "Attitudes Towards Assisted Suicide and Euthanasia Among Physicians in Washington State," *New England Journal of Medicine*, July 14, 1994, p. 89.

[6] *Compassion in Dying* v. *Washington*, 79 F. 3d 790 (1996).

[7] *Catechism of the Catholic Church* (Rome, Italy: Urbi et Orbi Communications, 1994), p. 531.

[8] *Luther's Small Catechism* (St. Louis: Concordia Publishing House, 1986), p. 36.

[9] *Institutes of the Christian Religion*, trans. Henry Beveridge (Grand Rapids, MI: Wm. B. Eerdmans Publishing Company, 1993), p. 347.

VI America's Heart Disease

[1] Euthanasia, A Review of Richard Coleson's "The Glucksberg & Quill Amicus Curiae Briefs: Verbatim Arguments Opposing Assisted Suicide" Fr. Joseph C. Howard, Jr., M. Div., American Bioethics Advisory Commission, Website. Updated: NA, Accessed: 18 October 1999, no page. http://www.all.org/abac/jchool.htm

[2] Ibid., no page.

3 "World Update: Netherlands," *International Anti-Euthanasia Task Force*, IAETF Update, 13:2 (April-June 1999). Webpage Accessed: 18 October 1999. http://www.iaetf.org/lua15.htm#84

4 *Suicide: A Christian Response*, Timothy J. Demy and Gary P. Stewart, eds. (Grand Rapids, MI: Kregel, 1998), p.121.

5 Gary Langer, Senior Polling Analyst, ABCNews.com, March 27, 1999. See http://abcnews.90.com/sections/politics/DailyNews/Kevorkian-poll 990327.html.

6 "Abortionist Was Clinton's Guest: One of 3 in US to Perform Procedure in Third Trimester," *Washington Times*, March 5, 1997.

7 These 49 instances occur in 42 verses: Exodus 20:13; Numbers 35:6,11,12,16 (twice), 17 (twice), 18 (twice), 19,21 (twice), 25,26,27 (twice), 28,30 (twice), 31; Deuteronomy 4:42 (twice), 5:17; 19:3,4,6; 22:26; Joshua 20:3,5-6; 21:13,21,27,32,38; Judges 20:4; 1 Kings 21:19; 2 Kings 6:32; Psalm 42:10; 62:3; 94:6; Proverbs 22:13; Job 24:14; Isaiah 1:21; Jeremiah 7:9; Ezekiel 21:22; Hosea 4:2; 6:9.

8 See Exodus 22:2. The implication here is that when a thief enters a home at night, it is more frightening, leading to a more drastic act of self-protection. In the daylight, the owner of the house would have more options, making an act of self-defensive homicide more difficult to justify.

9 For an excellent treatment of the Population Control movement and its myths, see Chapters 9 and 10 in *Love and Family*, by Mercedes Arzul Wilson (San Francisco: Ignatius Press, 1996).

10 'Disasters, economy benefiting charities" by John Long, *Washington Times*, December 6, 1999.

11 Richard Exley, *Blue Collar Christianity* (Tulsa: Honor Books, 1989), p. 13.

VII When the Vow Breaks . . .

1 Thomas Johnson, "The 'Family Hour': No Place for Your Children," *Parents Television Council Report*; January 1, 1997.

2 "Marriage," *The International Bible Encyclopedia*, 1956 edition, vol. III, p. 1997.

3 For an excellent treatment of this subject, see "Crimes," *International Standard Bible Encyclopedia*, 1956 edition, Vol. 2, pp. 745-748. I also recommend *Hard Sayings of the Bible* by Walter C. Kaiser Jr., *et al.*, Intervarsity Press, 1996.

4 Some of the names in this story have been changed to protect those who were not part of the interview process.

[5] David Horowitz, *Radical Son* (New York: The Free Press, 1997), p. 289.

[6] C. S. Lewis, *Mere Christianity* (New York: MacMillan Publishing Company, 1952), pp. 95-96.

[7] *Catechism of the Catholic Church,* Part 2, p. 400, paragraph 1603.

[8] *Westminster Confession of Faith,* (Glasgow: Free Presbyterian Publications, 1994), p. 104.

[9] Maggie Gallagher, *The Abolition of Marriage* (Washington, D.C.: Regnery Publishing, Inc., 1996), p. 31.

[10] Ibid.

[11] Ibid.

[12] "2 Studies Concur on Adverse Impact of Divorce on Kids: Abuse Found to Soar in Broken Homes," by Cheryl Wetzstein, *Washington Times,* June 8, 1997.

[13] Ibid.

VIII Collared Criminals and Trusty Thieves

[1] David O. Friedrichs, *Trusted Criminals: White Collar Crime in Contemporary Society* (Belmont, CA: Wadsworth Publishing Company, 1995), p. 116.

[2] Christine Hoff Sommers, "Teaching the Virtues," *Imprimis,* November 1991 (Hillsdale, MI: Hillsdale College), p. 1.

[3] "Crime in the United States," Uniform Crime Reports, Federal Bureau of Investigation, U.S. Department of Justice, Washington, D.C., 1997, released November 22, 1998, p. 29.

[4] "Nations of the World," *The World Almanac and Book of Facts, 1999* (Mahwah, NJ: Primedia References, Inc., 1998).

[5] Robert Wright, *The Moral Animal: Evolutionary Psychology and Everyday Life* (New York: Vintage Books, 1994), ch. 2.

[6] "A Meta-Analytical Examination of Assumed Properties of Child Sexual Abuse Using College Samples," American Psychological Association.

[7] For an exhaustive expose of the World Population Crisis myth and the psuedoscience that purports to support it, see various publications by the Population Research Institute, 5119A Leesburg Pike, Suite 295, Falls Church, VA, 22401. Web address: www.pop.org/index.html. See also, *The Birth Dearth* by Ben Wattenberg.

[8] "Gates, Tycoons' Largess Aims to Curb World's Birthrate," *Washington Times,* March 24, 1999.

9   For an excellent treatment of this subject, see Thomas G. West, *Vindicating the Founders: Race, Sex, Class and Justice in the Origins of America* (New York: Rowan and Littlefield Publishers, 1997).

10 For an expose of the false science of evolution, see Philip E. Johnson, *Reason in the Balance: The Case Against Naturalism in Science, Law, and Education* (Downers Grove: Intervarsity Press, 1995) and *Darwin on Trial* (Downers Grove: Intervarsity Press, 1993).

11 "The Social Costs of Gambling" by Jim Nesbitt, Newhouse News Service, March 16, 1998.

12 "Empty Dreams: The Social Significance of Gambling," *Focus on the Family*, 1994.

13 "The Social Costs of Gambling" by Jim Nesbitt, Newhouse News Service, March 16, 1998.

14 "The Need for a National Policy on Problem and Pathological Gambling in America," 1993, *Gambling Facts*, an occasional paper by the Ethics and Religious Liberty Commission of the Southern Baptist Convention, Nashville, Tennessee.

15 Letter to Mr. Jim Nicholson, Republican National Committee, and Governor Roy Romer, Democratic National Committee, from Representative Frank R. Wolf, April 3, 1998.

16 *Issues and Answers:* "Gambling, The Christian Life Commission of the Southern Baptist Convention," November 1993.

17 Christine Hoff Sommers, "Are We Living in a Moral Stone Age?" *Imprimis*, March 1998.

18 Robert I. Kahn, *The Ten Commandments for Today* (Garden City, NY: Doubleday and Company, 1964), p. 93.

IX Gossip, Rumors, and Innuendoes

1   *The Larger Catechism*, part of the *Westminster Confession of Faith*, 1646 Ed. (Glasgow: Free Presbyterian Publications, 1995), p. 230.

2   *Atlanta Constitution*, July 31, 1996, p. A-1.

3   George Stephanopoulos, *All Too Human: A Political Education* (Boston: Little Brown and Company, 1999), pp. 127-128.

X I Spy With My Little Eye

1   "Recommendations for Workplace Violence Prevention Programs in Late-Night Retail Establishments," Report of the U.S. Department of Labor, Occupational Safety and Health Administration, 1998.

[2] Sinedu Tadese stabbed Trang Ho to death on May 28, 1995. The story of this tragic episode at Harvard is told in *Halfway Heaven* by Melanie Thernstrom (New York: Doubleday, 1997).

[3] John Calvin, op. cit., p. 354.

[4] *The Five Books of Moses, A New Translation with Introductions*, op. cit., p. 21.

[5] Kathryn Spink, *Mother Teresa: A Complete Authorized Biography* (New York: Harper, 1997), p. 11.

[6] Ibid., p. xiv.

Epilogue

[1] "Atheists Meet With White House Officials," American Atheists Press Release, May 4, 1998.

[2] "Ministers Move to Intervene in Ten Commandments Case," American Family Association Press Release, March 15, 1999.

[3] I interviewed Mr. DiLoreto personally in Downey, California.

BIBLICAL REFERENCES

Aland, Kurt, Matthew Black, Bruce M. Metzger, and Allen Wikgren. *The Greek New Testament*. London: United Bible Societies, 1966.

Amplified Bible, The. Expanded Edition. Grand Rapids, MI: Zondervan, 1987.

Apocrypha. New York: Thomas Nelson & Sons, 1957,

Ben-Yehuda, Ehud. *Ben-Yehuda's Pocket English-Hebrew, Hebrew-English Dictionary*. New York: Washington Square Press, 1964.

Cassirer, Olive. *God's New Covenant: A New Testament Translation*. Grand Rapids, MI: William B. Eerdmans Publishing Company, 1989.

Fisch, Harold. Reviser and editor. *The Holy Scriptures*. Jerusalem: Koren Publishers Jerusalem Ltd., 1992.

Green Sr., Jay P. *Interlinear Hebrew-Greek-English Bible*. Grand Rapids, MI: Baker Book House Company, 1981.

Novak, Al. *Hebrew Honey*. Houston: J. Countryman Publishers, 1987.

Sacred Writings: Judaism: The Tanakh, The New JPS Translation. New York: Book-of-the-Month Club (and The Jewish Publication Society), 1985.

Snaith, Henry Smith. Supervisor. *Sefer Torah, Nabiim, Ketuvim*. London: The British and Foreign Bible Society, 1958.

Stern, David H. *Jewish New Testament*. Jerusalem, Israel and Clarksville, MD: Jewish New Testament Publications, 1989.

Strong, James, S. T. D., LL. D. *The Exhaustive Concordance of the Bible*. McLean, VA: MacDonald Publishing Company, n. d.

Thayer, Joseph Henry, D. D. *A Greek-English Lexicon of the New Testament*. New York, Cinncinnati, Chicago: American Book Company, 1889.

Vine, W. E., M. A. *An Expository Dictionary of New Testament Words*. Nashville and New York: Thomas Nelson Publishers, n. d.

Young, Brad H. *Jesus The Jewish Theologian*. Peabody, MA: Hendrickson Publishers, Inc., 1996.

Zodhiates, Th. D. Compiler and editor. *The Hebrew-Greek Key Study Bible*. Grand Rapids, MI: Baker Book House, 1984.

◢

APPENDIX

RELIGION IN THE PUBLIC

SQUARE

HONORABLE ROY S. MOORE

◣

THIS ARTICLE WAS ORIGINALLY
PUBLISHED AT
29 CUMB. L. REV. 347 (1999).

RELIGION IN THE PUBLIC SQUARE

HONORABLE ROY S. MOORE[+]

Few subjects attract controversy like the public profession of one's faith. This is especially true if that profession of faith is made by state or federal government officials in the public arena. Thus, the display of a plaque containing the Ten Commandments of God in a small courtroom in Etowah County, Alabama, and the opening of jury organizational sessions with voluntary prayer by clergy invited to that same court have attracted the attention of millions of people in the United States. These occurrences have sparked extensive public debate and controversy not only in the State of Alabama, but all across the nation.[1]

[+] © 1999 Roy S. Moore. Judge Moore is a circuit judge for the 16th Judicial District in Etowah County, Alabama. Credentials: Former Deputy District Attorney; Captain Military Police Corp, U.S. Army; Vietnam Veteran, Company Commander 188th MP Company; Graduate U.S. Military Academy West Point 1969; and University of Alabama School of Law, Juris Doctor Degree 1977.

[1] H.R. 74, 139th Leg., 2d Sess. (Del. 1998) (supporting Judge Roy Moore's display of the Ten Commandments in Court), *see also* H.R. Con. Res. 31, 105th Cong. 1st Sess. (March 3, 1997) (supporting the display of the Ten Commandments in all government office buildings); Senate Amendment 2252 to the Congressional Budget for the United States, S. Con. Res. 86, 105th Cong. 2d Sess. (April 3, 1998) (encouraging the public display of the Ten Commandments in the Supreme Court, U.S. Capitol Building, the White House, and courthouses across the nation); and Resolution of Support by the California Republican Assembly Annual State Convention March 8, 1998. On June 17, 1999, by a vote of 248-180, the United States House of Representatives approved an amendment to H.R. 1501, which preserves each state's right to display the Ten Commandments in schools, courthouses, and other public buildings.

This courtroom display of the Ten Commandments and voluntary clergy-led prayer precipitated the filing of legal actions in both federal and state courts in Alabama.[2] On July 7, 1995, the federal action filed by the Alabama Freethought Association in the District Court for the Northern District of Alabama was dismissed for lack of standing. The court held that the plaintiffs did not have a sufficient "nexus" with either the Ten Commandments plaque or the clergy-led prayer. Because the plaintiffs failed to show that they had been or were about to be injured in fact, the court ruled that no justiciable case or controversy existed. Following the district court's ruling, the State of Alabama filed a complaint in the state circuit court for Montgomery County, Alabama, seeking a declaratory judgment. The State named Etowah County Circuit Judge Roy Moore and the American Civil Liberties Union of Alabama as separate defendants. The circuit court held that both the Ten Commandments display and the practice of voluntary clergy-led prayer were unconstitutional practices under the First Amendment's Establishment Clause. On January 23, 1998, the Alabama Supreme Court set aside this judgment, dismissing the appeals from the circuit court's rulings on the grounds that no justiciable controversy existed. As a result of this dismissal, the Ten Commandments display and the practice of opening court sessions with voluntary clerk-led prayer continues in the Etowah County Court, but the constitutional issues raised by these practices remain unresolved.

As for the display of the Ten Commandments in the Etowah County courtroom, legal writers and commentators have carried the debate to the law reviews and other periodicals. In the December 1997 issue of the *South Texas Law Review*, for example, Brian T. Coolidge argued that the display of the Ten Commandments in a trial courtroom is a "dangerous" practice. Although Mr. Coolidge concedes that the message of the Commandments reflects universal teachings in civil society, the text makes explicit references to God, which in Mr. Coolidge's opinion makes the display inescapably unconstitutional.[3]

---

[2] See Alabama Freethought Ass'n v. Moore, 893 F. Supp. 1522 (N.D. Ala. 1995) (dismissed for failure of plaintiffs to show standing to prosecute); *see also* Alabama *ex rel.* James v. ACLU, 711 So. 2d 952 (Ala. 1998) (dismissed for lack of justiciable controversy).

[3] Brian T. Coolidge, Comment, *From Mount Sinai to the Courtroom: Why Courtroom Displays of the Ten Commandments and Other Religious Texts Violate the Establishment Clause*, 39 S. TEX. L. REV. 101 (1997).

Conversely, in an article published in the *Ohio Northern University Law Review*,[4] Jonathan P. Brose provides an excellent historical analysis of the history and meaning of the First Amendment of the United States Constitution. Brose persuasively reasons that the Establishment Clause was not meant to be a personal right, but a political one guaranteed to the states. The author suggests that, though the Fourteenth Amendment may have been designed to apply some of the restrictions of the Bill of Rights to state governments, the establishment provision was never among those rights.

I submit that the propriety of displaying the Ten Commandments in a court of law or engaging in voluntary prayer in a courtroom does not depend on Mr. Coolidge's selective incorporation analysis or even Mr. Brose's total denial of a relationship between the Establishment Clause and the Fourteenth Amendment. The real purpose of the First Amendment was and is to protect the states' and their citizenry's rights to acknowledge God according to the dictates of their conscience. If not for a desire to protect this unalienable right, the First Amendment would not have been ratified. Whether it is permissible under the First Amendment's Establishment and Free Exercise clauses to acknowledge God is certainly a question of immediate imperative. The extent to which the civil liberties and personal happiness of this generation and its posterity can be exercised hinge upon whether the First Amendment will be interpreted in a historical context or according to an activist judiciary. Clearly, the signers of the Declaration of Independence believed that God must be acknowledged and "that all men were created equal" and "endowed by their Creator with certain unalienable Rights," among which were "Life, *Liberty* and the Pursuit of Happiness."[5]

---

[4] Jonathan P. Brose, *In Birmingham They Love the Governor: Why the Fourteenth Amendment Does Not Incorporate the Establishment Clause*, 24 OHIO N.U. L. REV. 1 (1998).

[5] *The Declaration of Independence* para. 2 (U.S. 1776) (emphasis added).

Historically, academicians and political thinkers considered God to be the basis and grantor of all unalienable rights. In *A Summary View of the Rights of British America*, Thomas Jefferson stated that "[t]he God who gave us life gave us liberty at the same time; the hand of force may destroy, but cannot disjoin them."[6] In 1781, in his *Notes on the State of Virginia*, Query XVIII, Jefferson discussed slavery and in opposition asked: "And can the liberties of a nation be thought secure when we have removed their only firm basis, a conviction in the minds of the people that these liberties are of the gift of God? That they are not to be violated but with his wrath. . . ."[7]

It is fitting and proper, therefore, that I address this critical topic. Actions taken by me in my role as a circuit judge resulted in state and federal court suits over the display of the Ten Commandments and the continuance of a long-standing practice of inviting clergy from the community to begin jury organizational sessions with voluntary prayers. Since the Alabama Freethought Association's constitutional challenge to my actions in 1995, the debate has unrelentingly raged over whether such practices are permitted under the First Amendment. Throughout the debate my position on the matter has not only remained unchanged, but has even been bolstered by the ongoing discovery of historical evidence and legal scholarship supporting my position.

The display of the Ten Commandments in the Etowah County courtroom and the court's practice of opening jury organizational sessions in voluntary prayer have as their purpose the acknowledgment of that God upon whom the laws and government of the United States are based. Some may recoil at the forthright proposition that recognition by the state of the sovereignty of God does not violate the Constitution; however, an examination of the evidence clearly demonstrates that objections to official state acknowledgments of God are only a recent phenomenon in United States history. The purpose of this article is to examine the history, purpose, and meaning of the term "religion" as used in the First Amendment's

---

[6] THOMAS JEFFERSON, A SUMMARY VIEW OF THE RIGHTS OF BRITISH AMERICA 105-22 (9th printing Library of America 1774).

[7] THOMAS JEFFERSON, NOTES OF THE STATE OF VIRGINIA 163 (William Peden ed., Univ. of North Carolina Press 1954) (1787).

Establishment Clause and Free Exercise Clause, and the common misconceptions and misunderstandings surrounding that term. This article will also explain why the acknowledgment of God by the state and its citizens is not only right and proper under the First Amendment, but that to so acknowledge God is the very object and purpose of the First Amendment, indeed, the very reason for its existence.

THE MEANING OF RELIGION

The legal argument used by the courts to separate God from American public life rests upon the prohibition of an establishment of religion contained in the First Amendment to the United States Constitution. To begin to understand the role of the Establishment Clause, one must first examine the clause in relation to its companion provision, the Free Exercise Clause.

The relationship between these two clauses has been the topic of much debate. In his dissent in *Edwards* v. *Aguillard*,[8] Supreme Court Justice Scalia wrote:

> Our cases interpreting and applying the purpose test have made such a maze of the Establishment Clause that even the most conscientious governmental officials can only guess what motives will be held unconstitutional. We have said essentially the following: Government may not act with the purpose of advancing religion, except when forced to do so by the Free Exercise Clause, (which is now and then); or when eliminating existing governmental hostility to religion (which exists sometimes) or even when merely accommodating governmentally uninhibited religious practices, except that at some point (it is unclear where) intentional accommodations results [sic] in the fostering of religion, which is of course unconstitutional.[9]

As usual, Justice Scalia, in his unique but eloquent manner, captured the dilemma which the Court has created for itself. For many years, members of the Court have described the struggle to navigate "a

---

[8] 482 U.S. 578 (1987).

[9] *Edwards*, 482 U.S. at 636.

neutral course between the two religion clauses, both of which are cast in absolute terms, and either of which, if expanded to a logical extreme, would tend to clash with the other."[10]

But do the clauses "clash"? To claim that they do is to conclude that the Framers contradicted themselves in the first sixteen words of the First Amendment. What did our forefathers intend by prohibiting Congress from passing laws "respecting an establishment of religion," but also prohibiting Congress from passing laws "prohibiting the free exercise thereof"? To answer this question, it is essential that we know how the drafters of the First Amendment defined the word "religion."

Today, many do not think it important to know what religion means. Thus, few people bother to inquire. Rather than examining the plain meaning of the word religion and seeking to understand what the Framers meant by the term, others prefer to define the term in whatever way would most enable them to reach their desired goal. Some have even gone so far as to suggest a dual or "bifurcated" definition. For instance, Harvard law professor Laurence Tribe once suggested that some things are "clearly religious" and therefore banned in the public arena by the Establishment Clause, but protected in private by the Free Exercise Clause; and some things are "clearly non-religious [sic]" and therefore allowed in the public arena by the Establishment Clause, but not protected in private by the Free Exercise Clause. In between, Tribe contends, is a gray area that is "arguably religious or non-religious." Things in this category would be nonreligious for Establishment Clause purposes, but religious for free exercise clause purposes.[11] One would be foolish to think that our forefathers would use the word "religion" to mean one thing and something else six words later in the same sentence. The plain

---

[10] Walz v. Tax Comm'n, 397 U.S. 664, 668-69 (1970).

[11] *See* Kent Greenawalt, *Religion as a Concept in Constitutional Law*, 72 CAL. L. REV. 753, 813-15 (1984); *see also Peloza v. Capistrano Unified Sch. Dist.*, 37 F.3d 517, 521 n.5 (9th Cir. 1994) (citing in dictum); United States v. Allen, 760 F.2d 447, 450-51 (2d Cir. 1985).

meaning principle of legal construction holds that when a word is used twice in the same statute (here, in the same sentence) without differentiation, that word is presumed to have the same meaning in both places. By failing to adhere to any definition of religion, the United States Supreme Court has, in effect, achieved Professor Tribe's goal, manipulating the religion clauses to serve its own unstated policy ends.

Every judge, attorney, and professor of law should be more than curious as to why the modern high court has failed to define the term religion under the Establishment Clause. Numerous law review articles have been written on the subject,[12] and lower courts have been left to speculate as to the meaning of religion, usually concluding that the term is virtually impossible to define.[13] Nevertheless, the term religion was clearly understood by the men who wrote and approved the wording of the First Amendment to the United Constitution. James Madison, the fourth president of the United States and often called the Chief Architect of the Constitution, introduced the First Amendment on the floor of Congress in June 1789. Four years prior to the introduction of that amendment in the first Congress, Madison had been deeply involved in the question of religious freedom in Virginia, his own state. In 1785, Madison wrote a *Memorial and Remonstrance* against a bill proposed to establish a provision for teachers of the Christian religion. In that document, referred to by the Supreme Court in *Everson v. Board of Education*,[14]

---

[12] *See* Stephen D. Collier, *Beyond Seeger/Welsh: Redefining Religion under the Constitution*, 31 EMORY L.J. 973 (1982); Timothy L. Hall, *The Sacred and the Profane: A First Amendment Definition of Religion*, 61 TEX. L. REV. 139 (1982); Stanley Ingber, *Religion or Ideology: A Needed Clarification of the Religion Clauses*, 41 STAN. L. REV. 233 (1989); M. Elisabeth Bergeron, Note, *New Age or New Testament?: Toward a More Faithful Interpretation of "Religion,"* 65 ST. JOHN'S L. REV. 365 (1991); Julie A. Scheib, Note, *Secular Humanism as a Religion Within the Meaning of the First Amendment: Grove v. Meade School District*, 61 TUL L. REV. 453 (1986); Note, *Toward a Constitutional Definition of Religion*, 91 HARV. L. REV. 1056 (1978).

[13] Alvarado v. San Jose, 94 F. 3d 1223, 1227 (9th Cir. 1996).

[14] 330 U.S. 1, 63 (1947).

Madison clearly defined religion as "the duty which we owe to our Creator, and the manner of discharging it, [which] can be directed only by reason and conviction, not by force or violence."[15] By defining religion in such a manner, Madison adopted verbatim the first portion of the definition used by George Mason in the Virginia Bill of Rights of June 12, 1776.[16] Mason, often called the Father of the Bill of Rights, stated that:

> religion, or the duty which we owe to our Creator and the manner of discharging it, can be directed only by reason and conviction, not by force or violence; and, therefore, all men are equally entitled to the free exercise of religion, according to the dictates of conscience; and that it is the mutual duty of all to practice Christian forbearance, love, and charity toward each other.[17]

As a member of the committee to draft the Virginia Bill of Rights, Madison convinced his colleagues to substitute the phrase "[a]ll men are equally entitled to the free exercise of religion, according to the dictates of conscience," for the phrase "[t]hat all men should enjoy the fullest Toleration in the Exercise of Religion,"[18] the more restrictive language proposed by Mason. So the phrase "free exercise of religion," as well as the definition of the term religion, originated with the 1776 Virginia Bill of Rights.

Following the Constitutional Convention of 1787, the new Constitution was submitted to the states for ratification. Several states proposed a Bill of Rights to protect, among other things, freedom of conscience and freedom of religion. Utilizing the Virginia

---

[15] *Everson*, 330 U.S. at 64.

[16] *See* 7 THE FEDERAL AND STATE CONSTITUTIONS, COLONIAL CHARTERS, AND OTHER ORGANIC LAWS OF THE STATES, TERRITORIES, AND COLONIES, 3814 (Francis Newton Thorpe ed., 1st ed. 1909) (quoting section 16 of the Constitution of Virginia (1776)).

[17] *Id.*

[18] 1 JAMES MORTON SMITH, THE REPUBLIC OF LETTERS 50 (1995).

definition of religion and free exercise guarantee as models, Virginia, in its ratifying convention of June 1788,[19] and North Carolina, in its convention of August 1788,[20] both proposed the following:

> That religion, or the duty which we owe to our Creator, and the manner of discharging it, can be directed only by reason and conviction, not by force or violence, and therefore all men have an equal, natural and unalienable right to the free exercise of religion according to the dictates of conscience, and that no particular religious sect or society ought to be favored or established by law in preference to others.[21]

In 1833, Justice Joseph Story, a Harvard law professor who served on the United States Supreme Court from 1811 to 1845, recognized this definition of religion in his discussion of the meaning of the First Amendment of the Constitution. Justice Story stated that

> [i]t has been truly said, that "religion or the duty we owe to our Creator, and the manner of discharging it, can be directed only by reason and conviction, not by force or violence" . . . [and that] [t]he rights of conscience are, indeed, beyond the reach of any human power. They are given by God, and cannot be encroached upon by human authority, without a criminal disobedience of the precepts of natural, as well as of revealed religion.[22]

In sum, religion encompasses all of the duties owed to God and the manner of discharging those duties, both of which depended solely

---

[19] See *supra* note 16.

[20] *See* 5 THE FEDERAL AND STATE CONSTITUTIONS, COLONIAL CHARTERS, AND OTHER ORGANIC LAWS OF THE STATES, TERRITORIES, AND COLONIES 2802 (Francis Newton Thorpe ed., 1st ed. 1909) ("All men have a natural and inalienable right to worship Almighty God according to the dictates of their own consciences, and no human authority should in any case whatsoever, control or interfere with the right of conscience.")

[21]See *supra* note 16.

[22] JOSEPH STORY, 3 COMMENTARIES ON THE CONSTITUTION § 1870.

on individual conscience. Such duties to God were secured as rights against any laws prohibiting their performance.

For a court to preclude the acknowledgment of God is to infringe upon the rights of conscience and encroach upon those natural rights given by God. Justice Story considered such encroachment a criminal disobedience of the precepts of natural and revealed religion.[23] To deny the gift is to deny the giver. Furthermore, for the state to deny one's freedom of conscience to worship God is to deny God. The worship of God is a natural duty which cannot be denied by civil society, and therefore a right of man. James Madison summarized this point brilliantly in the *Memorial and Remonstrance*:

> [W]hat is here a right towards men, is a duty towards the Creator. . . . This duty is precedent both in order of time and degree of obligation, to the claims of Civil Society. Before any man can be considered as a member of Civil Society, he must be considered as a subject of the Governor of the Universe. And if a member of Civil Society, who enters into any subordinate Association, must always do it with a reservation of his duty to the general authority, much more must every man who becomes a member of any particular Civil Society, do it with a saving of his allegiance to the Universal Sovereign. We maintain therefore that in matters of Religion, no man's right is abridged by the institution of Civil Society, and that Religion is wholly exempt from its cognizance.[24]

According to Madison, all men are subject to God, and their duty to Him is superior to that owed to civil government simply because government authority is ordained by God. Thus, civil government was not to become entangled in questions of religion, or the duties which we owe to our Creator and the manner of discharging those duties. For this reason our forefathers declared that Congress shall

---

[23] *See id.*

[24] *Everson v. Board of Educ.*, 330 U.S. 1, 64 (1947) (quoting James Madison's Memorial and Remonstrance).

make no law respecting the establishment of *the duties which we owe to our Creator and the manner of discharging those duties*, or prohibiting the free exercise of *the duties which we owe to our Creator and the manner of discharging those duties*. As the Framers understood the term religion, there is no clash between the Establishment Clause and Free Exercise Clause. Indeed, there cannot be any such clash even when the clauses are expanded to their logical extreme. Civil society can have no interest in the form of one's worship or the articles of one's faith, because all assume that these rights were given by God.

In 1878, the Supreme Court addressed the meaning of religion in the First Amendment.[25] The Court referred to the definition used by Madison[26] and stated specifically that, because the word religion was not defined in the Constitution, the Court must discover its meaning by examining the historical antecedents of the First Amendment religion clauses.[27] A few years later, in 1890, the Supreme Court explicitly adopted the Virginia definition of religion as the one embodied in the First Amendment:[28]

> The term "religion" has reference to one's views of his relations to his Creator, and to the obligations they impose of reverence for His being and character, and of obedience to His will. . . . The First Amendment to the Constitution in declaring that Congress shall make no law respecting the establishment of religion or forbidding the free exercise thereof was intended to allow everyone under the jurisdiction of the United States to entertain such notions respecting his relations to his Maker and the duties they impose as may be approved by his judgment and conscience, and to exhibit his sentiments in such form of worship as he may think proper, not injurious to the equal rights of others, and to prohibit legislation for the support of any religious tenets or the modes of worship of any sect.[29]

---

[25] Reynolds v. United States, 98 U.S. 145 (1878).

[26] *See Reynolds*, 98 U.S. at 163.

[27] *Id.* at 162.

[28] Davis v. Beason, 133 U.S. 333 (1890), *abrogated by* Romer v. Evans, 517 U.S. 620 (1996).

[29] *Davis*, 133 U.S. at 342.

Succinctly stated, the First Amendment Establishment Clause was never intended to eliminate the necessary truth that government must recognize the sovereignty of God. To the contrary, God's sovereignty over nations is the very basis of the First Amendment religion guarantees, and without such sovereignty, these guarantees could not exist.

Why has the modern Supreme Court never embraced a definition of religion under the Establishment clause, even though the term was so well-defined by the historical antecedents of the First Amendment and the early Supreme Court cases involving that amendment? The answer is simply that to recognize the original meaning of religion would not conform to a secular worldview of society that some seek to establish, and that any other definition, if adopted by the Court, would go against logic and established precedent.

Since the 1960s, the Supreme Court has discussed "religion" and "religious" practices in many cases, although the meaning of the term "religion" under the Establishment Clause has never been addressed. For example, in a series of cases in 1965 involving conscientious objectors to involuntary military service, the Court found it necessary to determine the meaning of "religious training and belief." The Court stated that "[t]he test might be stated in these words: A sincere and meaningful belief which occupies in the life of its possessor a place parallel to that filled by the God of those admittedly qualifying for the exemption. . . ."[30] In other words, anything in which a person believed, or in which he professed a belief, which approximated a belief in God might qualify for an exemption—much different definition than the one controlling the term religion. Notwithstanding the clear textual difference between the language of the First Amendment and the Selective Service Act, the Court has acted as if the definitions are equivalent, giving rise to the dilemma that accommodating the free exercise of religion threatens a forbidden establishment of religion."[31]

---

[30] United States v. Seeger, 380 U.S. 163, 176 (1965).

[31] See, e.g., Welsh v. United States, 398 U.S. 533 (1970).

To avoid this dilemma, the current Supreme Court must once again recognize the original definition of "religion" under the Establishment Clause. Should the Court redefine religion along the lines of *Seeger*, it would radically change the true meaning of the First Amendment provisions regarding religion without any supporting precedent. By leaving religion undefined, the Court has opened the door to the erroneous assumption that, under the Establishment Clause, religion could include Buddhism, Hinduism, Taoism, and whatever might occupy in man's life a place parallel to that filled by God, or even Secular Humanism, which might be defined as man's belief in his own supremacy and sufficiency.[32] In such a case, God and religion are no longer distinguished in meaning, permitting the First Amendment to be used to exclude the very object it was meant to protect, namely the sovereignty of God over civil government.

SEPARATION OF CHURCH AND STATE

Although the phrase "wall of separation between church and state" does not appear in the Constitution of the United States, Declaration of Independence, Articles of Confederation, or any other official American document, many Americans have been led to believe that the First Amendment Establishment Clause requires our government to separate itself from anything relating to God. Such an interpretation of the meaning of the religion clauses of the First Amendment is simply erroneous. Nevertheless, no discussion of religion in the public square could be complete without addressing the true meaning of the term "wall of separation between church and state." In 1947, the Supreme Court stated that "[i]n the words of Jefferson, the clause against establishment of religion by law was intended to erect a wall of separation between Church and State. . . . That wall must be kept high and impregnable. We could not approve the slightest breach."[33]

---

[32] See Torcaso v. Watkins, 367 U.S. 488, 495 n.11 (1961).

[33] Everson v. Board of Educ. 330 U.S. 1, 16-18 (1947) (quoting Reynolds v. United States, 98 U.S. 145, 164 (1878)).

In an earlier case, the Court properly identified the origin of that phrase to be a letter dated January 1, 1802, sent by President Thomas Jefferson in reply to an inquiry from the Danbury Baptist Association. In that letter, Jefferson stated:

> Believing with you that religion is a matter which lies solely between man and his God; that he owes account to none other for his faith or his worship; that the legislative powers of the government reach actions only, and not opinions, I contemplate with sovereign reverence that act of the whole American people which declared that their legislature should make no law respecting an establishment of religion, or prohibiting the free exercise thereof, thus building a *wall of separation between church and state*.[34]

Relying upon this phrase, which appears in no relevant legislative or constitutional document, the Court has construed the Establishment Clause to forbid a simple prayer acknowledging God that was required by the New York Board of Regents in public schools in 1962,[35] the reading of the Bible in school classrooms in Maryland and Pennsylvania in 1963,[36] a display of a creche in the Allegheny County Courthouse in Pennsylvania during Christmas,[37] and the inclusion of invocations and benedictions in the form of prayer in graduation ceremonies in Rhode Island public schools.[38] Additionally, the Court declared unconstitutional a Rhode Island statute providing for the payment of salary supplements to teachers of secular subjects in non-public schools,[39] an Alabama law providing for a daily period of silence in public schools for meditation or voluntary prayer,[40] and a Louisiana statute providing for a balanced treatment of creation science and evolution science in public schools.[41] Rather than protect individual freedom, these cases deny the right of individuals to voluntarily engage in an activity solely because of its "religious" content, even though no one is coerced to participate in the activity.

---

[34] Reynolds v. United States, 98 U.S. 145, 164 (1878) (emphasis added) (quoting Thomas Jefferson's letter to the Danbury Baptist Association (Jan. 1, 1802)).

[35] *See* Engel v. Vitale, 370 U.S. 421 (1962).

[36] *See* School District v. Shempp, 374 U.S. 203 (1965).

[37] *See* County of Allegheny v. ACLU, 492 U.S. 573 (1989).

[38] *See* Lee v. Weisman, 505 U.S. 577 (1992).

[39] *See* Lemon v. Kurtzman, 403 U.S. 602 (1971).

[40] *See* Wallace v. Jaffree, 472 U.S. 38 (1985).

[41] *See* Edwards v. Aguillard, 482 U.S. 578 (1987).

A distinguished lawyer once said that during closing arguments in every case a thread of truth could be found running throughout the evidence, and if one could only find that thread, one would then see the truth. The same can be said for these cases interpreting the Establishment Clause of the First Amendment. They have but one object in common—the removal of the knowledge of God from our society. Did Jefferson contemplate such a removal or separation of God and government? By choosing the phrase "wall of separation between church and state," did he truly mean that the government should in no way support religion?

To understand what that phrase means, we must go back more than one hundred years before Jefferson wrote to the Danbury Baptist Association. In 1689, John Locke, a well-known English philosopher, wrote A Letter Concerning Toleration in which he clearly defined the proper relationship between church and state. Locke stated that he "esteem[ed] it above all things necessary to distinguish exactly the business of civil government from that of religion, and to settle the just bounds that lie between the one and the other."[42] Locke, after discussing the exact meaning of the term "church," concluded by stating that "the magistrate has no power to enforce by law, either in his own church, or much less in another, the use of any rites or ceremonies whatsoever in the worship of God. . . . And upon this ground I affirm that the magistrate's power extends not to the establishing of any articles of faith or forms of worship by the force of his laws."[43] Herein lies the true meaning of separation of church and state—government may never dictate one's form of worship or articles of faith. This does not mean that all public worship of God must be stopped; on the contrary, the free public worship of God was the very reason for a doctrine of separation of church and state.

According to the writings of Manasseh Cutler,[44] a Congressman from Massachusetts, on January 3, 1802 (just two days after the Danbury Baptist letter), then President Jefferson attended a church

---

[42] JOHN LOCKE, A LETTER CONCERNING TOLERATION 17 (1689).

[43] See id. at 19, 39.

[44] WILLIAM PARKER CUTTLER & JULIA PERKINS CUTTLER, LIFE JOURNALS AND CORRESPONDENCE OF REV. MANASSEH CUTTLER, LLD (1888).

service conducted by a well-known Baptist minister "in the House of Representatives"[45] and President Jefferson continued to attend such services during the remainder of his presidency. After the government moved to Washington in 1800, the same services were conducted regularly in the north wing of the Capitol building.[46] Ironically, today Jefferson's own words are used to forbid that which he found to be constitutionally permissible.

From 1807 to 1857, church services were conducted in Statuary Hall[47] and continued in the House until after the Civil War. Not only were worship services conducted in Congress, the services were also conducted in the War Office and the Treasury during Jefferson's administration.[48] Services were held in the old Supreme Court Chamber, located in the United States Capitol Building, from the very moment the government moved to Washington in 1800.[49] Obviously, neither Jefferson, nor any of the officials of the government, understood "separation of church and state" to mean that the federal government was precluded from recognizing the necessity of the public worship of God or from permitting active support of opportunities for such public worship.

During America's formative years, our Founders recognized that plainly the duty of civil government was to allow and encourage the public profession of faith in God, and this duty did not violate the separation between church and state. Justice Joseph Story wrote what is considered to be the leading exposition on the Constitution from the first half of the 1800s. In his treatise, Justice Story questioned whether any free government could endure if it fails to provide for the public worship of God. Specifically, he stated that

---

[45] See Id. at 118.

[46] See id. at 174.

[47] See JAMES H. HUTSON, RELIGION AND THE FOUNDING OF THE AMERICAN REPUBLIC 84 (1998).

[48] See id. at 89.

[49] See id. at 91.

"[i]t yet remains a problem to be solved in human affairs, whether any free government can be permanent, where the public worship of God, and the support of religion, constitute no part of the policy or duty of the state in any assignable shape."[50] Not only did Justice Story believe that the public worship of God and support of religion was a duty of the state, he also believed that faith in God was the basis of civilized society arid that no civilized society could or should be indifferent to religion, specifically to Christianity. He wrote:

> The promulgation of the great doctrines of religion, the being, and attributes, and providence of one Almighty God; the responsibility to him for all our actions, founded upon moral freedom and accountability; a future state of rewards and punishments; the cultivation of all the personal, social, and benevolent virtues; these never can be a matter of indifference in any well ordered community. It is, indeed, difficult to conceive, how any civilized society can well exist without them. And at all events, it is impossible for those, who believe in the truth of Christianity, as a divine revelation, to doubt, that it is the especial duty of government to foster, and encourage it among all the citizens and subjects.[51]

If God is the Giver of all human rights, the Source of all governmental authority, the Fountain of all national blessings, and the Author of the basic values that make a nation great, then prohibition of public worship of God in any manner, whether by its citizens in public institutions or by public officials in the exercise of the duties of their office, destroys the very foundation of government and violates the very essence of the meaning of separation of church and state.

The men who drafted the First Amendment did so to allow everyone the right to worship God according to the dictates of conscience. Today, however, the doctrine of "separation of church and state" distorts the very ends it was meant to protect. In a recent dissenting opinion, Chief Justice William Rehnquist said that the "'wall of separation between church and state' is a metaphor based on bad

---

[50] JOSEPH STORY, 3 COMMENTARIES ON THE CONSTITUTION § 1869.

[51] *Id.* at 1865.

242

history, a metaphor which has proved useless as a guide to judging. It should be frankly and explicitly abandoned."[52] Rehnquist also noted that "the greatest injury of the 'wall' notion is its mischievous diversion of judges from the actual intention of the drafters of the Bill of Rights."[53] Arguably, the doctrine has been abused, twisted, and taken out of context in recent Supreme Court decisions in order to prohibit the public worship of God. The opinions of earlier Justices of the Court reflect a radically different view of separation. In 1878, the Supreme Court explained the true meaning of "separation of church and state" by stating:

> That to suffer the civil magistrate to intrude his powers into the field of opinion, and to restrain the profession or propagation of principles on supposition of their ill tendency, is a dangerous fallacy, which at once destroys all religious liberty . . . that it is time enough for the rightful purposes of civil government for its officers to interfere when principles break out into overt acts against peace and good order. In these two sentences is found the true distinction between what properly belongs to the Church and what to the State.[54]

Instead of relying upon Jefferson's letter to the Danbury Baptists, the Court took these two sentences from Jefferson's Bill for Religious Freedom,[55] an official government document directly related to a historical antecedent of the First Amendment. In that document, Jefferson posited the foundation upon which his concept of separation of church and state rested: "Almighty God hath created the mind free, [and being the] holy author of our religion . . . yet chose not to propagate it by coercions. Coercions on either, as it was in His Almighty power to do. . . ."[56]

---

[52] Wallace v. Jaffee, 472 U.S. 38, 107 (1985).

[53] Id.

[54] See Reynolds v. United States, 98 U.S. 145, 163 (1878) (quoting Bill for Establishing Religious Freedom, 1 JEFF. WORKS 45; 2 HOWISON, HISTORY OF VA. 298).

[55] THOMAS JEFFERSON, THE STATUTE OF VIRGINIA FOR RELIGIOUS FREEDOM (1777).

[56] Id.

In 1878, the Supreme Court agreed with Jefferson's belief that the proper role of government did not encompass dictating how people should think or what they could or could not believe.[57] Recognition of godly principles and the acknowledgment of God were not considered to be an intrusion into freedom of conscience because it was God who had created the mind free. On the other hand, denial of the right to worship God in public institutions and by public officials would have been an unconstitutional intrusion because it would have been a denial of the freedom of conscience.

If the only basis for federal interference with the public worship of God is when it threatens to breach public order, the Supreme Court today would find it very difficult indeed to explain how a simple prayer acknowledging a Creator, a display of a creche at Christmas, or a statute which allows the teaching of creationism could be principles which break out into overt acts against peace and good order.

Some have argued that public prayer coerces unwilling citizens to participate. In the recent DeKalb County school prayer case, the United States District Court for the Middle District of Alabama held that student prayer at a graduation ceremony "may be effectively coercing students who do not wish to hear or participate in prayer to do so. . . ."[58]

To the contrary. The only coercion that has taken place in the DeKalb County school prayer case is a federal court order forbidding such activities. The Christian majority has been coerced into silence, simply because the minority might have to hear them. But nothing in the U.S. Constitution guarantees that a student will never have to hear disagreeable or offensive views because that student might feel peer pressure to participate. Peer pressure or public opinion are not the types of coercion the Framers intended to prohibit. By its plain text, the First Amendment only forbids the enactment of "any law."[59]

---

[57] *See Reynolds*, 98 U.S. at 163.

[58] Chandler v. James, 985 F. Supp. 1068, 1086 (M.D. Ala. 1997).

[59] U.S. CONST. amend. I.

No student should ever be forced by law to participate in prayer, but to stop the acknowledgment of God by prayer simply because another student might listen to something he does not wish to hear is as illogical as eliminating a school's mascot or motto because it may offend a student. Likewise, to conclude that student-led prayer before a football game is a "pervasive" religious activity and coercive is really but the intrusion of the federal magistrate's power into the field of opinion. Indeed, the federal judge in the DeKalb County case has required the county's school administrators and teachers to attend seminars requiring them to learn the judge's meaning of the First Amendment religion clauses. This is the very thing that Jefferson referred to as an "ill tendency" and as a "dangerous fallacy which at once destroys all religious liberty because he being of course judge of that tendency will make his opinions the rule of judgement and approve or condemn the sentiments of others only as they shall square with or differ from his own."[60]

For a court to deny to the people the unalienable right to acknowledge God is an infringement of that "natural right"[61] upon which the Bill for Establishing Religion [sic] Freedom was based and represents a destruction of the foundation upon which the doctrine of separation of church and state exists. As President Lincoln said in his 1863 Proclamation Appointing a National Fast Day:

> [I]t is the *duty* of nations as well as of men to own their dependence upon the overruling power of God, to confess their sins and transgressions in humble sorrow yet with assured hope that genuine repentance will lead to mercy and pardon, and to recognize the sublime truth, announced in the Holy scriptures and proven by all history that those nations only are blessed whose God is the Lord.[62]

---

[60] THOMAS JEFFERSON, THE STATUTE OF VIRGINIA FOR RELIGIOUS FREEDOM (1777) .

[61] *Id.*

[62] JAMES D. RICHARDSON, A COMPILATION OF THE MESSAGES AND PAPERS OF PRESIDENTS 1789-1902 (1907) (emphasis added).

If it be true that the First Amendment was never meant by our founding fathers to preclude the acknowledgment of God in schools, public institutions, and other facets of public life, and if the doctrine of separation of church and state has been twisted and wrongfully applied to deny the very freedom of conscience that doctrine was meant to preserve, then what motivates the courts to act with utter disregard to our history, our heritage, and the meaning, intent, and purpose of the First Amendment to the Constitution?

The intentions of the drafters of the First Amendment to the Constitution and the Framers of the Constitution of the United States is clearly evident; one need only look to their actions. When the First Congress met in April 1789, one of their first actions was to appoint chaplains in both Houses of Congress. From April 1789 to this date, Congress has recognized God by the appointment and payment from government funds of a chaplain to open each House of Congress and each session with prayer. America's first president, George Washington, and each President since, with the possible exception of one, has been administered an oath of office with his hand on the Holy Bible, that oath ending in the phrase "So Help Me God." Finally, the first Chief Justice to the United States Supreme Court, John Jay, in May 1790 specifically authorized opening court sessions with prayer by invited clergy.[63] Thereafter, all of the early justices of that Court observed that practice. Even today the United States Supreme Court opens with prayer, "God Save The United States And This Honorable Court." Truly, as the Court itself has observed, such "actions reveal [America's founders'] intent."[64]

Those wishing to remove the knowledge of God from the public arena frequently argue that the Fourteenth Amendment, by incorporating the First Amendment, prohibits state acknowledgment of

---

[63] See DOCUMENTARY HISTORY OF THE SUPREME COURT OF THE UNITED STATES 1789-1800 (Columbia University Press, Volume II).

[64] Marsh v. Chambers, 463 U.S. 783, 790 (1983).

God in public life. But the sovereignty of God has nothing to do with the relationship between the Fourteenth Amendment and the Establishment Clause. Presidents proclaim days of fasting and prayer, the Congress has chaplains and prayers, and the federal courts open with invocations which acknowledge God. With all three branches of the federal government recognizing the providence of God, it is incongruous for a state government, including its public schools, to be restricted from doing so. Not even its strongest advocates would argue that the First and Fourteenth Amendments prohibit the states from acknowledging God in ways that are permitted to all three branches of the federal government. As the United States Supreme Court stated in 1983 while upholding the right of the Nebraska Legislature to open with prayer: "In applying the First Amendment to the states through the Fourteenth Amendment, . . . it would be incongruous to interpret the Clause as imposing more stringent First Amendment limits on the states than the draftsmen imposed on the Federal Government."[65]

Indeed, America's forefathers gave thanks to God for the Constitution *on the very day* that they approved the wording of the First Amendment. On September 25, 1789, a joint committee of both Houses was directed to wait upon the President and request that he recommend to the people of the United States a day of public Thanksgiving and Prayer to be observed by acknowledging with grateful hearts, the many signal favors of Almighty God, especially by affording them an opportunity peaceably to establish a Constitution of government for their safety and happiness.[66] Shortly before that resolution, Congress passed the Northwest Ordinance, Article III, of which declared in part: "Religion, morality, and knowledge, being necessary to good government and the happiness of mankind, *schools and the means of education shall forever be encouraged.*"[67]

---

[65] *Id.* at 783.

[66] GALES & SEATON'S HISTORY, CONG. REC. (September 25, 1789).

[67] Northwest Ordinance of 1787, ch. 8, 1 Stat. 50 (1789).

The Northwest Ordinance, an organic law of the United States government and one of the most foundational pieces of legislation ever adopted by Congress, is most relevant in showing Congress's intent because it became law one month prior to congressional approval of the First Amendment. To the members of our first Congress, there was a necessary relationship between our schools and the encouragement of a dutiful relationship to God. The words of that Ordinance were later incorporated into the constitutions of various new states, including Ohio (1802), Mississippi (1817), Kansas (1858), and Nebraska (1875). Our forefathers clearly intended to base our government on a belief in God and believed that schools were the proper place to encourage religions and moral development.

But what is the *intent* today? Since the early 1960s when prayer and Bible reading in public schools were excluded by the Court, there has been a consistent effort to remove any recognition of God from public schools and public life. In 1962, when the United States Supreme Court removed the twenty-two word prayer of the New York Board of Regents in *Engel v. Vitale*,[68] the Court *completely ignored precedent*, failing to cite one case in support of its decision. Speaking for the Court in *School District of Abington Township, Pa. v. Schempp*,[69] Justice Clark stated: "Finally, in *Engel v. Vitale*, only last year, these principles were so universally recognized that the Court, without the citation of a single case and over the sole dissent of Mr. Justice Stewart reaffirmed them."[70] The Court in *Engel* found New York's twenty-two word prayer to be a "religious" activity."[71] However, the Establishment Clause does not address the term "religious activity," but rather the term "religion."[72] Although religion and religious activity may at first glance sound similar, in fact they

---

[68] 370 U.S. 421 (1962).

[69] 374 U.S. 203 (1963).

[70] School District v. Schempp, 374 U.S. 203, 221-22 (1963).

[71] *Engel*, 370 U.S. at 424.

[72] U.S. CONST. amend. I.

are very different. Religious activities may include many activities that would not of themselves constitute a religion. For example, prayer and Bible reading might be characterized as religious activities, but they do not constitute religions and are not limited to any specific religion, or even to religious people. People who do not consider themselves religious may read the Bible to gain wisdom or may even routinely engage in prayer. To use the term religious, instead of "religion," is to enlarge the prohibition of the First Amendment to preclude the very object the amendment was designed to preserve. How did the Supreme Court accomplish this feat, transforming the original intent of America's founders into a rule of its own making according to its own intent? Simply stated, the court did so by changing the role of the judiciary in American government, departing from the original intent of a judicial branch limited to saying what the law is, to making the law case-by-case.

In his concurring opinion in *Harper v. Virginia Dept. of Taxation*,[73] Justice Scalia observed that John Marshall's concept of the judicial role, shared by succeeding generations of American judges until very recent times, was understood to be limited to stating what the law is, not what the law shall be.[74] Scalia noted:

> That original and enduring American perception of the judicial role sprang not from the philosophy of Nietzsche but from the jurisprudence of Blackstone, which viewed *retroactivity* as an inherent characteristic of the judicial power, a power "not delegated to pronounce a new law, but to maintain and expound the old one."[75]

Justice Scalia could justifiably apply the further reasoning of Sir William Blackstone that when a "former determination is most evidently contrary to reason . . . [or] . . . contrary to the divine law, [a judge overruling that decision would] not pretend to make a new

---

[73] 509 U.S. 86 (1993).

[74] *Harper*, 509 U.S. at 107 (Scalia, J., concurring).

[75] *Id.* (quoting 1 WILLIAM BLACKSTONE, COMMENTARIES *69).

law, but to vindicate the old one from misrepresentation."[76] *This principle of retroactive decision making is a basic distinction between the judicial and legislative power and should be used to reverse the misinterpretation of the First Amendment to the United States Constitution, thus restoring the recognition of a Divine Creator upon which the First Amendment is based.*

In *Engel* the United States Supreme Court expounded a new law without precedent, and overnight the term "religion" was equated with the acknowledgment of God. In so doing, the Court exceeded the authority of the judiciary by declaring the law to conform to their personal view of what the world should be. They chose to declare what the law should be, as opposed to what the law is, based upon fixed absolute standards.

For over one hundred seventy years before 1962, prayer had occurred in the schools of our land; yet without the citation of a single case, that practice was abruptly ended. This fact evidently bothered Justice William O. Douglas, who wrote to his associate, Justice Hugo Black:

> As you know, I have had troubles with No. 468 - *Engel v. Vitale.* . . . I am inclined to reverse if we are prepared to disallow public property and public funds to be used to finance a religious exercise. If, however, we would strike down a New York requirement that public school teachers open each day with prayer, I think we could not consistently open each of our sessions with prayer. That's the kernel of my problem.[77]

Whatever their intent may have been, the practical effect of the Justices' decisions in *Engel* and *Schempp* has been to limit and reduce the acknowledgment of God in public schools. The effort to remove the knowledge of God from our public schools continues today. The

---

[76] *Id.* (quoting 1 WILLIAM BLACKSTONE, COMMENTARIES *69-70).

[77] Justice William O. Douglas, *To Hugo LaFayette Black*, in THE DOUGLAS LETTERS 200 (Melvin I. Urofsky ed., 1987).

Dekalb County, Alabama, decision is only one example of a nation-wide trend.[78] Under this federal court order, students are prohibited from vocal prayer and from giving each other religious materials, and even denied the right to discuss *anything of a devotional/inspirational nature*.[79] These restrictions stand in stark contrast to the practices and procedures allowed during the first 150 years of our existence.

Even as late as 1954, President Dwight David Eisenhower, in an address to Congress regarding the addition of "under God" to the official Pledge of Allegiance, remarked:

> From this day forward, the millions of our school children will daily proclaim in every city and town, every village and rural schoolhouse, the dedication of our Nation and our people to the Almighty. To anyone who truly loves America, nothing could be more inspiring than to contemplate this rededication of our youth on each school morning, to our Country's true meaning.[80]

Congress, by adding the proposed phrase to the Pledge of Allegiance, stated that it was doing so to acknowledge the sovereignty of God over the United States of America and to recognize that God's sovereignty is the basis for the nation's commitment to individual human dignity, individual human worth, and individual human rights. Thus, the Committee on the Judiciary of the United States Congress reported in support of placing "under God" in the Pledge of Allegiance:

> At this moment of our history the principles underlying our American Government and the American way of life are under attack by a system whose philosophy is at direct odds with our own. Our American Government is founded on the concept of the individuality and the dignity of the human being. Underlying this concept is the belief that the human person is important because he was created by God and endowed by Him with certain inalienable rights which no civil authority may usurp. The inclusion of God in our pledge therefore would further acknowledge the dependence of our people and our Government upon the moral directions of the Creator.[81]

---

[78] *See* Chandler v. James, 985 F. Supp. 1062 (M.D. Ala. 1997).

[79] *See id.* at 1063.

[80] Statement by the President, 83d Cong., 2d Sess. 8618 (1954).

[81] Joint Resolution, 83d Cong., 2d Sess. (1954).

As for compliance with the First Amendment's religion clauses, Congress elaborated:

> It should be pointed out that the adoption of this legislation in no way runs contrary to the provisions of the first amendment [*sic*] to the Constitution. This is not an act establishing a religion or one interfering with the "free exercise" of religion. A distinction must be made between the existence of a Religion as an institution and a belief in the sovereignty of God.[82]

Consistently, throughout the 1950s, Congress and the President acted in accordance with this understanding of the First Amendment. In 1952, by Act of Congress, a day was set aside for the people to unite by "turn[ing] to God in prayer and meditation. . . ."[83] In 1955, the phrase "In God We Trust" was placed on all monies to reflect "the spiritual basis of our way of life,"[84] and in 1956 those same words were made the National Motto of the United States.[85]

If the radical separationists have their way, that which the President and Congress intended to accomplish in the 1950s will soon be outlawed from the nation's public schools, and perhaps even from public life. Yet neither the federal law nor the First Amendment has changed. All that has changed is the Supreme Court's attitude towards official acknowledgments of God. Beginning with the 1960 prayer and Bible reading cases and continuing with various additional rulings demanding religious neutrality in the public square, the Court has substituted its intent for that of the Framers and of Congress and the President. If this judicial trend continues, soon the intentions of a few will become the deception of many.

DECEPTIVE COURT TESTS

The Supreme Court contrived a number of deceptive and obtuse "legal tests" for application in First Amendment cases, which create the appearance of constitutional principle and are touted as critical

---

[82] *Id.*

[83] H.R.J. Res. 382, 82d Cong., 2d Sess. (1952).

[84] Joint Resolution, 84th Cong., 2d Sess. (1955).

[85] Joint Resolution 85th Cong., 2d Sess. (1956).

tools for deciphering which conduct and practices are permitted under the First Amendment's religion clauses. The fact of the matter is that these tests merely serve to obfuscate the original intent of the First Amendment's religion clauses and to transform such clauses in furtherance of the Court's political agenda of "religious neutrality" and advancement of secular humanism. This point is best illustrated by an examination of the current evolving tests devised by the high Court in Establishment Clause jurisprudence.

For many years, the Court has used the *Lemon* test by which it measured a statute, act or practice under the Establishment Clause. Consisting of three parts, the test required a government act or practice 1) to have a "secular purpose," not a religious one, 2) to have, as its primary or principal effect, neither the advancement nor inhibition of religion, and 3) to pose no excessive government entanglement with religion.[86] Almost universally taught in America's law schools, the *Lemon* test neither applies nor advances the true purpose of the Establishment Clause. With no definition of religion to control its application, the test is easily manipulated to destroy the very object and purpose of the religion clauses of the First Amendment. In fact, the first prong alone, which requires that a government policy be divorced from any religious foundation, puts the test at odds with the original purpose of the Establishment and Free Exercise Clauses.

Without a belief in God, neither the Establishment Clause nor the Free Exercise Clause would have been proposed. Thus, the preamble to Thomas Jefferson's Statute for Religious Freedom, the Establishment Clause's precursor, begins with a historical statement rooted in the book of Genesis—"[w]ell aware that Almighty God hath created the mind free"[87]—and rests upon a principle rooted in the teachings of Jesus Christ—"that all attempts to influence it [the mind] . . . by civil incapacitations . . . are a departure from the plan of the

---

[86] Lemon v. Kurtzman, 403 U.S. 602, 612 (1971).

[87] THOMAS JEFFERSON, THE STATUTE OF VIRGINIA FOR RELIGIOUS FREEDOM (1777).

holy author of our religion."[88] This Bible-based public policy principle enabled James Madison, in debate on the floor of Congress on
August 15, 1789, to explain the religion clauses in secular language.[89]

Both Jefferson and Madison knew that neutrality about God was not
possible in a nation founded upon the laws of nature and of nature's
God.[90] Nevertheless, lower courts continue to cling to the *Lemon* test
despite the fact that the United States Supreme Court has repeatedly
departed from its use in various cases.[91] No longer using *Lemon* as the
preeminent test for establishment clause cases, the Court is now
searching for other tests. Not unexpectedly, these tests have as little
relevance to the First Amendment as does the Lemon test.

At least two of the present members of Supreme Court, Justice
O'Conner and Justice Souter, have used an "endorsement" test which
questions whether or not a reasonable person would view the activity
in question as a government endorsement.[92] In 1994, the United
States Court of Appeals for the Ninth Circuit stated that a hypothet-
ical observer would be "informed as well as reasonable; we assume that
he or she is familiar with the history of the government practices at
issue. . . ."[93] Two years later, that same court upheld the ruling of a
district court that the erection of a ten ton, twenty-five foot high
bronze and concrete sculpture in the form of a coiled serpent, the
Aztec god Quetzacoatl, costing the City of San Jose $400,000 in
addition to transportation and installation costs, would not be
perceived by a reasonable observer as an endorsement of religion.[94]

---

[88] *Id.*

[89] GALES & SEATON'S HISTORY OF DEBATES IN CONGRESS, Aug. 15, 1789.

[90] THE DECLARATION OF INDEPENDENCE para. 1 (U.S. 1776).

[91] *See, e.g.,* Rosenberger v. Rectors and Visitors of the Univ. of Va., 515 U.S. 819 (1995); Capitol Square Review and Advisory Bd. v. Pinette, 515 U.S. 753 (1995); Board of Educ. v. Grumet, 512 U.S. 687 (1994); Zobrest v. Catalina Foothills Sch. Dist., 509 U.S. 1 (1993), Lee v. Weisman, 505 U.S. 577 (1992); Lynch v. Donnelly, 465 U.S. 668 (1984); Marsh v. Chambers, 463 U.S. 783 (1983).

[92] Capitol Square Review and Advisory Bd. v. Pinette, 515 U.S. 753, 778 (1995).

[93] Kreisner v. City of San Diego, 1 F.3d 775, 784 (9th Cir. 1993).

[94] *See* Alvarado v. City of San Jose, 94 F.3d 1223, 1225 (9th Cir. 1996).

One may, and rightfully should, find it difficult to understand how a small, privately financed copy of the Ten Commandments on a schoolhouse wall in Kentucky,[95] and a framed panel of the Ten Commandments on a courthouse in Georgia[96] were adjudged unconstitutional under the Establishment Clause, but a ten ton bronze and concrete statute of an Aztec god, costing a municipality $400,000 and over which a ceremony was performed, was considered constitutional under that same Clause. Apparently the only religion which is prohibited under the Establishment Clause, if one uses the endorsement test, is the religion upon which the nation is founded. Although the endorsement test appears to be designed to require the government to be "religiously neutral" in practice, it only requires the government to be neutral regarding Christianity.

To avoid this hypocritical stance of the more liberal justices on the Court, Justice Anthony Kennedy has landed upon the "coercion" test. As used by Justice Kennedy in *Lee* vs. *Weisman*,[97] the coercion test does little to illuminate the truth. This test poses the question of whether or not a person feels coerced by a particular religious practice.[98] Not only does the test require a workable definition of "coercion," but it must identify the class of persons who can be coerced. Is it the "reasonable person" or a reasonable schoolchild, adult juror, prison inmate, etc.? In *Weisman* Justice Kennedy distinguished prayer at school graduation exercises from prayer at other public gatherings by asserting that students would be "psychologically coerced" by peer pressure to participate.[99] As Justice Scalia pointed out in his dissent, however, psychology does not supply a foundation upon which to base constitutional law: "I find it a sufficient embarrassment that our Establishment Clause jurisprudence regarding holiday displays . . . has come to 'requir[e] scrutiny more commonly associated with interior decorators than with the judiciary'. . . . But interior decorating is a rock hard science compared to psychology practiced by amateurs."[100]

---

[95] *See Stone* v. *Graham*, 449 U.S. 39 (1980).

[96] *See Harvey* v. *Cobb County*, 811 F. Supp. 669 (N.D. Ga. 1993).

[97] 505 U.S. 577 (1992).

[98] *Id.*

[99] *Id.* at 596.

[100] *Id.* at 636 (quoting American Jewish Congress v. Chicago, 827 F.2d 120, 129 (7th Cir. 1987)).

The province of the judiciary is not to analyze the mind of man, much less that of children, to determine the motives and intent of their every action. To encourage respect for the beliefs which have formed the foundation of our law and government is not, in any sense, the establishment of religion. To recognize the sovereignty of God by the allowance of public worship is not only proper, but is also a duty of the state and cannot be perceived as coercion. As Justice Joseph Story pointed out in his *Commentaries* on the Constitution, "[T]he duty of supporting religion, and especially the Christian religion, is very different from the right to force the consciences of other men, or to punish them for worshiping God in the manner, which, they believe their accountability to [H]im requires."[101] The founding documents and charters of the original thirteen colonies, as well as the Declaration of Independence, assume a Divine Creator. As Mr. Justice Douglas aptly stated in *Zorach v. Clauson*,[102] "[W]e are a religious people whose institutions presuppose a Supreme Being."[103] Justice Douglas continued by stating that "[w]hen the state encourages religious instruction or cooperates with religious authorities by adjusting the schedule of public events to sectarian needs, it follows the best of our traditions"; for by doing so the state "respects the religious nature of our people. . . ."[104] To allow the worship of God by school children is not a coercion of those who may not believe, but stand by in respectful silence. To forbid such public worship is in a very real sense to prefer "those who believe in no religion over those who do believe."[105]

In Mr. Jefferson's Bill for Establishing Religious Freedom, he defined "true coercion" when he stated that "to compel a man to furnish contributions of money for the propagation of opinions which he

---

[101] JOSEPH STORY, 3 COMMENTARIES ON THE CONSTITUTION 1870.

[102] Zorach v. Clauson, 343 U.S. 306, 313 (1952).

[103] *Id.* at 313.

[104] *Id.* at 313-14.

[105] *Id.* at 314.

disbelieves and abhors, is sinful and tyrannical."[106] Many believe that being compelled to pay taxes to support a school system that does not allow the public acknowledgment of God and that propagates evolution, abortion, and homosexuality is not only sinful and tyrannical, but true coercion. The use of the coercion test as elaborated by the Court today leads to a legal quagmire and is no more a valid guide to understanding the true meaning and purpose of the First Amendment than is the endorsement test or *Lemon* test.

Only reluctantly has the Supreme Court abandoned the *Lemon* and such related tests. In 1983, the Supreme Court utilized a "historical analysis" test[107] to uphold the practice of the Nebraska Legislature opening legislative sessions with prayer. Noting that colonial legislatures had prayer and chaplains, as did the Continental Congress, the early state legislatures, and the very same Congress which passed the First Amendment in 1789, the Court stated that an unbroken practice was not something to be lightly cast aside.[108] Of course, the propriety of an act for First Amendment determination depends not on the number of years it has existed, but rather on its substantive evaluation under the original meaning and purpose of that Amendment.[109] However, in determining what that true meaning and purpose is, the actions of the Congress that adopted the First Amendment, as well as those of the states which ratified it, are very relevant and instructive.[110]

To understand the First Amendment, courts must look to the original definition of the terms used in the First Amendment and the practices of those who drafted and approved it. In other words, courts must utilize a textual or original intent approach, not novel tests which are more like weathervanes to find direction. If the historical precedent test of *Marsh* had been applied to school prayer cases in the 1960s, the result almost certainly would have been very different.

---

[106] THOMAS JEFFERSON, THE STATUTE OF VIRGINIA FOR RELIGIOUS FREEDOM (1777).

[107] Marsh v. Chambers, 463 U.S. 783, 790-92 (1983).

[108] *See id.*

[109] *See id.* at 709-91.

[110] *See id.*

From the beginning, prayer in school was a regular practice across our land.[111] Only by ignoring history in the *Engel* case was the Court able to cast the regular practice of school prayer lightly aside.[112]

With history, text, and purpose cast aside, and no consensus on the High Court for a test other than the much maligned *Lemon* test, lower courts remain free to employ *Lemon* to fit their purposes. As Justice Anthony Scalia noted in his concurring opinion in 1993 in the *Lamb's Chapel* case:

> Like some ghoul in a late-night horror movie that repeatedly sits up in its grave and shuffles abroad, after being repeatedly killed and buried, *Lemon* stalks our Establishment Clause jurisprudence once again, frightening the little children and school attorneys of Center Moriches Union Free School District. Its most recent burial, only last Term, was, to be sure, not fully six feet under. . . . Over the years, however, no fewer than five of the currently sitting Justices have, in their own opinions, personally driven pencils through the creature's heart. . . . The secret of the *Lemon* test's survival, I think, is that it is so easy to kill. It is there to scare us (and our audience) when we wish it to do so, but we can command it to return to the tomb at will. When we wish to strike down a practice it forbids, we invoke it; when we wish to uphold a practice it forbids, we ignore it entirely. Sometimes, we take a middle course, calling its three prongs "no more than helpful signposts." Such a docile and useful monster is worth keeping around, at least in a somnolent state; one never knows when one might need him.[113]

In 1998 in DeKalb County, Alabama, the *Lemon* "ghoul" has again been called back from the grave to scare little school children, their parents, teachers, and attorneys for the school board.[114] Once

---

[111] *See supra* text accompanying notes 75-79.

[112] Engel v. Vitale, 370 U.S. 421 (1962).

[113] Lamb's Chapel v. Center Moriches Union Free Sch. Dist., 508 U.S. 384, 398-99 (1993) (citations omitted).

[114] Chandler v. James, 985 F. Supp. 1062, 1085 n.28, 1087 (M.D. Ala. 1997).

again, the federal district court has breathed life into *Lemon* in order to strike down a practice the court wishes to forbid. When *Lemon* has served its purpose, it will again be put to rest, to be resurrected whenever the next master calls. As such, the people of DeKalb County are being intimidated by "monitors" appointed by the court and by indoctrination programs consisting of a "mandatory in-service training session,"[115] and are thereby coerced into abandoning customs and traditions which they have held dear from time immemorial.

But what is to come of those practices which have been left for yet another day? When will *Lemon* again be brought to life to remove from our public acknowledgment such mottos as "In God We Trust" on our money, "One Nation Under God" in our Pledge of Allegiance, and "So Help Me God" in our oaths? Will *Lemon* continue to stalk our First Amendment jurisprudence until every vestige of God is removed from our public life, and every public display of faith is annihilated? Must we wait until prayer is heard no more in our hallowed halls of justice and every school child is made afraid to mention the name of God for fear of being reported to a principal or a judge by a court appointed monitor? The time has come to cast away these deceptive tests for the Establishment Clause and thereby realize its true purpose and meaning—to promote the knowledge of God through freedom of conscience.

CONCLUSION

"[I]t is proper to take alarm at the first experiment on our liberties."[116] Borrowing these words from James Madison's 1785 *Memorial and Remonstrance against Religious Assessments*, Justice Hugo Black in the 1962 *Engel* case invoked Madison's warning against a twenty-two word prayer which read, as follows: "Almighty God, we acknowledge our dependence upon Thee, and we beg Thy blessings

---

[115] *Id.* at 1067-68.

[116] Engel v. Vitale, 370 U.S. 421, 436 (1962) (quoting James Madison, *Memorial and Remonstrance Against Religious Assessments, in* WRITINGS OF MADISON 183, 185-86).

upon us, our parents, our teachers and our Country."[117] This prayer, composed by the New York Board of Regents for voluntary recitation by school children and their teachers at the opening of each school day,[118] was hardly a "first experiment" on the liberties of school children and their families. To the contrary, it was patterned after the long-standing public tradition of invoking the guidance of Divine Providence in the conduct of government business since the founding of the American Republic.[119] To this day, prayers similar to that composed by the New York Board of Regents continue to be made in the halls of state legislatures and Congress, at inaugurations of Presidents and Governors and in America's courtrooms, including the United States Supreme Court. Indeed, the impeachment trial of President Clinton began in the United States Senate with an invocation by the Senate Chaplain seeking God's guidance.

By depriving America's school children of the privilege of prayer, the Court has not stopped a first experiment on their liberties, but denied to public school children the right to engage in a civic activity that goes to the very heart of the American way of life, reflected in the nation's motto "In God We Trust." What Representative Louis C. Rabaut of Michigan stated in support of the inclusion of "under God" in the Pledge of Allegiance is equally applicable to the continuation of prayer in school: "[T]he children of our land, in the daily recitation of the pledge [of allegiance] in school, will be daily impressed with a true understanding of our way of life and its origins."[120]

Prior to 1962, no public acknowledgment of God had ever been considered to be an establishment of religion. If it were, the National Motto, the Pledge of Allegiance, the National Anthem, and every piece of United States currency would be unconstitutional; yet the courts have not struck down these practices. Even the Declaration of Independence fails every prong of the *Lemon* test simply because this

---

[117] *Id.* at 422.

[118] *See id.*

[119] *See supra* p. 40.

[120] Statement of Louis C. Rabaut, 83d Cong., 2d Sess. (1954).

nation was established upon a belief in God, not secular neutrality toward God. The intent of our Founding Fathers was to promote and preserve a belief in God, and therefore government and God were inseparably intertwined.

James Madison stated that it is proper to take alarm at the first experiment on our liberties when a tax could be placed on the citizenry to support a preferred Christian denomination in violation of one's unalienable and God-given rights of freedom of conscience.[121] How much more is it an "experiment on our liberties" to forbid the acknowledgment of the One from Whom our rights are received?

In 1962, and to this day, the United States Supreme Court had usurped the power of the states to acknowledge the Creator, a power and right preserved to the people under the First and Tenth Amendments of the United States Constitution. In doing so, the Court has directly contradicted the wishes of the people expressed by Congress in 1954, 1955, and 1956. In case after case, the Supreme Court has incorrectly held that a connection between state government and God is inappropriate. It is time now to pay heed to the words of Madison, which Justice Black ignored in *Engel*: "The freemen of America did not wait til usurped power had strengthened itself by exercise and entangled the question in precedents. They saw all the consequences in the principle and they avoided the consequences by denying the principle. We revere this lesson too much, soon to forget it."[122]

When government interferes in any way with man's dutiful relationship with God, it interferes with freedom of conscience. The First Amendment to the United States Constitution was adopted to preserve the right to worship God according to the dictates of conscience and to prevent government interference with that right.

---

[121] *See* Engel v. Vitale, 370 U.S. 421, 436 (1962) (quoting James Madison, *Memorial and Remonstrance Against Religious Assessments, in* WRITINGS OF MADISON 183, 185-86).

[122] James Madison, *Memorial and Remonstrance Against Religious Assessments, in* WRITINGS OF MADISON 183, 185-86).

The intent of our Founders was never to prohibit the public acknowledgment of God, for to do so would have been a denial of the basis upon which our freedoms are secure. To restrict a display of the Ten Commandments in a court of law, to forbid opening courts with prayer, or to deny children the right of voluntary participation in prayer is a denial of the acknowledgment of God in violation of the United States Constitution and the First Amendment.

ABOUT THE AUTHOR

Rev. Rob Schenck is a missionary to elected and appointed officials in Washington, D.C., where he directs Operation Save Our Nation, an effort to bring the Word of God to bear on the hearts and minds of those who make public policy in America. Since 1995, Rob has recruited teams of pastors and church leaders who travel to Washington to present members of Congress, the White House, and the federal courts with beautiful stone artwork tablets of the Ten Commandments as a reminder of the standard to which God holds all of us to account.

Rob and his twin brother, Paul, met Jesus Christ at age 16. The Schencks have been preaching since they were 19. Rob holds a diploma in Bible and Theology from Buffalo (New York) School of the Bible and a Master of Arts in Christian Ministry from Faith Evangelical Lutheran Seminary, Tacoma, Washington. He is an ordained minister of the Evangelical Church Alliance. His brother, the Reverend Dr. Paul Schenck, is a minister in the Reformed Episcopal Church and serves a parish in nearby Baltimore County.

The Schencks work together in Washington, D.C., where their outreach office is located on Pennsylvania Avenue, midway between the White House and the United States Capitol. Their ministry recently purchased a historic Victorian townhouse adjacent to the United States Supreme Court for use as a ministry center to the judicial branch of government.

Rob appears regularly in the national secular and Christian media. His candid and personal insights on government personalities and activities have placed him at the center of many Washington news conferences. He has been seen on The News Hour with Jim Lehrer, Nightline, CNN, C-SPAN, Fox Network's Hannady and Combs, and the 700 Club. *Life, Time, Newsweek, U.S. News and World Report,* and *Christianity Today* have carried reports of his ministry endeavors as well as editorials on his leadership. *The New York Times, The Chicago Tribune, The Houston Chronicle* and *The Los Angeles Times* have all carried feature stories on his work. His biography was the front cover story of the *Washington Times* magazine and the *Baltimore Sun's* biography was one of the most extensive ever published in that paper. *The Washington Post* recently ran a special religion report on his Capitol Hill outreach.

Rob's communication style, humor, and unique perspective on Washington, D.C., will inspire and challenge your heart to become part of the solution to our national problems.

You may contact Rev. Schenck at the following:

Rev. Rob Schenck
Scheduling Office
8813 Commerce Court
Manassas, VA 20110
703-257-5593

or write to him c/o PRSchenck@aol.com

Additional copies of this book and other book titles
from **ALBURY PUBLISHING** are
available at your local bookstore.

ALBURY PUBLISHING
P. O. Box 470406
Tulsa, Oklahoma 74147-0406

For a complete list of our titles,
visit us at our website:

www.alburypublishing.com

For international and Canadian orders,
please contact:

Access Sales International
2448 East 81st Street
Suite 4900
Tulsa, Oklahoma 74137
Phone 918-523-5590   Fax 918-496-2822

THE TEN COMMANDMENTS

PROJECT

The Ten Words That Will Change A Nation is the "textbook" for the Ten Commandments Project, an effort to re-introduce the American people to the Great Words of Sinai. You are invited to be a part of this exciting mission to bring back the Ten Commandments to American public life. You may do this in four ways:

1. Purchase additional copies of *The Ten Words That Will Change A Nation* and give them as gifts to your family, friends, and co-workers.

2. Purchase sets of beautiful stone artwork tablets of the Ten Commandments for display in your church, home, place of employment, or even your vehicle.

3. Sponsor a presentation of the Ten Commandments to an elected or appointed official in Washington, D.C., or in your own state capital or local community.

4. Encourage young people to organize for National T-Day when students across the United States wear t-shirts with the Ten Commandments on them.

To request more details on the Ten Commandments Project, call 1-800-551-2930, or visit out website at www.tencommands.org!